Africana Paradigms, Practices, and Literary Texts: Evoking Social Justice

CLENORA HUDSON-WEEMS, PhD

Cover image © Shutterstock.com

www.kendallhunt.com
Send all inquiries to:
4050 Westmark Drive
Dubuque, IA 52004-1840

Copyright © 2021 by Kendall Hunt Publishing Company

ISBN: 978-1-7924-6191-0

All rights reserved. No part of this publication may be reproduced, stored in a retrieval system, or transmitted, in any form or by any means, electronic, mechanical, photocopying, recording, or otherwise, without the prior written permission of the copyright owner.

Published in the United States of America

To All Africana People—May God Bless Us and prepare the world for bountiful blessings that will ultimately benefit all—Men, Women, and Children everywhere.

Contents

Foreword	*Judge Joe Brown*	ix
Preface	*Benjamin W. Jones*—Medical Student, University of Kansas *Jamica Jacobs*—Biological Sciences, Sen, McNair Scholar, MU	xi
Introduction	*Clenora Hudson-Weems, PhD*	xvii
PART I	**Africana Theories: Inter-Cultural/Inter-Disciplinary Movements**	**1**
Chapter 1	Africana Womanism: Authenticity and Collectivity in Securing Social Justice—*Clenora Hudson-Weems, PhD*	3
Chapter 2	Afrocentricity and Transformation: Understanding a Movement—*Molefi Kete Asante, Phd*	23
Chapter 3	Black Women Adult Educators—The Utterers of Black Leadership Preparation: Africana Womanism and the Afrocentric Praxis—*Jacqueline Roebuck Sakho, EdD*	33
PART II	**Africana Moments & Persuasions in Re-Shaping Our Lives**	**51**
Chapter 4	The Essential James Baldwin: Life and Literature, At Home and Abroad—*Pamela D. Reed, PhD*	53
Chapter 5	The African American Literary Tradition—*Clenora Hudson-Weems, PhD*	69
Chapter 6	The Significance of HBCUs: The Social, Academic, & Career Determining Benefits of HBCUs—*Sharon H. Porter, EdD*	95

v

Chapter 7	Africana Studies and Economics, In Search of a New Progressive Partnership—*James B. Stewart, PhD*	105
Chapter 8	When Will We Learn? It's Not Their Heads, It's Their (Broken) Hearts—*S. Renee Mitchell, EdD*	115
PART III:	**Evolutionary Movements: Beliefs, Ideas and Action**	**135**
Chapter 9	Networks of Steel: How Reparations for European Enslavement of Africans Unite the African Diaspora—*Raymond A. Winbush, PhD*	137
Chapter 10	"The Modern Civil Rights Movement" (1994)—*Clenora Hudson-Weems, PhD*	147
Chapter 11	End Emmett Till Continuums: Beyond George Floyd, Breonna Taylor, and Ma'Khia Bryant—*Ngeri Nnachi, JD, MPPL*	163
Chapter 12	Nourish to Flourish: Maroonage—Woodsonian Philo-Praxis and the Education of Black Children—*Lasana D. Kazembe, PhD*	171
Chapter 13	Be Woke! Black America and the Holy Trinity—A SERMON—*Rev. Debra Walker King, PhD*	183
Conclusion		191
Coda	SANKOFA—Learn the lessons of the past in order to move forward for a successful future	197

Reflections on Our Past, Present, and Future Possibilities

From Filmscript—*Emmett's Liberation/Whitten's Redemption* 197

THE CHRONICLE OF HIGHER EDUCATION

"Professor Seeks to Make Film About Lawyer Who Defended Racist Murderers"—by Jennifer Ruark 213

COLUMBIA DAILY TRIBUNE

"The Civil Rights Movement, Then and Now: Anti-Racism to Stop the Emmett Till Continuum in a 5-Step Solution"—Clenora Hudson-Weems 214

Epilogue	*Maurice Green, PhD*—Founding Manager/Director, Black PhD (Network & Black Doctoral Network)	
	Alveda C. King, Hon. Dr.(hc)—Niece of Dr. Martin Luther King, Jr. & Dir. of Civil Rights for the Unborn; author of King Rules: Ten Truths for You, Your Family, and Our Nation to Prosper)	
	Kamika Lynette Bell, MEd—Executive Director, Catalyst for Change, Inc. & Girls with Pearls	215
Afterword	*Gail F. Baker, PhD*	219
Abstracts		221
Editor & Contributors		231
Appendix		233
Index		239

Foreword

Contributed by:
Judge Joe Brown, JD

Protecting womanhood and promoting manhood: These things humans have been about forever, as they are inherent in the process of breeding and providing for the next generations of the species. At the root of this human cycle is man and woman, working together to build and maintain families. These fundamental concerns and aspects of humanity are presently at risk in a world in which extended families are gradually fading away with each passing year. This is particularly true in the Africana community.

The current climate is such that what needs to be said cannot be stated bluntly without incurring censorship, approbation from the ensnared and reflexive rejection by the propagandized. That said, the code that follows is perhaps necessary to escape the vigilant algorithms that would restrict a direct message. Is this politically correct novelty of a "fluid" lifestyle and worldview a valid thing—or a fevered dream of delusional narcissists? Is this a sound development, or something that has festered in a transient safety bubble; an impermanent feature reflecting a temporary hiatus in the harsh reality of existence?

Humanity's ability to manipulate nature has secured the species a unique position; it has become a force of nature, a thing that can significantly alter the environment and bring about extinction events. This ability to consciously manipulate and manage the planet to a significant degree has brought things to a nexus point. It would seem that the United States has become the arbiter of this process; it certainly is in the forefront of humanity's planetary dominance.

The National problems are many; preeminent is the long-standing contradictions and inequities of the racial dynamic it has with its formerly enslaved citizenry. The traditional normative worldview sums itself with this observation: The human house will soon fall if it is divided. Men and Women need each other—if only to secure procreation and the proper rearing of offsprings. Masculinity is not only descriptive of condition and nature, but proscriptive of internal control.

Earth remains a very dangerous place to live; natural and human hazards cannot be escaped, even if human nature has allowed the species to impose safe conditions and circumstances in some small regions of human habitation. Maintenance of those conditions is dependent upon vigilance and continued attention to the inherent necessities of our favorable circumstances. The traditional Yin/Yang balance cannot be suppressed without disaster. Liberty, freedom, and safety are earned and the acquisition of the first two are not safe. Being a free people is a dangerous thing, fraught with hazard; freedom is inherently dangerous. The direct and collateral consequences of the process of earning and maintaining a free condition are dire. Freedom and Liberty are not things that a people are entitled to; they are not entitlements but rewards for those who would make the necessary sacrifices. This historic reality has been replaced by a too great sense of presumptive entitlement—unaccompanied by a sense of duty and obligation.

Time will tell if this attitude of entitlement to safety is sound or ill-advised; functional—or extreme disfunction; enlightenment or perversion and decadence that leads to an inevitable downfall. Duty, honor, obligation, responsibility, accountability, dependability; purpose, focus; morality, ethics, courage, and bravery—are these things still a necessary adjunct to the successful navigation of adversity? Have we reached a utopian status wherein these heretofore fulfilling virtues are no longer necessary? Or (as many well understand) are they still necessities when it comes to human prosperity and collective wellbeing?

The olden values have taken us from cave and hut to monumental architecture and space platforms. Where will we go now? What will the balance become? What will be the mix? Our streets are filled with senseless violence, and we are losing both our individual and collective purpose, cause, and focus. We must bring ourselves back to an understanding that restores our drive, reflective in that absence in our children today. We must rediscover the pleasure in purpose if we are to maintain our collective humanity. These are some of the pertinent issues that are evoked in this timely and important volume, highlighting critical concerns for ultimate human survival.

This multilayered book is a powerful blueprint, which gives us milestones and guidance from the mind and soul of a wise Woman, one who has carefully selected a phenomenal cadre of astute scholars in myriad areas of expertise in order to bring this significant text to full fruition. The forward pathway for the peoples of the African Diaspora is set out within these pages. The urgent message is both prescriptive and required reading for those seeking theoretical, cultural, and literary perspectives, both historical and contemporary on the Africana experience. Hence, we would do well to absorb the vital information presented herein.

JoeB
(Judge Joe Brown)

Preface

Contributed by:
Benjamin Jones—Medical Student, University of Kansas
Jamica Jacobs—Biological Sciences, Senior, McNair Scholar, MU

I   *"Of all the forms of inequality, injustice in health care is the most shocking and inhumane."*—Martin Luther King Jr., March 1966

Social justice is a term that has always meant something to me. Since high school, I have always felt a calling to advocate for myself and others as best I can. As a Black man pursuing medicine, I've educated myself on many of the healthcare barriers that negatively affect the black community, and as I launch my medical training at the University of Kansas, I am committed to making a difference, particularly for Black people because of our racial status. While I've learned extensively about the worlds of research and science, no class has had a greater impact on my growth as a young man than my African Diaspora Literature and Theory class, designed and taught by Dr. Clenora Hudson-Weems, whose specialization reveals the literary power to inform the world of unlimited messages, creatively mirroring Black life. It is Black life, too long and too often neglected, that the editor, and her chosen colleagues alike, have graced this book with priceless information for all to witness.

The editor of this book, Dr. Hudson-Weems, with her enthusiasm for Africana history, art, and literature, has an amazing ability to introduce students to an entire Africana world, and her colleagues have joined her in their own specific fields of study. The knowledge of historical figures and current events, earlier introduced in my Africana class, has given me information that I will remember for life, for her teaching and guidance have likewise inspired me to see the need for social justice from a medical lens, social justice being the threshold of this edited volume. I am here reminded of Toni Morrison's *Home*, set in the 1950s, surrounding the Korean War, with protagonist Frank Money being called back home to rescue his little sister, Cee. Her employer and physician, Dr. Beauregard Scott, had been experimenting on her in the form of eugenics, sterilization, a practice suspicious of still existing even today. As Dr. King's words allude, "there is an alarming amount of racial inequalities in health care." My African Diaspora Literature class has given me the knowledge and enlightenment to recognize that I can not only be a Black physician, but a Black physician who can work to make improvements in healthcare inequalities for all, including Blacks. This book, *Africana Paradigms, Practices, and Literary Texts: Evoking Social Justice*, and its focus on social justice, will surely continue to enlighten my quest for social justice, as it will for many others. The brilliant chapters herein on Afrocentricity, Africana Womanism, Black Empowerment, and more, offered by the perceptive authors here, will give us all the tools necessary to advocate for marginalized communities. I hope to take their knowledge and inspiration to help fight for social justice in medicine. Granted, there is a lot of work to be done, but the knowledge I have gained under Dr. Hudson-Weems' tutelage is certainly a good place to start. Through her teaching and writing, which certainly apply to her fellow contributors as well, we are all given the power to make a difference. Through mentorship, outreach, and service, I plan on helping to eradicate many of the inequalities in medicine, healthcare, education, and society. Unquestionably, valuable insights and lessons to be learned from this book will continue to inspire me, and many others, to work for a brighter future for all humankind.

> II. "... We're all in it together; Family-Centrality—that's it; we're going nowhere without the other." (Hudson-Weems, "Africana Womanism: I Got Your Back, Boo" 2009)

Joining in on the course, Africana Womanism blessed me with the feeling of timelessness, with relatable African-centered materials, rooted in the past that mandated bringing the information and the right methodology together. Much like the theory itself, that treats any and all issues in what Dr. Hudson-Weems calls an "interconnected" fashion, the authors represented in this book strongly interconnect on key issues, as they explore some of the same things, but with different focuses, depending upon their specific areas of expertise. This is the theory and practice of Dr. Hudson-Weems for her interdisciplinary/intercultural course, whereby in teaching the theory, she begins by highlighting the 18 distinct features for the Africana Womanist. But it goes far beyond being just a paradigm. It is a way of life, which enabled me to see the true nature of each as a collective multigenerational pillar.

As I look back on my life, I realize that I have been impacted by these elements defining me as an active Africana womanist, reinforcing the power of family-centrality, which, in the end, makes life itself happen. For example, it took my mother, Gloria J. Dudley Robinson, and the whole community for me to be able to be in college and have the opportunity to be introduced to such a phenomenon that gave me a safe space where I felt comfortable and unjudged, a pleasant relief in my academic journey, in colliding with my personal life. Even though I was just her student, my knowledge was never belittled, only enhanced, for the class structure was enriching and required all students to engage by implementing our ideas in a "call and response" manner. This class gave me a new perspective on how to improve my sense of self by defining myself and securing my own authentic identity, ultimately manifesting in what I want regarding my future goals, really fundamental to my identity.

The lives of many people are reflected throughout this textbook. The relationships that one can develop with an authentic curriculum, such as offered in this textbook, will transcend its pages, as this could incite a desire to not only take action, but to develop a hunger for deepening one's knowledge of social justice.

In conclusion, the past year has shown the desperate need we have for a better justice system, including a better healthcare system and much more, strongly emphasizing Social Justice. Courses designed to help all, as it has done for the both of us, are very beneficial, for we can now better understand our "interconnectedness" in working together toward true Social Justice on all fronts. As students in our designated field of the sciences, we can better appreciate now our subject connection with others, and can embrace our efforts as copartners, together working to bring about true "justice for all." This is what the editor and her contributors do. In return, we are able to continue the dialogue with information and tactics needed for future generations through intellectualism, leadership, and action, knowing, at last, that "We'll all in it together" and this reality we pledge to uphold forever.

Introduction

Contributed by:
Clenora Hudson-Weems, PhD

> "Until the lions have their history, tales of hunting will always glorify the hunters."
>
> (**An African Proverb**)

While the focus of this multidisciplinary volume, entitled *Africana Paradigms, Practices & Literary Texts: Evoking Social Justice*, highlights the rich world of Africana people in quest for our God-given birthright to true freedom for our families and communities, I am reminded of the Sledge Sisters' famous Rhythm & Blues top single, "We Are Family." As an Africana family, we must come and stick together for Victory for all of our people, which need not necessarily stop there. In the Routledge Fifth Edition of the 1993 classic, *Africana Womanism: Reclaiming Ourselves*, the author notes that

> There is much to be gained by all on both sides when "the other" involves himself/herself in correcting the dehumanization of a fellow human being. For example, Harriet Beecher Stowe, . . . author of the classic nineteenth-century novel, *Uncle Tom's Cabin*, demonstrates how slavery not only dehumanizes Blacks, but Whites as well, via her characterization of one of the main protagonists, Simon Legree, whose white privilege reduced him to a sub-human level, a monster. (110)

The above quotation projects a positive reality wherein the so-called "privileged" could also gain more, for it is more to life's happiness than mere physical rewards. The economic exploitation of African Americans during slavery, and the continuing eras of racial dominance, result in the making of an egregious, monstrous recipient of endless callous, though lucrative, grand self-serving material benefits. Yet, we live in our world of human diversity of many ethnicities, wherein one must forever be cognizant of the fact that we are all members of the Human Race, and thus, are entitled to the same rights and privileges, demanding that policies/laws be put in place for just equity for all.

The Constitution of the United States reflects the ideal of a true Democratic Republic (American Democracy), although the creators and signers of the **United States Declaration of Independence** (July 4, 1776) —Thomas Jefferson, Benjamin Franklin, John Adams, Roger Sherman, and Robert R. Livingston—did not have the best interest of African Americans in mind, as they had strategically classified Blacks as only 3/5 human being. Needless to say, however, we are well cognizant of the fact that we were and remain a great people, full-fledge human beings sanctioned by God, the Father from the beginning of time. Although too often relegated to the status of "hidden figures," many know that many of our attributes have been concealed, kept from the world for countless reasons. But as William Cullen Bryant, lawyer and poet, asserts in "The Battlefield,"—"Truth, pressed to earth, shall rise again." That powerful truth was later quoted by Dr. Martin Luther King, Jr. as he made his prophetic proclamation in his speech toward the end of the 1965 Selma (Alabama) March—"No lie can live forever. We shall overcome." Indeed, once the whole truth is totally realized, wherein racism is debunked at last, Africana people will soar to the top of an unimaginable existence, having demanded respect, recognition, and long-overdue benefits as fellow human beings.

This comprehensive collection of essays, written by an array of highly visible researchers, authors, visionaries, and public intellectuals, has made possible a magnificent body of materials, indeed, invaluable, which could ultimately lead to workable resolutions to today's continuing problems, particular relative to racism and how it has made the richest of the country and others as well, financially set for life and then affording their off-springs a lavish life via Generational Wealth. And what an awesome job for the contributors, who have brought these truths to the surface, beginning with the **Foreword**, written by the illustrious *Judge Joe Brown, JD*—TV Personality of CBS 15-year Syndicated Court Show—*Judge Joe Brown* (Hollywood, California), the worldwide longest-running TV Court Show during its time (1998–2013); the **Preface**, coauthored by my remarkable former students/mentees, *Benjamin Jones,* Medical Student, University of Kansas and **Jamica Jacobs**, Biological Sciences senior, McNair Scholar, UMC; the **Epilogue**, by *Maurice Green, PhD*—Founding Manager/Director, Black PhD Network and Black Doctoral Network, *Alveda C. King, HonDr. h.c.*—Niece of Dr. Martin Luther King, Jr., Director of Civil Rights for the Unborn, and author of *King Rules: Ten Truths for You, Your Family, and Our Nation to Prosper,* and *Kamika Lynette Bell, MEd*—Executive Director, Catalyst for Change, Inc & Girls with Pearls; and **Afterword**, by *Gail F. Baker*, **PhD**—Provost and Vice President of Academic Affairs, University of San Diego—co-author of *Exploding Stereotypes.* The insightful chapters were meticulously crafted by the following: *Molefi Kete Asante, PhD*—Creator/Advancer—*Afrocentricity*, Professor/Founding Chair, Department of Africology, Temple University, General Editor, *Journal of Black Studies* and author of *The Afrocentric Idea*, and *The History of Africa; The Quest for Eternal Harmony*; *Jacqueline Roebuck Sakho, EdD*—Department of Leadership Studies & Adult Education, School of Education, North Carolina A&T State U; *Pamela D. Reed, PhD*— Founding Executive Director of the Africologic Institute and Associate Professor of English, Virginia State University and Featured Blogger, *Diverse: Issues in Higher Education*; *Sharon Hargro Porter, EdD*—Executive Director, Next in Line to Lead Aspiring Principals Leadership Academy,

Introduction   xvii

and Editor-in-Chief, *Vision & Purpose LifeStyle Magazine*; **James B. Stewart, PhD**—Past President National Council of Black Studies, Vice Provost (ret.) and Professor Emeritus, School of Labor and Employment Relations, Penn State University, and author of *Flight: In Search of Vision*; **S. Renee Mitchell, EdD**—Award-Winning 25-year Former Newspaper Journalist, national award-winning program for Black youths—*I Am M.O.R.E.* (Making Ourselves Resilient Everyday) and 2-time nominee for *The Pulitzer Prize*; **Raymond Arnold Winbush, PhD**—Research Professor and Director of the Institute for Urban Research, Morgan State University, and author of *Should America Pay? Slavery and The Raging Debate on Reparations*; **Nkgeri Nnachi, JD, MPPL**—Doctoral Dissertator, University of Maryland–Baltimore County, and author of "Our Father Didn't Show Up to Court for the Child He Ruined" (*The Atlantic*, 2016); **Lasana D. Kazembe, PhD**—Executive Director, Third World Press, Assistant Professor, Indiana University–Purdue University Indianapolis, and editor of *Keeping Peace*; **Debra Walker King, PhD**—Professor of English and UF Term Professor—2019 to 2022, University of Florida, and author of *African Americans and the Culture of Pain*; **Keena Day, MA**—Doctoral Candidate, University of Dayton; Director of Humanities Instructions & Fine Arts, DSST Public Schools; with her Contemporary Remix of Margaret Walker's "For My People"; as well as **myself**, Professor, Creator of *Africana Womanism*, Establisher of Till as Catalyst of the Civil Rights Movement, Film Writer, and author of *Africana Womanism: Reclaiming Ourselves*, *Emmett Till: The Sacrificial Lamb of the Civil Rights Movement*, and co-author (with Dr. Wilfred D. Samuels, University of Utah) of *Toni-Morrison*. Without the phenomenon insights, and resolute commitments to Africana people for the perseverance of our legacy for future generations, this book of a plethora of knowledge and passion could not have been realized.

Thank God for the vision and for gifting me with the perceptive ability and enthusiastic spirit to select the best and most committed, diligent, passionate academic and human rights activists for such a grand mission herein put forth. You can be assured that all of the participants, and their seminal roles in the making of this worthy creation, have performed immeasurably to bring forth a truly meaningful initiatives for public review and execution as a final step for Social Justice for Africana people. With this, I humbly welcome all to join us in celebrating a wonderful experience with love and respect for all, as well as lessons to be learned and possible solutions to burning issues, long overdue for final corrections, including a possible racial healing.

In the meantime, let us be ever mindful of the critical issues surrounding not only the Coronavirus and vaccinations against it, but the formidable force against humanity, manifested in the ongoing murders of Blacks, and subsequent demonstrations and deep conversations, at last, brought to the surface for debate for possible solutions. For these burning concerns, the demand for Social Justice remains even today critical issue, but on a higher plateau with what I have deemed "Emmett Till Continuums," now painfully serving to expose racist practices. I am here reminded of the antilynching crusader herself, Ida B. Wells-Barnett, who dedicated her life to bringing forth Social Justice for Blacks in her endless efforts to end such crimes against nature, against African Americans in particular. She executed her efforts through media exposure, as owner of a local newspaper situated in Memphis, Tennessee, in the deep south where every level of racial dominance was not only practiced, but legal—*de fact/ de jour!* Many Africana Academicians, like those represented in this significant edited volume, have dedicated their lives, their careers to changing the reality of Africana people, strongly moving forth to bring to ultimate fruition true freedom from the musty bondage of cruel and unfounded racial dominance, representing unthinkable acts in order to validate base white supremacy. Needing a healing to a sickness that begs for relief, the 1921 Tulsa massacre is a symbol of the depths of the pain that yet reigns today, 100 years later! We seek Victory Now via unveiling truths about who Africana people really are in all dimensions in order to finally debunk racism forever!

Part I
Africana Theories: Inter-Cultural/Inter-Disciplinary Movements

Hudson-Weems, who named and refined a new terminology and paradigm relative to the true role of Africana women . . . introduced Africana Womanism [which] . . . addresses the particular needs and desires relative to Africana women's unique lives revolving around their worldview and thus, is distinct from all other female-based theories because it prioritizes the triple plight—race, class, and gender—of Africana women. . . . Unlike feminism or black feminism, [it] is family-centered rather than female-centered and is concerned first and foremost with race empowerment rather than female empowerment.

(Clenora Hudson-Weems, PhD—"The African American Literary Tradition" in *The African American Experience*)

The Afrocentric idea is distinguished by five characteristics . . . the principal features of the Afrocentric theory since its inception in the late 1970s. . . . The aims of Afrocentricity as regards the cultural idea are not hegemonic. Afrocentrists . . . express an ardent belief in the possibility of diverse populations living on the same earth without giving up their fundamental traditions . . . The Afrocentric idea is essential to human harmony [which] represents a possibility of intellectual maturity. . . It is an attitude, a location, an orientation. . . . The Afrocentrist seeks for the African person the contentment of subject, active, agent place.

(Molefi Kete Asante, PhD—"Afrocentricity and Transformation: Understanding a Movement" in *Contemporary Africana Theory*)

Chapter 1
Africana Womanism: Authenticity and Collectivity in Securing Social Justice

Contributed by:
Clenora Hudson-Weems, PhD

Lift Every Voice and Sing by James Weldon Johnson

The powerful lyrics of James Weldon Johnson's "Life Every Voice and Sing," considered the Black National Anthem, later set to music by his brother, J. Rosamond, at the turn of the twentieth century, stand as an excellent representation of the call for collectivity on the part of Blacks in our pursuit of freedom, determined to fight "till victory is won." This motto has defined our national liberation struggle for centuries and will continue for the ultimate justice for all. It commands that African Americans hold true to our needs via respecting our roots with regards for true Africana life. Emerging from a vast body of thought and action coming from multigenres (music, poetry, orations, novels, movies, essays, etc.), authentic Black life should be effectively preserved for documentation purposes in enabling invaluable instructive truths.

In today's world of evolving ideals and concepts, confusion and delusion, political and religious persuasions, and much more, it is virtually impossible to ignore the fact that things are rapidly changing, some with questionable agendas that do not necessarily speak directly to the betterment of our society. Therefore, in order to create and secure a better society, one wherein love and happiness inseparably reside, security and friendship, as well as an overall good will for all hail, we must put in place ways by which these realities can prevail. And the literary text, dramatically reflecting life itself, is only one of many venues wherein one is introduced to and hopefully learns from the history of past experiences needed to imagine a different and better future for all, including Africana people. What, then, is Africana Womanism and how does it inform our society today?

> Hudson-Weems, who named and refined a new terminology and paradigm relative to the true role of Africana women . . . introduced Africana Womanism [which] . . . addresses the particular needs and desires relative to Africana women's unique lives revolving around their worldview

and thus, is distinct from all other female-based theories because it prioritizes the triple plight—race, class, and gender—of Africana women.... Unlike feminism or black feminism, [it] is family-centered rather than female-centered and is concerned first and foremost with race empowerment rather than female empowerment (Hudson-Weems, "The Literary Tradition" 135).

It is true, that our ultimate success, including our social, economic, religious, and political persuasions, depends inevitably upon a Collective Movement, one which unselfishly embraces the entire family—men, women, and children. It permeates all activities dedicated to the true Africana Womanist, with a particular allegiance to an authentic worldview for her people. The 18 distinct characteristics of Africana Womanism represent how this goal can be best realized in bringing to full fruition, via first loving ourselves and each other, our God-given birthright as free human beings for the survival of our future generations.

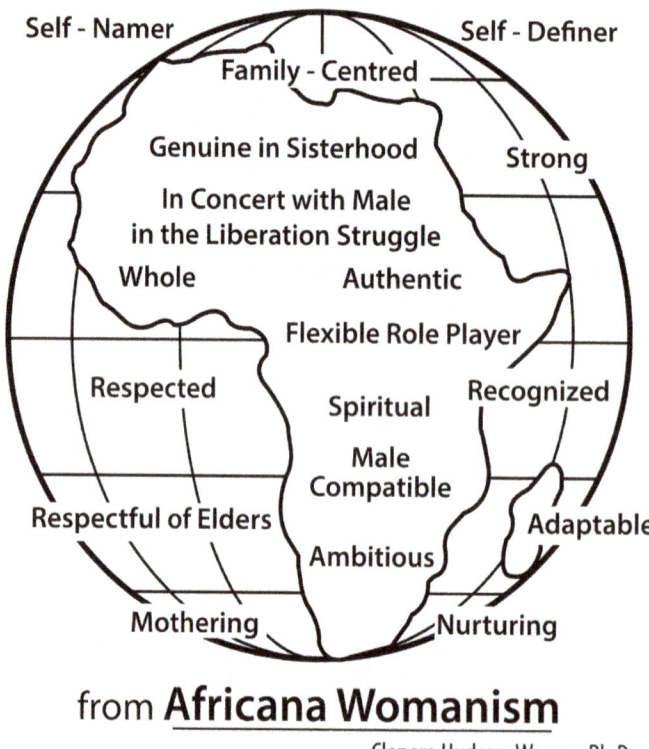

from **Africana Womanism**
Clenora Hudson-Weems, Ph.D.

As validated by two Namibian writers, Angela Cowser and Sandra I. Barnes in "From Shack Dwellers to Home-Owners," the practicing of the 18 Africana Womanism elements daily is one way to elevate one's life, with an obvious mandate for collectivity. Firming upholding what could be considered seminal missions for the Africana woman, below are those tenets, with commentary on how they work for the good of the Africana family, to be used as a yardstick for improving our communities:

1. Remain authentic in securing the responsibility of **Self-Naming** and **Self-Defining** as the first steps in derailing her needs and those of her community.

Chapter 1: Africana Womanism: Authenticity and Collectivity in Securing Social Justice 5

2. Insist upon placing the family, which includes men, women, and children, at the center—**Family-Centrality**, not female centrality, for human survival.
3. Remain true to the role of **Genuine Sisterhood**; she must be there for her challenging moments, ultimately emerging as true supporting winners.
4. Understand that our spiritual, emotional, and psychological **Strength** (internal strength) far exceeds our physical strength, indeed, needed for aiding in the making of a secure and successful people, both individually and collectively.
5. Continue our collective mission, remaining **In Concert with the Male in the Struggle** for our families/communities.
6. Realize our dimensions, a multidimensional **Whole**, well rounded being, one who naturally represents more than a single ideal.
7. Insist upon an **Authentic** existence, which is culturally connected, as we can only be really happy when we love and respect ourselves and our people.
8. Appreciate the fact that the woman is a **Flexible Role Player**, who operates within both the homeplace with her family, and the workplace as an employee–employer, without sacrificing either role in her quest to fulfill both.
9. Realize that her demand for both **Respect** and **Recognition** requires that the reciprocal nature of both be practiced. This means that in order to *get* these pleasures, one must also *give* them as well—a genuine game of fair play.
10. Put God first, for clearly there is that Divine Being who created everything in the universe and thus, the successful operation of all must necessarily come from Him! This is **Spirituality** personified!
11. Understand the importance of **Male Compatibility**, which involves the male, the flip side of the coin, without whom, the human race, as we know it, will become extinct. Still, one's personal preference remains one's own business.
12. Insist that we remain **Respectful of Elders**, realizing that they have paved the way for us to move forward. And the legacy continues!
13. Know that she is **Adaptable**, needing no "room of one's own" (Virginia Woolf) in order to realize her goals in life. For example, her kitchen and table become her office and desk when she shifts to the demands of her career.
14. Appreciate that we are more successful when we work together. Thus, the Africana woman is **Ambitious**, realizing that it takes "2 to tango" to create a secure harmonious existence as we strive for Generational Wealth, "together!"
15. Stand resolute in upholding her duties and responsibilities to the children and our future generations. She must be **Mothering and Nurturing**, for molding character and caring for the physical and emotional needs of the children are critical for the continuation of a wholesome people/society.

Three of them stand as pairs, such as **Mothering** and **Nurturing**, two major cornerstones of Africana Womanism, relative to the role of the Africana womanist.

The end of the first decade of the twentieth-first century, 2010, marked a powerful global moment for Africana Womanism, which was later documented, with its many ideas and lessons to be learned and handed down for generations to come. In October of that year, a defining event occurred on the campus of the University of Zimbabwe, where the first International Africana Womanism Conference, hosted by the university, convened. Dr. Itai Muhwati—then Chair of the Department of Literature and Languages, now Dean of Faculty—and his colleagues coordinated the grand event. Hundreds of presenters and attendees came from not only universities throughout the continent of Africa, including several universities throughout Zimbabwe, the University of South Africa and the University of Botswana, but from universities in the United States as well, including California State University, the University of Oklahoma, Delaware State University, the University of Missouri, and so on. Moreover, participants outside of Academia were represented as well, such as *The Honourable Joice Mujuru*, Vice President of the Republic of Zimbabwe, who delivered the Opening Welcome for hundreds who came from far and near to be a part of this historic coming together of men and women alike to discuss our destiny as African people and what was needed to make our quest a reality. We strongly proposed that we forge a way to secure each other in our collective journey toward ultimate victory.

Two years later, the 2012 publication of select papers presented by some 65 global presenters (both men and women) during the conference made its debut. The comprehensive volume, *Rediscoursing: Africana Womanism in the Search for Sustainable Renaissance: Africana Womanism in Multi-disciplinary Approaches*, was edited by Dr. Muwati et al. It was a dynamic compilation of articles representing an illuminating and engaging three-day dialogue on interconnected critical issues for global Africana people. In the Foreword to the book, I stated that

> The historic Africana Womanism conference, initiated, organized and hosted by the University of Zimbabwe, convening on October 27–29, 2010, advancing to a higher plateau, the relativity of an important all-inclusive paradigm considering crucial global issues on all fronts. . . . accepted the charge for actively engaging in the urgent struggle for human survival against the odds of race, class and gender oppression, the cornerstone for prioritization for Africana Womanism (xii–xiii).

In the Introduction, the editors took a strong position in support the significance of Africana Womanism in the modern-day struggle for human rights of all Africana people:

> "Because of the value of womanhood in Africa's development, women's activism and struggles need to be part of the broader effort to rid society of all injustice. Indeed, women need to broaden their struggle to go beyond female-centeredness and embrace, for example, a gender and family-centered perspective that tackles the human rights of the entire family" (xviii).

As conceptualizer of Africana Womanism, I delivered the Opening Plenary, which became the opening chapter for the book, entitled "Ending De-womanization, De-feminization and De-humanization via Self-naming, Self-definition and Genuine Sisterhood." In the Introduction, the editors/conference coordinators assessed that my focus served as

Chapter 1: Africana Womanism: Authenticity and Collectivity in Securing Social Justice 7

> a bulwark against the continuing abuse and dehumanization of women
> ... [as it] confronts black men who demonstrate flagrant disrespect and
> disregard for women (xx).

They had earlier stated that

> Africana Womanism liberates the enslaved and distorted African cultural space and draws pedagogically nourishing perspectives on African womanhood and gender that can be utilized by people of African descent in their attempts to deal with challenges affecting their existence. It takes "its model from Africana women warriors and moves on to create a paradigm relative to this age-old legacy of Africana women's activism." (Hudson-Weems 2001, 137) (Foreword xvii).

Needless to say, the book, an outgrowth of the conference, had successfully documented the deep discussions surrounding the destiny of global Africana people. It was, indeed, a victorious culmination of over 2½ decades (1985–2010) of research, proving to be an unpremeditated organic preparation for a truly memorable moment in our collective history.

Although the journey of over three decades has been quite challenging, it has been very exciting and rewarding in its quest for a just and authentic existence for all Africana people. According to Muwati and Mguni in Chapter 7—"An Anatomy of Negative Male–Female Relations: A Human Rights Issue" (Muwati and Mguni xxii), the dynamics of male–female relationships deeply impact upon the family. The quest for true happiness and security for the family requires that we "re-educate society on the importance of living, working and producing together as men and women." This becomes a sacred legacy, which must be handed down for generations, as we embrace our mission and commitment, the very *raison d'être* of Africana Womanism, strategically designed to bring all Africana people together, despite centuries of brutal global racial dominance. For this reason,

> Both the woman and her male counterpart must come to an agreement that each must respect and protect each other as a part of a necessary collective for the betterment of not only our communities, but for the world communities at large. . . . [Perceptively] critic, activist and author, Audrey Lorde, notes that Black men and women demonstrate that we have inherited a "shared racist oppression . . . joint defenses and joint vulnerabilities" (Lorde 228) . . . Admittedly, we are "In It Together" . . . Our collective battle against the antagonistic forces, reflecting our restless world of confusion and uncertainty, will no doubt continue until basic freedom for all is realized (Hudson-Weems, *Africana Womanism*, 5th ed. 113).

To that end, Africana Womanism strongly reflects the "interconnectedness" of Africana men and women confronting all matters of race, class, and gender within the context of life experiences, beautifully meshed together like woven fabric, in this collective mission for global Africana survival. Quite different from the later creation of "intersectionality," which separates the parts in its analysis for sake of focusing, a separation and division from each other, interconnectedness has always demonstrated how all parts come together, and has held true for Africana people, dating back to African antiquity. This legacy must continue until true parity for all is realized. Chapter 8 of *Africana Womanism*, my analysis of Toni Morrison's *Beloved*, is entitled "Morrison's *Beloved*: All Parts Equal," whereby the very title itself clearly suggests that there exists a natural interconnection between all parts of all our life experiences. Further invalidating the need for "intersectionality" in assessing the practice and action of Africana people, Dr. Mark Christian asserts in the Afterword to *Africana Womanism: Reclaiming Ourselves*, Fifth Edition that

> The current academic fad phrase is "intersectionality" as if those of us in the Africana discourse never considered the myriad of issues encountered by our communities. "Race," class and gender, and the prioritization therein, have always been key issues for comprehending *Africana Womanism* (Christian 131).

Moreover, in one of the leading anthologies for the study of Africana American literature, *Call and Response: The Riverside Anthology of the African American Literary Tradition*, the editors concluded that all our experiences are, in fact, interconnected for Black women activists:

> Of all the theoretical models, Hudson-Weems's best describes the racially based perspective of many black women's rights advocates, beginning with Maria W. Stewart and Frances W. Harper in the early nineteenth century. (1379)

This impressive anthology includes ideas and experiences found in some of the ancient African Proverbs, African American Work Songs, Spirituals, Sermons, Prayers, Folk Tales, Poetry, Slave Narratives, Letters, Orations, Essays, Music, Plays, Fiction, and much more. The slave narratives are of particular significance, relative to the African American experiences, as that genre dates back to the inception of the African American literary tradition, wherein we witness the narratives of great narrators like Olaudah Equiano, Linda Brent, and Frederick Douglas, to name a few. They reflect the reputed beginnings of the African American slave experience in 1619, marked by the first official landing of the slave ship in Jamestown, Virginia, although it has been since documented that the actual first slave ship landed on these shores nearly a century before in 1526.

Because many view the slave narrative as signaling the inception of the Africana American literary tradition, and moreover, since Africana womanism is rooted in African antiquity, it is important to pause for an explication of the coming together of these two entities. Dr. April Langley offers a convincing Africana womanist reading of the male slave narrator himself in *The Interesting Narrative of the Life of Olaudah Equiano or Gustavus Vassa, the African*. In highlighting Equiano's journey, taking him through the obvious physical trials and tribulations, Dr. Langley identifies those transforming experiences, which evolve to his ultimate position as co-partner with the female companion, thus enabling us to witness, too, his

Chapter 1: Africana Womanism: Authenticity and Collectivity in Securing Social Justice

> . . . conversions from African nobleman to African slave, from African slave to Atlantic slave, from Atlantic flaneur, from Atlantic flaneur to Christian . . . from husband and father to African American and British ancestor. . . . Equiano's re-visioning and re-visiting of dominant political and spiritual discourses through sub-dominant lenses is illustrative of his complication and deployment of gendered critiques of racial oppression that do not rely solely on Western-derived notions of gender. In her theory of Africana womanism, Hudson-Weems delineates the primary concerns of African men and women thus: "The African womanist, focusing on her particular circumstances, comes from an entirely different perspective, one that embraces the concept of collective struggle for the entire family in its overall struggle for liberation survival, thereby resolving the question of her place in the venue of women's issues" (Langley, "Equiano's Landscapes" 46–47; Hudson-Weems, Africana Womanism 44).

That said, in the headnote to Hudson-Weems' article, "Africana Womanism: An Historical, Global Perspective for Women of African Descent," the editors stated the following relative to their position on the theory of Africana Womanism:

> "The first African American woman intellectual to formulate a position on Africana womanism was Clenora Hudson-Weems, author of the 1993 groundbreaking study *Africana Womanism: Reclaiming Ourselves*. Taking the strong position that Black women should not pattern their liberation after Eurocentric feminism but after the historic and triumphant woman of African descent, Hudson-Weems has launched a new critical discourse in the Black Women's Literary Movement" (Hill et al., *Call and Response* 1735).

On the matter of terminology, Africana Womanism and Africana-Melanated Womanism, they are basically on the same page, explicating the dynamics of the identity of a committed body, resolute in the dedication to the family. A modified version of Africana Womanism, the term African-Melanated Womanism evolved much later, which in actuality is more of a terminological evolution, than a conceptual distinction. It established a more overt notion of an all-inclusive Africana global concept in the revolutionary theoretical paradigm, maintaining family centrality, which is rooted in its beginnings, dating back to African antiquity, many centuries before the terminology itself was introduced.

> Therefore, I did not create the phenomenon in and of itself, but rather observed Africana women, documented our reality, and [named and] refined a paradigm relative to who we are, what we do, and what we believe in as a people (Hudson-Weems, "Self-Naming" 449).

In the mid-1980s, the original term, Africana Womanism, earlier called Black Womanism, was created for the express purpose of naming and defining all women of African descent in her ongoing quest for authentic existence. She remained "In Concert with Her Male

Counterpart in the Struggle," one of the seminal characteristics of Africana Womanism. Addressing issues confronting her family is itself the global move toward securing our true freedom, for the lives of all Africana people have been relegated for centuries to a sub-level position. Hence, it was critical that an authentic paradigm be established, with its own authentic name and definition, needed for an Afrocentric perspective wherein we place Africa at the center of the analysis of people of Africa and the African diaspora (Asante, *The Afrocentric Idea* 1987). We must be situated within the realm of our own urgent concerns, with the insistence upon our own set of priorities. Such an analysis enables the needs of African people in general to be properly addressed, as the end goal for all Africana people is to have a fair and an equal level of existence in the eradication of an unjust system, monopolized and dominated by a selfish controlling dominant culture.

According to Dr. Ama Mazama, an Afrocentric scholar of Guadeloupe, in her article, "The Afrocentric Paradigm,"

> Clenora Hudson-Weems coined the term Africana Womanism in 1987 out of the realization of the total inadequacy of feminism and the like theories (e.g. Black feminism, African womanism, or womanism) to grasp the reality of African women, let alone give us the means to change that reality (Mazama 400–401).

Dr. Molefi Kete Asante, who coined the term Afrocentricity, succinctly corroborates Mazama's sentiments in the Afterthought in Hudson-Weems' sequel Africana Womanism book, *Africana Womanist Literary Theory*. Here he defines Africana Womanism as an Afrocentric movement of the significant participation of the female, who

> is critical to a full understanding of the substantive contributions of women scholars to our total liberation. It is true, as Ama Mazama has observed, that Africana womanism seeks to correct the total inadequacy of feminism to appreciate the reality of African women. In fact, what Hudson-Weems demonstrates is that no transformation can take place without a rethinking of the way Africana women have been viewed and view themselves in the Western world (Asante 138–139).

As the definitive Afrocentric scholar, Dr. Asante has written countless volumes on this ever-evolving concept. However, despite his clarion call for authenticity, there are those who fail to appreciate this need and support it, which in the final greatly weakens the overall movement with such a dilution. Dr. Adele Newson-Horst notes that

> Notwithstanding Hudson-Weems's long-standing insistence upon self-naming and self-defining, many Back women scholars, who have built their careers on aligning themselves with feminist theory, insist upon making feminist theory fit Black women's activities. Hudson-Weems questions in "Cultural and Agenda Conflicts in Academia: Critical Issues for Africana Woman's Studies" (*WJBS* 1989): [that] "procrusteans have mis-labeled Africana women activists, like Sojourner Truth and other

prominent Africana women freedom fighters such as Harriett Tubman, and Ida B. Wells, simply because they were women." (*Contemporary Africana Theory* 361; *WJBS* 186).

With this illumination, followed through by the execution of authentic acts and authentic ways of being—the elimination of centuries of ethnic inequality, which is a painful and incomprehensible reality that unjustifiably violates any human reasoning for true humanity—the mandate for social justice now escalating at a faster speed than ever is clearly in order for bringing about a final closure.

And we can achieve this goal effectively via collectivity. As the ancient African proverb strongly advocates, "It takes a village to raise a child," which is an excellent analogy for the perfect prescription for resolving the global battle of Africana people against racial dominance. We must unyieldingly and collectively fight against racism, with full knowledge that whether in the United States, South America, the Caribbean Islands, Europe, Canada, or elsewhere, clearly white supremacy and racial dominance have dominated the scene. Even in Africa, the original birthplace of Africana people, and perceived to be that of people in general, Africana people have been informed and dominated by the other. A more obvious example is the assigned position of Blacks in South Africa, where Africaners, not Africans, are the rulers of the land wherein the privileged population, although a vast minority group, ironically dictate the laws and rules guiding that region and its Black majority population. Therefore, this phenomenon is critical, as time is well overdue for Africana people to unanimously reclaim total control over both our lives and our land for our children.

It cannot be stated enough that due to the pervasiveness of racism worldwide, Africana people everywhere must come together in a global movement dedicated to a fair, just, and rewarding society for all its people. Because Africana women, by their very nature, are family centered, a defining feature of Africana Womanism, we cannot be easily separated from the men and children in our lives. Our very existence, in terms of interacting with each other and combatting daily confrontations, is interconnected. In describing the lives and activities of Africana women and life in general, we stand as a unit, one that is best described as an integrated part of a whole that should be neither delinked nor analyzed as separate entities with separate priorities. In other words, the lives and concerns of Africana people and their destinies are interconnected as a viable part of each other, as demonstrated in Sojourner Truth's powerful and much quoted 1852 self-actualization oration, "And Ain't I A Woman":

> "Da man ober dar say dat women needs to be helped into carriages and lifted ober ditches, and to have the best place everywhere. Nobody eber helped me into carriages, or ober mud puddles, or give me any best place. And Ain't I a Woman?" (Truth)

Indeed, she is! However, while the race factor for her and Blacks in general comes first, as "her oration demonstrates the primacy of overcoming racial obstacles before addressing the absurdity of female subjugation," she must consider all three parts of her identity as a collective (Hudson-Weems, "Africana Womanism: An Historical Global Perspective" 1736–37). To be sure, it is because of the fact that she is Black that she is denied the common privileges of white women, but she knows too well that she is also a woman, and thus, a victim of patriarchal limitations as well. In this notable speech, which has erroneously been referred to by many as a "the feminist manifesto," she dramatically prioritizes her triple plight as race, class, and gender. Her race is an obvious, as she expresses herself in a distinct dialect, identified as the Black vernacular, which Dr. Robert Williams calls "Ebonics." In "Ebonics: Re-Claiming and Re-Defining Our Language," he, too, calls for the need for defining ourselves, which could and should include our Black verbal expressions (*Contemporary Africana Theory, Thought and Action* 241–250). From first identifying herself as Black, Sojourner Truth then moves to identify her status as economically disadvantaged, apparently due to her race. While the question of gender—meaning virtually nothing relative to her being among this *white* community of women—is that final blow for women in general, due to a long-established patriarchal system, Sojourner, in an ironic twist, interestingly closes her famous oration on that note.

Continuing the dialogue on the importance of male and female compatibility in advancing our overall struggle against racial dominance is South African journalist, Gracious Madondo, in "Why Africa Relates to Africana Womanism," in *The Southern Times: The Newspaper for Southern Africa*. She contends that

> . . . unlike the Western rooted feminist approach to literature . . . Africana womanism speaks of male and female compatibility, where men and women co-exist together without conflict, [realizing that] the real cause of inequalities in Africa [is] colonialist patriarchal tendencies (Madondo 2018).

This is one of many publications appearing across the continent of Africa that emphasizes this fact. Even in the literary arena, authors emphasize this phenomenon in their novels. For example, Mariama Bâ, Senegalese writer and author of the first African publishers' Noma Award-Winning novel, So *Long a Letter*, highlights interdependence, one of the features of Africana male–female relationships embodied in her protagonist. Ramatoulaye asserts that she "cannot imagine life without a man," despite the fact that all male–female relationships are not perfect and that the system of polygamy, inauthentic to African life, actually came to Africa with the invasion of colonialism by European. It represents the ugly system that reduces women to the low status of an underling:

> Bâ's attack on a polygamous society that subjugates women, and her interest in the rights of Africana women in *So Long A Letter* does not justify categorizing it as a feminist novel. To begin with, the author dedicates the book "To all women and men of good will," thereby demonstrating her natural inclination to include men as a very important part of women's lives. Moreover, it is not so much the subject itself of female subjugation in the novel, but rather the way in which the protagonist treats the problem that distinguishes the novel from typical feminist writings. According to Acholonu, feminist fiction "aims essentially at establishing a feminist kingdom which spurns compromise between the sexes." [2] However, instead of attacking the male directly, the author

attacks the patriarchal system, one to which the male, too, becomes subject. But more important, it must be reiterated that the concerns for women and women issues are not the exclusive venue of the feminist alone. Quite the contrary, the Africana womanist, too, is interested in the welfare and position of the woman; however, her treatment of those issues are different. For instance, the Africana womanist does not treat the woman as one divorced from the need for a traditional family nucleus, which is, after all, tantamount to traditional Africana society. Instead, the Africana womanist presents the woman, even though oftentimes victimized, as one who is inextricably connected to a family unit, which ultimately defines her true meaning and purpose in today's world, ridden with chaos and confusion (Hudson-Weems, *Africana Womanism* 62).

Many in South America, too, such as Brazil and the Caribbean, wherein positive Africana Womanism research and commentaries reside, offer ongoing dialogues about authentic Africana existence. The global family centered paradigm demonstrating the applicability of Africana Womanism in our world is, indeed, rapidly growing. Dr. Antonio Tillis contributes to the dialogue in his seminal article, "Nancy Morejón's 'Mujer Negra': An Africana Womanist Reading" (Tillis 2001). In Dr. Doris Gilliam's doctoral dissertation, "I Have to Know Who I Am: An Africana Womanist Analysis of Afro-Brazilian Identity in the Literature of Mirian Alves, Esmeralda Ribeiro and Conceição Evaristo," she presents a thorough examination of the identity of the Black woman in literature (Gilliam 2013). She, like Tillis, uses Africana Womanism as an appropriate, authentic tool of analysis, the former focusing on the prioritization of the race factor in the interpretation of the Cuban poet, while the latter opens up with self-naming and self-defining, the two critical features representing the first steps in identifying who we are as an Africana people, which is contrary to the assigned identity given us by the dominant culture.

In the United States, Nobel Laureate, Toni Morrison, in a short, but profound statement, comments on this issue of the importance of self-naming and self-definition, gleamed through the narrator's observation in *Beloved*— "Definitions belonged to the definers, not the defined" (Morrison's *Beloved* 190). Hudson-Weems elaborates of this long-standing negativity of such an existence:

> Toni Morrison's narrator in *Beloved* aptly articulates the forced position of the Africanan during slavery as one who is defined not by self, but rather by the dominant culture—the definer. It is a peculiar predicament, one that Africanans have been experiencing for centuries. This situation must be challenged and changed if Africana people the world over are to realize true parity. It is in this vein that the Africana woman is being reclaimed, renamed and redefined. (Hudson-Weems, *Africana Womanism*, 5th Fifth ed. 35).

Clearly, the system had licensed the dominant culture with the right to dictate the legitimate. Our mission, then, in theorizing our identity, must necessarily challenge that inaccurate norm, substituting, instead, what is authentic and appropriate for us. This, then, becomes a compelling act, one of theorizing the true nature of our existence. As literature reflects life, analyses of how the 18 descriptors of Africana Womanism play out in literary texts are quite successful and plentiful.

Beginning here with a truly dynamic Post-Civil War and Reconstruction writer, Anna Julia Cooper (1858–1964), Dr. Larese Hubbard, a perceptive literary critic of early writers of this era, has done substantive Africana womanist readings of Cooper, particularly regarding her book, *A Voice from the South* (1892). In Dr. Hubbard's "Anna Julia Cooper and Africana Womanism: Some Early Conceptual Contributions," appearing in *Black Women, Gender, and Families*, she does a counter analysis of the author who has been erroneously referred to my many as a prefeminist, much like many other Black women writers/activists, such as Ida B. Wells.

A journalist and Anti-Lynching Crusader for Social Justice, Wells, born on July 16, 1861 in Holly Springs, MS, made her lifetime commitment to Social Justice for her people following the March 9, 1892 brutal lynching of her dear friend, Thomas Moss, and his two business partners, Calvin McDowell and William Henry Stewart.

> His spirit in smoke ascended to high heaven.
> His father, by the cruelest way of pain,
> Had bidden him to his bosom once again;
> The awful sin remained still unforgiven.
> All night a bright and solitary star
> (Perchance the one that ever guided him,
> Yet gave him up at last to Fate's wild whim)
> Hung pitifully o'er the swinging char.
> Day dawned, and soon the mixed crowds came to view
> The ghastly body swaying in the sun:
> The women thronged to look, but never a one
> Showed sorrow in her eyes of steely blue;
> And little lads, lynchers that were to be,
> Danced round the dreadful thing in fiendish glee.
>
> (Claude McKay, 1920)

This sonnet is evocative of the fate of the three and moreover, the attitude of the whites (men, women and children) surrounding the occasion, as interpreted by Hudson-Weems in "Claude McKay: Black Protest in Western Traditional Form":

"The Lynching" … depicts a Black Christ figure sacrificed by an antagonistically hostile and insensitive White mob. [In contrast], it is the star, not a fellow creature, that expresses a sense of sympathy for the lynchee. … The little children, the supposedly embodiment of innocence, happily and fearlessly dance around the gruesome figure. … This type of insidious attitude is cyclical; the practice of implanting these attitudes in the minds of the offspring only renders the despicable perpetuation of lawful" inhumanity in the American system. (Hudson-Weems, *WJBS*, Spring 1992, 2–3)

Yoked with the sin of being born black, these three men were not allowed to be ambitious. Because they opened up a grocery Store, People's Groceries, in their neighborhood on Mississippi Blvd. and Walker in Memphis, TN, feared of possibly becoming competition to another grocery store in that community by its white proprietor, they were lynched. And

Chapter 1: Africana Womanism: Authenticity and Collectivity in Securing Social Justice

because the first priority of the brave, family-centered Africana Womanist, Ida B. Wells, was the safety of the entire family (men, women and children), not just herself and the female in general who naturally need the protection of the male counterpart, she rose to the occasion, demonstrating an equal concern about her male companions. In exposing the historic lynching in her newspaper, *The Memphis Free Speech and Headlight*, and during national and international engagements where she spoke out vehemently against this phenomenon, she was exiled from Memphis, threatened to be lynched should she ever return (Willis, *The Memphis Diary of Ida B. Wells*, 1995). It was not until the symbolic "Home-Coming" that this international icon, along with her Chicago descendants, her great-great granddaughter, Michelle Duster (Author), and great-great grandson, Dan Duster (Keynote Banquet Speaker), was welcomed back. The week-long celebration in her honor—beginning on July 11, 2021, organized by The Memphis Memorial Committee (including Elaine Turner, owner of Heritage Tours), and chaired by the Rev. Dr. Lasimba M. Gray—culminated on her birthday, July 16, in the unveiling of an Ida B. Wells bronze statue, erected in the new Ida B. Wells Plaza, located on the corner of the famous Beale Street and 4th Street.

Cooper and Wells are clearly kindred spirits. The former articulates the drive behind the very nature of the interconnectedness of the African man and woman, given the inseparable bond between the two as expressed in her book *A Voice from the South*: "Woman's cause is man's cause. We rise or sink together, dwarfed or Godlike, bound or free." In a preoccupation with the demands of our on-going liberation struggle during the time of reconstruction following the Civil War and the Emancipation Proclamation, the Dr. Hubbard insisted upon the importance of remaining a family-centered, race defending collective. She relies upon the characteristics of Africana Womanism in assessing Cooper, whose strong proclamation says it best, powerfully acted out by Ida B. Wells' life-time commitment to our life-saving factor, "In It Together," via supporting each other. We must protect that reality and hold to it, solid validation that Ida B. Wells-Barnett is the embodiment of the Africana Womanist, her very *raison d'être* for existence. Moreover, we must also insist upon this priority of the race factor for Africana people in securing our ultimate victory, always driven by the parental practice of spiritual reliance upon God for direction and support (Charles and Hilda Williams, "Pre-Africana Womanist: Ida B. Wells-Barnett").

In a leap "from slavery to freedom," demonstrating how this sentiment plays out relative to the Africana male–female struggle for total emancipation, we focus on Claude McKay, a Harlem Renaissance writer and master sonneteer. In his powerful poem, "If We Must Die," written following World War I when Blacks returned to the United States, only to be reminded of the reality that despite the myriad sacrifices they had made during their tenure on foreign lands as supportive Americans, they were the targets of wide-spread brutal attacks as lynchees, disrespected and invariably not regarded and thus, not treated as fellow human beings. Their commitment to change this reality, expressing Black pride and demanding the continuation of the legacy of collectivity and interconnectedness, is ever evident. To be sure, the emphasis on the decade strong, proud Blacks of the Harlem Renaissance of the 1920s is crystalized in the popular persona, "The New Negro," one who would return any insult given, rather than simply acquiesce. Hence, he stands as the embodiment of a strong Black man, boldly taking a stand in McKay's memorable sonnet, "If We Must Die," wherein the poet strategically casts, in an uncustomary format of antithetical elements—Black protest in a western tradition form, the sonnet:

> If we must die—let it not be like hogs
> Hunted and penned in an inglorious spot,
> While round us bark the mad and hungry dogs,
> Making their mock at our accursed lot.
> If we must die—oh, let us nobly die,
> So that our precious blood may not be shed
> In vain; then even the monsters we defy
> Shall be constrained to honor us though dead!
> Oh, Kinsmen! We must meet the common foe;
> Though far outnumbered, let us show us brave,
> And for their thousand blows deal one deathblow!
> What though before us lies the open grave?
> Like men we'll face the murderous, cowardly pack,
> Pressed to the wall, dying, but fighting back!

This position is a natural one, one which Harlem Renaissance's most prolific poet, Langston Hughes, anticipates in his poem, "A Dream Deferred/Harlem."

Indeed, an explosion of some sort, in the form of a riot or retaliation, will inevitably evolve, as the victim must in some way take some protective form of action. These two Harlem Renaissance authors vividly depict the inferred victim as "the new Negro, the militant, who must bravely and unapologetically stand "erect against their [American's] hate." This is articulated in yet another of McKay's memorable sonnets, "America," wherein he expresses an ironic, oxymoronic patriotic posture of love for his country in the midst of racial disfavor:

> Although she feeds me bread of bitterness,
> And sinks into my throat her tiger's tooth,
> Stealing my breath of life, I will confess
> I love this cultured hell that tests my youth.
> Her vigor flows like tides into my blood,
> Giving me strength erect against her hate,
> Her bigness sweeps my being like a flood.
> Yet, as a rebel fronts a king in state,
> I stand within her walls with not a shred
> Of terror, malice, not a word of jeer.
> Darkly I gaze into the days ahead,
> And see her might and granite wonders there,
> Beneath the touch of Time's unerring hand,
> Like priceless treasures sinking in the sand.
>
> (McKay)

With the dehumanization/brutalization of Blacks, the persona's projection of an inevitable fate that America will suffer—tragically "sinking in the sand"—stands out as a warning that if injustice continues, there will be a day of reckoning. Despite all, time included, according to Debra Walker King in *African Americans and the Culture of Pain*, "we still

Chapter 1: Africana Womanism: Authenticity and Collectivity in Securing Social Justice 17

have open sores, injuries bleeding from ongoing assaults of racism and prejudice, blatant and inadvertent stereotyping, defensiveness, denial, and racial hurt" (160). One is here reminded of the deep, profound wounds, emotional as well as physical, that Blacks continue to suffer, such as revealed in Morrison's Pulitzer Prize-Winning novel, *Beloved*, wherein the fragile predicament of the woman is presented. Her vulnerable status cries out for emotional protection during her moments of emotional insecurities:

> "That anybody white could take you whole self for anything that came to mind. Not just work, kill or maim you, but dirty you. Dirty you so bad you couldn't like yourself anymore" (Morrison, *Beloved* 251)

That support will come in the form of a collective initiative on the part of the male counterpart, coming forth during the private moments of his female counterpart. He must protect her, giving her a sense of worthiness when she is left with a feeling of absolute no self-esteem. Clearly, we need each other to strengthen ourselves emotionally, as well as physically. Physical and emotional support is also evidenced in another of Morrison's novels, *Home*, in which the protagonist, Frank Money, is called back home to rescue his sister, Cee, from the clutches of her employer and physician, Dr. Beauregard Scott, an unrepentant Confederate. Endangering her life, the doctor incessantly engages in racist experiments in eugenics, rendering Cee both infertile and near-death; however, her loving brother saves her. Cee could not have survived had Frank not hastily come to her rescue, no more so than Blacks in general during slavery could have survived without the support of each other, led by God. How collective is this Movement—God, man and woman, indeed, a time-tested reality through the centuries?

An excellent companion piece for these inspiring selections is Maya Angelou's powerful poem, "Still I Rise."

Further Africana womanist readings of later twentieth century writers include many national and international Africana womanist novelists. In the analyses of some of these writers, Dr. Betty Taylor Thompson joins as yet another perceptive contributor for the 2001 *The Western Journal of Black Studies* Special Issue on Africana Womanism, for which I served as guess editor. In her article, "Common Bonds from Africa to the U.S.: Africana Womanist Literary Analysis," she contends that "there is a distinct link between the concerns of African and African American women writers in the characters, themes, and women's issues and concerns that appear in their fiction, dramas, and essays" (Thompson 177). Here, she does close readings of such award-winning novels as Toni Morrison's *Song of Solomon* and *Beloved*, Gloria Naylor's *Bailey's Café*, Flora Nwapa's *Efuru*, Mariama Bâ's *So Long a Letter*, and Tsitsi Dangarembga's *Nervous Conditions*, to name a few.

Exemplar Africana womanist novelists are also represented in *Africana Womanism: Reclaiming Ourselves*, wherein the focus for Part II of the book is the application of Africana Womanism theory to five Africana womanist novels: Zora Neale Hurston's *Their Eyes Were Watching God*, Mariama Bâ's *So Long a Letter*, Paule Marshall's *Praisesong for the Widow*, Toni Morrison's *Beloved*, and Teri McMillan's *Disappearing Acts*. In the sequel Africana Womanism book, *Africana Womanist Literary Theory*, an Africana Womanist's reading of Sister Souljah's *No Disrespect* is introduced, entitled "Sister Souljah's *No Disrespect*: The Africana Womanist's Dilemma." All of these novels offer powerful authentic interpretations, demonstrating the presence of the eighteen characteristics of the Africana

Womanist to varying degrees, as they move through life as true, proud Africana womanists.

And the list continues with many Africana womanist representations both inside and outside of the United States, as well as inside and outside of the Academy, while demonstrating and promoting the presence of our strong commitment to our authentic missions, demeanor, and overall persona. These women hail from the world of politics, entertainment, the media, and so on, many of whom are everyday mothers and wives, who have committed themselves to the elevation of the global Africana community. To be sure, the myriad studies utilizing the Africana womanist tool of analysis in the study of Africana people in general is not only found in the United States, but throughout the African diaspora, sufficient enough to make the point that Africana Womanism is alive and well, strongly representing an authentic theoretical methodology, proven to be a powerful useful tool of analysis in accurately assessing Africana life, its historical and its cultural dynamics covering all dimensions of life. The following poem recapitulates the essence of the overall ways and mannerism of true Africana/Africana-Melanated Women:

"Africana Womanism: I Got Your Back, Boo" (2009)

Don't you know by now, girl, we're all In It Together!
Family-Centrality—that's it; we're going nowhere without the other
That means the men, the women, and children, too,
Truly collectively working—"I got your back, Boo."

Racism means the violation of our constitutional rights,
Which creates on-going legal, and even physical fights;
This 1st priority for humankind is doing what it must do,
Echoing our 1st lady, Michelle—"I got your back, Boo."

Classism is the hoarding of financial privileges,
Privileges we must all have now in pursuit of happiness.
Without a piece of the financial pie, we're doomed to have a coup;
Remember—protect the other—"I got your back, Boo."
Sexism, the final abominable sin of female subjugation,
A battle we must wage right now to restore our family relations.
All forms of sin inevitably fall under 1 of the 3 offenses.
Africana Womanism, "I Got Your Back, Boo," corrects our common senses.

This four-stanza poem, in which the race, class, and gender factors are prioritized, can serve as a model today for all to come together in a collective struggle. As we follow the lead of the father of the modern Civil Rights Movement of the 1950s and the 1960s, Dr. Martin Luther King, Jr., we must continue to stride toward freedom, as the global icon himself so eloquently calls for in his book, *Stride Toward Freedom*.

All being said, it is clear that more than anything, we desire to leave an authentic legacy for our future generations to have as they continue a legacy of saving our thoughts as well as our pride, integrity, and survival tactics needed to eliminate the ongoing threat to our existence. Imagine how powerful it would be to see our own identifying and strategizing ways of empowering ourselves to create victories for ourselves, instead of succumbing to the dominant culture's negative evaluations of our worth, and the limitations continuously inflicted upon us as their means of maintaining their superiority complex. And what a victory, when we at last are of one accord and mind! To finally know that their assigned inferiority–superiority identifiers for Blacks and whites respectively are incorrect and nonexistent—a great victory, indeed, with the realization that we are a beautiful Africana people, endowed with God-given intelligence and abilities, which must be acknowledged.

As fellow human beings, we, too, aspire to ultimately realize our dreams of greater heights: "Ah, but a man's reach should exceed his grasp, or what's a heaven for?" (Tennyson's "Adrea del Sarto"). The problem is that in the case of Blacks, we often fall short of our goals resulting from impasses set forth by the dominant culture. As Dr. Mark Christian, editor of *Integrated But Unequal: Black Faculty in Predominately White Space*, so apply notes in his Conclusion,

> "all are equal, but some are more equal than others." That is the reality, we are supposedly all treated equally, but the outcome of such "equality" is skewed most often favorably toward those from the White cultural groups, and those who assimilate to such (229).

We must, therefore, call a halt once and for all to anything that prohibits us from achieving what is our, including the right to secure and celebrate who we really are and moreover, what course of action we should be taking. And we can do this as a strong Africana people, working together—Men, Women, Children—In Concert in a global stride toward Victory for our own. This is the ultimate goal of true Africana Womanism! Moreover, by extension, isn't this precisely what the quest for human/civil rights is all about in the first place—the humanity of all humankind?

Bibliography

Asante, Molefi Kete. *The Afrocentric Idea*. Temple UP, 1987.

Asante, Molefi Kete. The Afterword in *Africana Womanist Literary Theory* by Clenora Hudson-Weems. Africa World Press, 2004, pp. 137–139.

Christian, Mark. The Afterword in *Africana Womanism: Reclaiming Ourselves*. 5th ed., Routledge, 2019; 1st ed., 1993.

Christian, Mark. *Integrated But Unequal: Black Faculty in Predominately White Space.* Africa World Press, 2012.

Cooper, Anna Julia. *A Voice from the South: By a Woman of the South.* Oxford UP, 1988.

Gilliam, Doris. "I Have to Know Who I Am: An Africana Womanist Analysis of Afro-Brazilian Identity in the Literature of Mirian Alves, Esmeralda Ribeiro and Conceição Evaristo." 2013. Florida State University, PhD dissertation.

Hill, Patricia Liggins, et al. *Call and Response: The Riverside Anthology of the Africana American Literary Tradition.* Mifflin Company, 1998.

Hubbard, Larese. "Anna Julia Cooper and Africana Womanism: Some Early Conceptual Contributions." *Black Women, Gender, and Families*, vol. 4, no. 2, 2010, pp. 31–53.

Hudson-Weems, Clenora. "Africana Womanism: An Historical Global Perspective for Women of African Descent." *Call & Response: The Riverside Anthology of the Africana American Literary Tradition.* Houghton Mifflin Company, 1998, pp. 1735–39.

Hudson-Weems, Clenora. "Africana Womanism: An Overview." *Out of the Revolution: The Development of Africana Studies,* eidted by Delores Aldridge and Charlene Young, Lexington Books, 2000, pp. 205–17.

Hudson-Weems, Clenora. *Africana Womanism: Reclaiming Ourselves*, 5th ed., Routledge, 2019; 1st ed., 1993.

Hudson-Weems, Clenora. *Africana Womanist Literary Theory.* Africa World Press, 2004.

Hudson-Weems, Clenora. "Claude McKay: Black Protest in Western Traditional Form." *The Western Journal of Black Studies*, vol. 16, no. 1, 1992, pp. 1–5.

Hudson-Weems, Clenora. "Cultural and Agenda Conflicts in Academia: Critical Issues for Africana Women's Studies." *The Western Journal for Black Studies*, vol. 13, no. 4, 1989, pp. 185–89.

Hudson-Weems, Clenora. Foreword in *Rediscoursing African Womanhood in the Search for Sustainable Renaissance: Africana Womanism in Multi-disciplinary Approaches*, edited by Itai Muwati, et al., College Press Publishers, 2012, pp. xii–xv.

Hudson-Weems, Clenora. "Self-Naming and Self-Definition: An Agenda for Survival." *Sisterhood, Feminisms and Power: From Africa to the Diaspora*, edited by Obioma Nnaemeka, Africa World Press, 1998, pp. 449–52.

Hudson-Weems, Clenora. "The African American Literary Tradition." *The African American Experience: An Historiographical and Bibliographical Guide*, edited by Arvah E. Strickland and Robert E. Weems, Jr., Greenwood, 2001, pp. 116–43.

King, Debra Walker. *African Americans and the Culture of Pain.* U of Virginia P, 2008.

Langley, April. "Equiano's Landscapes: Viewpoints and Vistas from the Looking Glass, the Lens, and the Kaleidoscope." *The Western Journal of Black Studies*, vol. 25, no. 1, 2001, pp. 46–60.

Madondo, Gracious. "Why Africa Relate to Africana Womanism." *The Southern Times: The Newspaper for Southern Africa*, 19 July 2018.

Mazama, Ama. "The Afrocentric Paradigm: Contours and Definitions." *Journal of Black Studies,* vol. 31, no. 4, 2001, pp. 387–405.

Morrison, Toni. *Beloved.* Alfred A. Knopf, 1987.

Muwati, Itai, and Mguni, Zifikile. "An Anatomy of Negative Male-Female Relations in Mabasa's Novel *Ndafa Here?* A Human Rights Issue." *Rediscoursing African Womanhood in the Search for Sustainable Renaissance: Africana Womanism in Multi-disciplinary Approaches*. College Press Publishers, 2012, pp. 50–62.

Muwati, Itai, Mguni, Zifikile, Gwekwerere, Tavengwa, Magosvongwe, Ruby. *Rediscoursing African Womanhood in the Search for Sustainable Renaissance: Africana Womanism in Multi-disciplinary Approaches*. College Press Publishers, 2012.

Newson-Horst, Adele S. "*Mama Day*: An Africana Womanist Reading." *Contemporary Africana Theory, Thought and Action: A Guide to Africana Studies*, edited by Clenora Hudson-Weems, Africa World Press, 2007, pp. 359–72.

Thompson, Betty Taylor. "Common Bonds from Africa to the U.S.: Africana Womanist Literary Analysis." *The Western Journal of Black Studies*, vol. 25, no. 3, 2001, pp. 177–84.

Tillis, Antonio D. "Nancy Morejón's 'Mujer Negra': An Africana Womanist Reading." *Hispanic Journal*, vol. 22, no. 2, 2001, pp. 483–94.

Truth, Sojourner. "And Ain't I a Woman." *Narrative of Sojourner Truth*. Arno and *New York Times*, 1968.

Williams, Robert L. "Ebonics: Re-Claiming and Re-Defining Ur Language." *Contemporary Africana Theory, Thought and Action: A Guide to Africana Studies*, edited by Clenora Hudson-Weems, Africa World Press, 2007, pp. 2241–250.

Applications, Exercises, Questions, Implications, and Challenges

1. What is Africana Womanism and its priorities in combatting racial dominance?
2. How does Africana Womanism differ from Africana-Melanated Womanism?
3. List all five female-based paradigms and how each differs from the other.
4. Is interconnectedness more suited for the Movement than intersectionality?
5. Can a man be considered or called an Africana Womanist? Why or why not?
6. List the eighteenth distinct characteristics of Africana Womanism.
7. List the fifteen positive/negative elements of male/female relationships.
8. How can Africana Womanism empower the Africana community?
9. Why is Family-Centrality essential to the liberation movement?
10. List some twenty-first century figures to compliment earlier writers herein.

Class Discussions and **Oral Reports** on two timely African American Novels representing the significance of key themes, that is, the Prison Industrial System and Eugenics, today and thus, are very appropriate and much-needed for debate now. These hot topics can be approached as we engage in close Africana Womanist Readings of the two Award-Winning novelists—**Toni Morrison** and **James Baldwin**:

1. Although James Baldwin's novel-turned movie *IF BEALE STREET COULD TALK*, differs in a few ways from the original 1970s book publication, the salient characteristics of Africana Womanism yet ring out loudly, such as male–female compatibility in the struggle against racism. Point out a few instances of this and more, also utilizing the movie version of the novel, which can be seen on *YouTube*.
2. Toni Morrison's **Home** will be augmented by an interview with the novelist herself on her twenty-first century masterpiece; it can be accessed from *YouTube*.

Chapter 2
Afrocentricity and Transformation: Understanding a Movement

Contributed by:
Molefi Kete Asante, PhD

Afrocentricity is an intellectual perspective deriving its name from the centrality of African people and phenomena in the interpretation of data. Maulana Karenga, a major figure in the Afrocentric Movement, says "it is a quality of thought that is rooted in the cultural image and human interest of African people." The Afrocentric school was founded in the late twentieth century with the launching of the book *Afrocentricity*, where theory and practice were merged as necessary elements in a rise to consciousness. Among the early influences were Kariamu Welsh, Abu Abarry, C. T. Keto, Linda James Myers, J. A. Sofola, and others. Afrocentricity examined some of the same issues that confronted a group calling themselves the Black Psychologists who argued along lines established by Bobby Wright, Amos Wilson, Na'im Akbar, Kobi Kambon, Wade Nobles, Patricia Newton, and several other psychologists. African American scholars trained in political science, history, and sociology such as Leonard Jeffries, Tony Martin, Vivian Gordon, Kwame Nantambu, Barbara Wheeler, James Turner, and Charshee McIntyre, greatly influenced by the works of Yosef Ben-Jochannan and John Henrik Clarke, had already begun the process of seeking a non-European way to conceptualize the African experience prior to the development of Afrocentric theory.

On the other hand, Afrocentricity found its inspirational source in the philosophy of Kawaida, a concept founded by Maulana Karenga in the 1960s, that establishes a set of values—Nguzo Saba, the Seven Principles—guiding an African-centered way of engaging and viewing the world. Kawaida's long-standing concern that the cultural crisis is a defining characteristic of twentieth century African reality in the diaspora, as the nationality crisis is the principal issue on the African continent. Afrocentricity sought to address these crises by repositioning the African person and reality from the margins of European thought, attitude, and doctrines to a centered, positively located place within the realm of science and culture.

Afrocentricity finds its grounding in the intellectual and activist precursors who first suggested culture as a critical corrective to a displaced agency among Africans. Recognizing that Africans in the diaspora had been deliberately deculturalized and made to accept the conqueror's codes of conduct and modes of behavior, the Afrocentrist discovered that the interpretative and theoretical grounds had also been moved. Thus, synthesizing the best of Alexander Crummell, Martin Delaney, Edward Wilmot Blyden, Marcus Garvey, Paul Robeson, Anna Julia Cooper, Ida B. Wells-Barnett, Larry Neal, Carter G. Woodson, Willie Abraham, Frantz Fanon, Malcolm X, Cheikh Anta Diop, and the later W. E. B. DuBois, Afrocentricity project an innovation in criticism and interpretation. It is in some senses a paradigm, a framework, and a dynamic. It is not a worldview, however, and should not be confused with Africanity, which is essentially the way African people—any African people—live according to customs, traditions, and mores of their society. One can be born in Africa, follow African styles, and modes of living, and practice African religion arid still not be Afrocentric; to be Afrocentric one has to have a self-conscious awareness of the need for centering. Thus, those individuals who live in Africa and recognize the decentering of their minds because of European colonization may self-consciously choose to be demonstratively in tune with their own agency. If so, this becomes a revolutionary act of will that cannot be achieved merely by wearing African clothes or having an African name.

School of Thought

Among contemporaries, the works of Maulana Karenga, Abu Abarry, Chinweizu, Ngugi wa Thiong'o, J. A. Sofola, Ama Mazama, Aboubacry Moussa Lam, Terry Kershaw, Walter Rodney, Leachim Semaj, Danjuma Modupe, Kwame Nantambu, Errol Henderson, Runoko Rashidi, Charles Finch, Nah Dove, Marimba Ani, Aisha Blackshire-Belay, Theophile Obenga, and Oba T'shaka have been inspiring in defining the nature of the principal Afrocentric school of thought. The principal motive behind their intellectual works seems to be the use of knowledge for the cultural, social, political, and economic transformation of African people by suggesting the necessity for a recentering of African minds in a way that brings about a liberating consciousness. Indeed, Afrocentricty contends that there could be no social or economic struggle that would make sense if African people remained enamored with the philosophical and intellectual positions of white hegemonic nationalism as it relates to Africa and African people. At base, therefore, the work of the Afrocentric school of thought is a political one, in the sense that all social knowledge has a political purpose. No one constructs or writes about repositioning and recentering merely for the sake of self-indulgence; none could afford to do so because the African dispossession appears so great and the displacing myths so pervasive that simply to watch the procession of African peripheralization is to acquiesce in African decentering.

The Afrocentrist contends that passion can never be a substitute for argument as argument should not be a substitution for passion. Afrocentric intellectuals may disagree over the finer points of interpretation and over some facts, but the overall project of relocation and reorientation of African action and data has been the rational constant in all Afrocentric work. Interest in African people is not sufficient for one's work to be called "Afrocentric." Indeed, Afrocentricity is not merely the discussion of African and African American issues, history, politics, or consciousness; any one may discuss these issues and yet not be an Afrocentrist. Furthermore, it is not a perspective based on skin color or biology and should not be confused with melanist theorists, who existed before the Afrocentrists, and whose emphasis tends to be on biological determinism. Danjuma Modupe of Hunter College has posited agency, centeredness, psychic integrity, and cultural fidelity as the minimum four theoretical constructs that are necessary for a work to be called Afrocentric. Thus, what is clear is that neither a discussion of the Nile Valley civilizations (an argument against white racial hierarchy) nor of how to develop economic productivity in African American communities is sufficient for a discourse to be considered Afrocentric. Operations that involve the Afrocentric framework, identified by the four theoretical constructs, represent an Afrocentric methodology. As in every other case, the presentation of theory and methodological considerations implies avenues for criticism. Those criticizing Afrocentricity are more effective when the criticism derives from the definitions established by the proponents of Afrocentricity themselves; otherwise, it is possible for criticism to devolve into low-level intellectual sniping at points considered irrelevant by most Afrocentrists. For example, the debate over extraneous issues such as "was Aristotle black?" or "was Cleopatra black?" has nothing at all to do with Afrocentricity. What is more relevant for the Afrocentrist is the question, "what is the *location* of the person asking such questions or the location of the person needing to answer them?"

The Emergence

Although a number of writers and community activists growing out of the Black Power Movement of the 1960s had increasingly seen the need for a response to marginality, Afrocentricity did not emerge as a critical theory and a literary practice until the appearance of two small books by the Amutefi Publishing Company in Buffalo, New York. The press published Kariamu Welsh's *Textured Women, Cowrie Shells, Cowbells, and Beetiesticks* in, 1978 and Molefi Kete Asante's book *Afrocentricity* it 1980. These were the first self-conscious markings along the intellectual path of Afrocentricity, that is, where the authors, using their own activism and community organizing, consciously set out to explain a theory and a practice of liberation by reinvesting African agency as the fundamental core of African sanity. Welsh's book was a literary practice growing out of her choreographic method/technique known as *umfundalai*, projected in her dances at the Center for Positive Thought, which she directed. On the other hand, the book *Afrocentricity* was the first time that the theory of Afrocentricity had been launched as an intellectual idea. It was written from observations and textual analyses of what intellectual activists such as Welsh, Maulana Karenga, and Haki Madhubuti were doing with social transformation in community organizations. Rather than use political organization for the sake of organization, they had articulated a cultural base to the organizing principle. This had a more telling effect on and a more compelling attraction to African people. Based on the lived experiences of African people in the Caribbean, Africa, and elsewhere in the diaspora, the Afrocentric idea had to be concerned with nothing less than the relocation of subject–place in the African world after hundreds of years of living on the imposed and ungrounded terms of Europe.

Unlike the Negritude Movement to which the Afrocentric Movement is often compared, Afrocentricity has not been limited to asking artistic questions. Indeed, the cultural question as constructed by the Afrocentrists is not merely literature, art, music, and dance, but the entire process whereby Africans are socialized to live in the modern world. Thus, economics is a cultural question as much as religion and science in the construction of the

Afrocentrists. This is why Afrocentrists tend to pose three sets of questions. How do we see ourselves and how have others seen us? What can we do to regain our own accountability and to move beyond the intellectual and cultural plantation that constrains our economic, political, and scientific development? What allied theories and methods may be used to rescue those African ideas and ideas that are marginalized by Europe and thus in the African's mind as well? These have become the crucial questions that have aggravated our social and political worlds and agitated the brains of the Afrocentrists.

Five Distinguishing Characteristics

As a cultural configuration, the Afrocentric idea is distinguished by five characteristics. Essentially, these have remained the principal features of the Afrocentric theory since its inception in the late 1970s:

1. An intense interest in psychological location as determined by symbols, motifs, rituals, and signs.
2. A commitment to finding the subject–place of Africans in any social, political, economic, architectural. Literary, or religious phenomenon with implications for questions of sex, gender, and class.
3. A defense of African cultural elements as historically valid in the context of art, music, education, science, and literature.
4. A celebration of centeredness and agency and a commitment to lexical refinement that eliminates, pejorative about Africans or other people.
5. A powerful imperative from historical sources to revise the collective text of African people.

While numerous writers have augmented and added to the central tendency of the Afrocentric theory, it has remained concerned with resolving the cultural crisis as a way of achieving economic, political, and social liberation. A group of thinkers including Ama Mazama, Abu Abarry, Aisha Blackshire-Belay, Kariamu Welsh-Asante, Clenora Hudson-Weems. Miriam Maat Ka Re Mo'hges, Katherine Bankole, Cynthia Lehman, Ayi Kwei Armah, Terry Kershaw, Clovis Semmes, Danjuma Modupe, Nilgun Anadolu Okur, C. T. Keto, Molefi Asante, and their students have located the terms of Afrocentricity in the vital areas of linguistic, historical, sociological, and dramatic interpretations of phenomena. This tendency has been called the Temple Circle of Afrocentricity. For example, Abarry has examined orature and libation oratory in African cultural history in connective ways, thus avoiding the disconnected discourses usually found about Africa. Others such as Mekada Graham and Jerome Schiele have concentrated on the social transformative aspects of centrality, believing that it is possible to change the conditions of the socially marginalized by teaching them to see their own centrality and thus empower themselves to confront their existential and material situations. Afrocentrists believe that there is a serious difference between commentary on the activities of Europeans, past and present, and the revolutionary thrust of gaining empowerment through die reorientation of African interests. There is no rush to discover in Europe the answers for the problems that Europe created for the

African condition, psychologically, morally, and economically. Afrocentrists do not shun answers that may emerge in the study of Europe but what Europeans have thought and how Europeans have conceived their reality can often lead to further imprisonment of the African mind. Thus, Afrocentrists call for the liberation of the mind from any notion that Europe is teacher and Africa is pupil; one must contest every space and locate in that space the freedom for Africa to express its own truths. This is not a biologically determined position. It is a culturally and theoretically determined one. That is why there are now Afrocentrists who are European and Asian, and one can find Africans who are not Afrocentric. The new work on Du Bois by the Chinese Afrocentrist Ji Yuan and the work of Cynthia Lehman on the Egyptian texts are examples of non-Africans exploring the various dimensions of centeredness in their analyses of African phenomena. It is consciousness, not biology that decides how one is to apprehend the intellectual data because the key to the Afrocentric idea is orientation to data, not data themselves. Where do you stand when you seek to locate—that is, interrogate—a text, phenomenon, or person?

Objectivity-Subjectivity

Perhaps because of the rise of the Afrocentric idea at a time when Eurocentric scholars seemed to have lost their way in a dense forest of deconstructionist and postmodernist concepts challenging the prevailing orthodoxies of the Eurocentric paradigm, we have found a deluge of challenges to the Afrocentric idea as a reaction to postmodernity. But it should be clear that the Afrocentrists, too, have recognized the inherent problems in structuralism, patriarchy, capitalism, and Marxism with their emphasis on received interpretations of phenomena as different as the welfare state and E. E. Cummings' poetry. Yet the issues of objectivity and subject–object duality, central pieces of the Eurocentric project in interpretation, have been shown to represent hierarchies rooted in the European construction of the political world.

Afrocentrists claim that the aim of the objectivity argument is always to protect the status quo, because the status quo is never called upon to prove its objectivity, only the challengers to the status quo are asked to explain their objectivity. And in a society where white supremacy has been a major component of the social, cultural, and political culture, the African will always be in the position of challenging the white racial privileged status quo, unless, of course, he or she is co-opted into defending the economic, literary, critical, political, social, or cultural status quo. In each case, the person will be defending the reality created by Eurocentrists.

It is the subversion of that configuration that is necessary to establish a playing field based on equality. To claim that those who take the speaker or subject position vis-B-vis others counted as audiences and objects on the same footing is to engage in intellectual subterfuge without precedence. On the other hand, it is possible—as the Afrocentrists claim—to create community when one speaks of subject–subject, speaker–speaker, audience–audience relationships. This allows pluralism without hierarchy.

As applied to race and, racism, this formulation is clear in its emphasis on subject–subject relationships. Of course, this subject–subject relationship is almost impossible in a racist system or in the benign acceptance of a racist construction of human relationships as may be found in the American society and is frequently represented in the literature of several scholars who have African ancestry but who are clearly uncomfortable with the fact. White supremacy cannot be accommodated in a normal society and therefore when a writer or scholar or politician refuses to recognize or ignores the African's agency, he or she allows for the default position, white supremacy, to operate without challenge and thus participates in a destructive mode for human personality. If African people are not given subject–place, then we remain objects without agency, intellectual beggars without a place to stand. There is nothing essentially different from this enslavement than the previous historical enslavement except out inability to recognize the bondage. Thus, you have a white-subject and black-object relationship expressed in sociology, anthropology, philosophy, political science, literature, and history rather than a subject–subject reality. It is this marginality that is rejected in the writings of Afrocentrists.

Diopian Influence

The late Cheikh Anta Diop did more than anyone else to reintroduce the African as a subject in the context of African history and culture. It was Diop's singular ambition as a scholar to reorder the history of Africa and to reposition the African in the center of his or her own story. This was a major advance during the time that so many African writers and scholars were rushing after Europe to prove Europe's own point of view on the rest of the world. Diop was confident that the history of Africa could not be written without throwing off the falsifications of Europe. Doing this was not only politically and professionally dangerous but it was considered to be impossible given the hundreds of years of accumulated information in the libraries of the West.

To begin with, Diop had to challenge the leading scholars of Europe, meet them in their intellectual home arena, defeat their arguments with science, and establish Africa's own road to its history. That he achieved his purpose has meant that the scholars who have declared themselves Afrocentrists have done so with the example of Diop marching before in splendor. His key contention was that the ancient Egyptians laid the basis of African and European civilization and that the ancient Egyptians were not Arabs or Europeans, but as Diop would say "Black Africans" to emphasize that there should be no mistake. These "Black Africans" of the Nile Valley gave the world astronomy, geometry, law, architecture, art, mathematics, medicine, and philosophy. The ancient African Egyptian term *seba* first found in an inscription on the tomb of Antef I from 2052 B.C.E. had as its core meaning in the *MedU Neter,* the "reasoning style of the people."

What Diop taught his students and readers was that Europe pronounced itself the categorical superior culture and therefore its reasoning often served the bureaucratic functions of "locking" Africans into a conceptual cocoon that at first glance seems harmless enough. Nevertheless, the prevailing positions, often anti-African, were supported by this bureaucratic logic. How can an African liberate himself or herself from these racist structures? Afrocentrists take the position that this is possible, essential, but can only happen if we search for answers in the time–space categories that are antihegemonic. These are categories that place Africa at the center of analysis of African issues and African people as agents in our own contexts. Otherwise, how can we ever raise practical questions of improving our situation in the world? The Jews of the Old Testament asked, How can you sing a new song, in a strange land? The Afrocentrists ask, How can the African create a liberative philosophy from the icons of mental enslavement?

Afrocentricity as a Corrective and Critique

There are certainly political implications here because the issue of African politics throughout the world becomes one of securing a place from which to stand, unimpeded by the interventions of a decaying Europe that has lost its own moral way in its reach to enslave and dispossess other people. This is not to say that all Europe is bad and all Africa is good. To even think or pose the issue in that manner is to miss the point. For Africans and Native Americans, Europe has been dangerous. It is five hundred years of danger, and I am not now talking of physical or economic danger, though that history is severe enough, but of psychological and cultural danger, the danger that kills the soul of a people. I surmise that a people's soul is dead when it can no longer breathe its own air, or speak its own language, and when the air of another culture seems to smell sweeter. Following Frantz Fanon, the Afrocentrists argue that it is the *assimiladoes,* the educated elite, whose identities and affiliations are often killed first. Fortunately, their death does not mean the people are doomed; it only means they can no longer be trusted to speak what the people know because they are dead to the culture, to the human project.

Therefore, Afrocentricity stands as both a corrective and a critique. Whenever African people, who collectively suffer the experience of dislocation, are relocated in a centered place (that is with agency and accountability), then we have a corrective. By recentering the African person as an agent, we deny the hegemony of European domination in thought and behaviour and then Afrocentricity becomes a critique. On one hand, we seek to correct the sense of place of the African, and on the other hand, we make a critique of the process and extent of the dislocation caused by the European cultural, economic, and political domination of Africa and African peoples. It is possible to make an exploration of this critical dimension by observing the way European writers have defined Africa and Africans in history, political science, anthropology, and sociology. To condone the definition of Africans as marginal, "fringe" people in the historical processes of the world, including the African world, is to abandon all hope of reversing the degradation of the oppressed.

Thus, the aims of Afrocentricity as regards the cultural idea are not hegemonic. Afrocentrists have expressed no interest in one race or culture dominating another; they express an ardent belief, in the possibility of diverse populations living on the same earth without giving up their fundamental traditions except where those traditions invade other people's space. This is precisely why the Afrocentric idea is essential to human harmony. The Afrocentric idea represents a possibility of intellectual maturity, a way of viewing reality that opens new and more exciting doors to human understanding. I do not object to viewing it as a form of historical consciousness, but more than that, it is an attitude, a location, an orientation. To be centered is to stand some place and to come from some place; the Afrocentrist seeks for the African person the contentment of subject, active, agent place.

Principal Concepts

Afrocentricity represents a reaction against several tendencies. It spurns the limited analysis of Africans, in the Americas as Europeans as well as the notion that Africans in the Americas are not Africans. Rather, it concentrates on what Afrocentrist Danjuma Modupe of Hunter College calls the Condition-Effects-Alleviation Complex and the global formation. Modupe contends that the communal cognitive will is activated by cultural fidelity to that will, but cultural fidelity to that will is also fidelity to Afrocentricity itself. He is one of the leading proponents of the view that Afrocentric consciousness is necessary for psychological liberation and cultural reclamation. This view is shared by numerous Afrocentrists.

There are four areas of inquiry in Afrocentricity: cosmological, axiological, epistemological, and aesthetics. A person seeking to locate a person, event, or phenomenon will have to utilize one of these forms for inquiry. Accordingly, the Afrocentrist places all phenomena within one of these categories. The term cosmological refers to the myths, legends, literatures, and oratures that interact at a mythological or primordial level with how African people respond to the cosmos. How are racial or cultural classifications developed? How do we distinguish between Yoruba and African Brazilian? How do gender, class, and culture interact at the intersection of science? The epistemological issues are those that deal with language, myth, dance, or music; for example, as they confront the question of knowledge and proof of truth. What is the rational structure of Ebonics as an African language, and how does it present itself in the African American's behavior and culture? *Axiology* refers to the good and the beautiful as well as to the combination that gives us right conduct within the context of African culture. This is a value issue. Since Afrocentricity is a transgenerational and transcontinental idea, as Van Home of the University of Wisconsin–Milwaukee suggests, it utilizes aspects of the philosophies of numerous African cultures to arrive at its ideal. "Beauty is as beauty does," is considered an African American adage, but similar proverbs, statements, and sayings are found throughout the African world where beauty and goodness are often equated. *Aesthetics* as an area of inquiry is closely related to the issue of value. Afrocentrists have isolated, as in the work of Kariamu Welsh-Asante, seven senses of the Afrocentric approach to aesthetics: polyrhythm, dimensionality and texture, polycentrism, repetition, curvilinearity, epic memory, wholism. Welsh-Asante contends that these elements are the leading aspects of any inquiry into African plastic art, sculpture, dance, music, and drama. A number of Afrocentric scholars have delved into a discussion of ontology, the study of beingness, as another issue of inquiry. This should not be confused with the idea of personalism in the original Afrocentric construction of philosophical approaches to Afrocentric cultural theory (critical methodology) and Afrocentric methodology (interpretative methodology). In my earlier writings on Afrocentricity, I contended that the European and Asian worlds might be considered materialistic and spiritualistic whereas the dominant emphasis in the African world was personalism. This was not to limit any cultural sphere but to suggest the most prominent ways that large cultural communities respond to their environments.

Maulana Karenga has identified seven areas of culture. These cultural elements are frequently used by Afrocentrists as well as practitioners of Kawaida when conceptualizing areas of intellectual organization. They are history, mythology, motif, ethos, political organization, social organization, and economic organization. Used most often in the critical analysis of culture, these organizing principles are applied to fundamental subject fields of social, communication, historical, cultural, economic, political, and psychological fields of study whenever a student wants to determine the relationship between culture and a given discipline.

The Discipline of Africology

Finally, the Afrocentrists have determined that a new discipline, Africology, emerges from the various treatments of data from the Afrocentric perspective. Africology is defined as the Afrocentric study of African phenomena. It has three major divisions: cultural/aesthetics, social/behavioral, and policy/action. Under cultural/aesthetic, the scholar can consider at a minimum three key elements to culture and aesthetics: epistemic, scientific, and artistic dimensions. In terms of epistemic dimensions, the Afrocentrist examines ethics, politics, psychology, and other modes of behavior. The scientific dimensions include history, linguistics, economics, and other methods of investigation. The artistic dimension involves icons, art, motifs, symbols, and other types of presentation.

Bibliography

Achebe, Chinua. *Things Fall Apart*. Heineman, 1957.

Asante, Molefi Kete. *Afrocentricity*. Africa World Press, 1988.

———. *The Afrocentric Idea*. Temple UP, 1987.

———. *Kemet, Afrocentricity and Knowledge*. Africa World Press, 1990.

———. *Malcolm X and other Afrocentric Essays*. Africa World Press, 1993.

Asante, M. K., and Abarry, Abu. *African Intellectual Heritage*. Temple UP, 1996.

Asante, M. K., and Asante, Kariamu, editors. *African Culture: The Rhythms of Unity*. Africa World Press, 1990.

Asante, M. K., and Mattson, Mark. *African American Atlas*. Macmillan, 1998.

Baker, Houston. *The Journey Back: Issues in Black Literature and Criticism*. University of Chicago Press, 1980.

Blackshire-Belay, Carol Aisha, editor. *Language and Literature in the African American Imagination*. Greenwood Press, 1992.

Cerol, de Marie-Josée. *Introduction of Guateloupean Creole*, 1991.

Chinweizu. *Decolonising the African Mind*. Pero, 1987.

Diop, Cheikh Anta. *The African Origin of Civilization*. Lawrence Hill, 1976.

———. *Civilization or Barbarism: An Authentic Anthropology*. Translated from the French by Yaa-Lengi Meema Ngemi, edited by Harold J. Salemson and Marjolin de Jager. Lawrence Hill, 1991.

———. Drake, St. Clair. *Black Folk Here and There: An Essay in History and Anthropology*. Vol. 1, Center for Afro-American Studies, 1987.

Forbes, Jack D. *Africans and Native Americans*. University of Illinois Press, 1993.

Gates, Henry Louis, Jr. *The Signifying Monkey*. Oxford UP, 1988.

Harris, Joseph. E., editor. *Global Dimensions of African Diaspora*. Howard University, 1982.

Holloway, Joseph E. and Vass, Winifred K. *The African Heritage of American English*. Indiana UP, 1993.

Jean, Clinton M. *Behind Eurocentric Veils: The Search for African Realities.* University of Massachusetts Press, 1991.

Kambon, Kobi. *The African Personality in America: An African Centered Framework.* Nubia Nation Publications, 1992.

Karenga, Maulana. *Introduction to Black Studies,* 2nd ed., University of Sankore Press, 1993.

———. *Kawaida Theory.* University of Sankore Press, 1995.

Keto, C. Tsehloane. *The Africa-Centered Perspective of History.* K. A. Publications, 1989.

Marable, Manning. *African and Caribbean Politics: From Kwame Nkrumah to Maurice Bishop.* Verso, 1987.

Martin, Tony. *Race First: The Ideological and Organizational Struggles of Marcus Garvey and the Universal Negro Improvement Association,* 1st ed., The Majority Press, 1986.

Morrison, Toni. *Beloved.* Random House, 1990.

Myers, Linda James. *Understanding the Afrocentric Worldview.* Kendall-Hunt, 1988.

Nascimento, Abdias do. *Racial Democracy in Brazil: Myth or Reality.* Sketch Publishing, 1977.

Nascimento, Elisa Larkin. *Pan-Africanism and South America: Emergence, of a Black Rebellion.* Afrodiaspora, 1980.

Ngugi wa Thiong'o. *Decolonising the Mind.* Heinemann, 1987.

———. *Moving the Centre: The Struggle for Cultural Freedoms.* Curry/Heineman, 1993.

Okur, Nilgun. *Contemporary African American Drama: From Black Arts to Afroentricity.* Garland Press, 1997.

Richards, Dona Marimba. *Yurugu: An Africa-Centered Critique of European Domination.* Africa World Press, 1993.

Rodney, Walter. *How Europe Underdeveloped Africa.* Howard UP, 1986.

Thompson, Vincent B. *Africa and Unity: The Evolution of Pan Africanism.* Longman, 1969.

Walters, Ronald. *Pan-Africanism in the African Diaspora: An Analysis of Modern Afrocentric Political Movements.* Wayne State UP, 1993.

Welsh, Kariamu. Textured Women, Cowrie Shells, Cowbells, and Beetiesticks. Amutefi Publishing Company, 1978.

Welsh-Asante, Kariamu. *African Dance.* Africa World Press, 1996.

Welsh-Asante, Kariamu, editor. *The African Aesthetic: Keeper of the Traditions.* Greenwood Press, 1993.

West, Cornel. *Race Matters.* Beacon Press, 1992.

Williams, Chancellor. *The Destruction of Black Civilization.* Third World Press, 1988.

Wilson, William Julius. *The Declining Significance of Race.* University of Chicago Press, 1985.

Woodson, Carter G. *The Mis-Education of the Negro.* Africa World Press, 1990.

Wright, Richard. *Native Son.* Harper and Row, 1966.

Ziegler, Dhyana, editor. *Molefi Kete Asante and Afrocentricity: In Praise and Criticism.* Winston-Derek, 1994.

Chapter 3

Black Women Adult Educators—The Utterers of Black Leadership Preparation: Africana Womanism and the Afrocentric Praxis

Contributed by:
Jacqueline Roebuck Sakho, EdD

Afrocentricity is the conscious process by which a person locates or relocates African phenomena within an African subject content or agency and action. It is therefore location as opposed to dislocation, centeredness as opposed to marginality (Asante, "Intellectual Dislocation" 97).

The Eurocentric view has monopolized the theoretical and epistemological development of adult education and leadership preparation programs, at the exclusion of Afrocentric theories broadly defined (Colin, "The Universal Negro Improvement Association," 1988; Johnson-Bailey; James and Farmer; Sheared, "An Africentric Feminist Perspective," 1991; Colin and Guy; Alfred; Smith; Sissel and Sheared; Flowers; Brigham; Ntseane) and specifically, Africana Womanism (Sheared, "*The Handbook of Race*"). Asante (Intellectual Dislocation) gives explicit directions when critiquing normative ideology and assessing "intellectual dislocation" of any intellectual text (97). The Afrocentric writer, thinker, and/or practitioner must conduct the work of locating one's cultural knowledge and intellect and then snatching one's centeredness from marginalization. In this truth is the discussion outline. Much is hidden with the intentional and deliberate act of marginalizing knowledge. I am unearthing Afrocentric knowledge and the potential impact on Critical Adult Education (CAE) to demonstrate that, "there is no absolute knowledge because of the communal involvement in knowledge construction and knowledge acquisition" (Ntseane, "Culturally Sensitive Transformational Learning" 307). In other words, knowledge is coconstructed while in proximity to others, to cultures and to systems. As an Africana Womanist Adult Educator, I bring Afrocentricity from the margins and center its location within CAE. Adult Education leadership preparation writ large has much to learn from Afrocentricity and an Africana Womanist in order to embody communal knowledge in leadership preparation practice. I enact Africana Womanism as practitioner of this discussion.

While school and education are often interchanged as synonymous, Dr. David Stovall argues that the practice of doing school in the twenty-first century is oppressive and a delivery system of white supremacy/racism; yet, education is/can serve as an act of resistance against the political economy and structures of doing "school" (Stovall 2016). Ntseane, makes an assertion from Bostwana culture and learning that applies here. Ntseane (Culturally Sensitive Transformational Learning) asserts, as Afrocentric writers, thinkers, and practitioners, what we have to deal with is that . . . "current education systems have limited or no adequate reference to the [African Diaspora] indigenous education that Africans already had prior to [Maafa][1]" (311). By deal with, we mean embody a practice of collective transformative agency (Dillard, "Leading with Her Life") bridging the historicity of Afrocentric knowledge about leadership preparation with cultural information (Asante, "Locating a Text" 2) across the collective knowledges of elders, parents, youth, and grassroots leaders. What does it mean to be a [Black woman adult] educator in the reawakening of racial violence against Black people[s], and in particular, Black women and youth? (Haddix et al., "At the Kitchen Table" 382). But even so, do we fully realize the present urgency? (Locke 1935, 109). At least for the moment, these issues and the problems they involve constitute critically an adult problem, with an adult remedy as their only immediate solution (Locke 1935, 107). What follows is an integrated discussion of CAE leadership preparation, locating my cultural knowledge as an Africana Womanist adult educator, and concluding with an imagining of Afrocentric Adult Educational Leadership.

(Re)Framing CAE

The etymological origins of the word prefix *re* date back to 1300 Anglo French. The intended use of *re* could indicate changing the chemistry of a word so to speak or, representing the undoing of a meaning. In this case to (re)frame, then, is to undo the purpose or intention of the role of adult education and leadership preparation specifically for the Historical Black Colleges & Universities (HBCU) adult leadership preparation. For Black adult learners, the concept of Adult Education leadership preparation can be traced back to the Catechism schools to prepare enslaved Africans with religious indoctrination and to increase their resale value. During the Civil War, Contraband schools were provided to those adult Africans who escaped from the enslavement in the south to be able to provide necessary learning to support the Union Army. Contemporarily, Adult Education for Black adults continued during the Great Depression era beginning with Dr. Alaine Locke. In fact, Hayden and DuBois (1977) describe his efforts and impact as that of a "drum major" of adult education for Black adult leadership. Locke critiquing of the field began in his 1934 address to the American Association of Adult Education (AAAE).

---

[1] Maafa—the capture, kidnapping, and enslavement of Africans in death camps called plantations as chattel labor to build an American Slave Society during what has become known globally as the Transatlantic Enslavement of Africans living on the Continent of African and indigenous to America.

I myself am convinced that the key to an intellectual interest is a strong emotional drive and that in Negro adult education we should boldly capitalize the motivation of racial interest and let the bogey of propaganda be hanged, if by this means we can get desirable results of serious sustained interest and effort (Locke 352).

The average adult is not merely surrounded by a multiplicity of facts which are confusing and meaningless to him without social and cultural understanding; he is influential in forming a public opinion which, by being intelligent or unintelligent, progressive or reactionary, definitely affects the crucial issues of our collective living (Locke, "Education for Adulthood" 108).

Indeed, the public mind has yet to mature (Locke, "Education for Adulthood" 105).

For the purposes of reframing Adult Education leadership preparation, I am beginning with CAE as the closet version from the field to Afrocentric thought and praxis. The practice of CAE is informed by the following adult learning praxis: *self-directed learning, critical reflection, experiential learning/learning as leadership* (Brookfield, "Self-Directed Learning" and *Becoming a Critically Reflective Teacher*). Therefore, the primary theory of action for CAE is *if* adult learners engage in CAE praxis as self-directed learners who actionize critical reflection *and* experiential knowledge *then*, they will enact transformative learning. This theory of action foregrounds the premise of CAE to "liberate the adult learning and teaching" by creating processes to challenge the ideologies of doing public school and contest the hegemonic narrative about education (Brookfield, *The Power of Critical Theory* 2004). Brookfield (Self-Directed Learning) argues self-directed learning guided by critical self-reflection can be reconceptualization as an . . . inherently political idea, an oppositional counter hegemonic force (229). Criticality of self-reflection begins with the individual's assumptions, beliefs, and behaviors in relationship to community and systems (1) instigating truth-telling about ideologies of oppression and injustice; (2) fostering the courage to dispute hegemony and its narratives; and (3) unearthing and exposing the hidden truth(s) about power as a necessity for revealing the true character of power. Experiential knowledge is identified in the literature on adult education as a major factor in how adults learn. It serves as a visual platform to "provide opportunities for aspiring leaders to retrieve, reflect, and infuse their experience into their learning, and provide context, variability and personalization for learning success" (Richardson 2015). The experiences that adults bring to a learning situation is identified in the literature on adult education as a major factor in how adults learn. Therefore, preparation programs should provide opportunities for aspiring leaders to retrieve, reflect, and infuse their experience into their learning, and provide context, variability and personalization for learning success (Richardson, "Making Learning Foundational," 2071). The act of retrieving experiences surpassing the boundaries of the Eurocentric view relating to what serves as experience not recognizing the cultural information as described early by Asante. Richardson ("Making Learning Foundational") advice for the CAE leadership preparation is that learners must be afforded the opportunity to retrieve experiences. The author cautions, however, care must be taken to incorporate opportunities for aspiring leaders to critically examine, reflect, and contextualize their learning. While it is important to build on aspiring leaders' existing views of and experiences with leadership, it is as important to allow for expanding one's view of leadership through additional knowledge and experience (2071).

In the present time of yet another awakening of sanctioned racial violence against Black people and their bodies, I make sense of my work in adult education and leadership preparation as "fugitive politic [–] insurgent scholarship [and practice] intended to contest, refute, and offer a different reality from that which is offered under the realities of White supremacy (Stovall 282). CAE considers adult [e]ducational leaders, like other members of the society, are born into a society that perpetuates racist behaviors through an organized system" (Gooden and O'Doherty 229). Pushing CAE around the corner toward Afrocentric thought and praxis and collective transformative agency to describe the ways in which both the preparation (instructor outcomes and process) and andragogy (the science of adult education: learners' process and needs) must first be decolonized and then, translated into Afrocentric Adult Education Leadership preparation activities. Brookfield (*Becoming a Critically Reflective Teacher*) critiques the theoretical rigor of the field for oppressing other worldviews and specifically Afrocentric thought about adult learning stating, "[g]iven that . . . [c]riticality's theory is undeniably Eurocentric [; then,] [w]hite European critical theorists are unlikely to reframe critical theory in the service of a different racial group" (Brookfield 274). As such, CAE as with all other Eurocentric theoretical frameworks must be decolonized (Asante, Ani, Dillard) and "(re)claimed" (Perlow et al. 5).

Africana Womanist Adult Educator

Clenora Hudson-Weems's research warns of the uncritical acceptance of dominant cultural theorizations. She argues

> . . . we take the Procrustean approach, via superimposing alien or outside theories and methodologies as a primary means of analyzing and interpreting our texts from a so-called legitimate, universally theoretical perspective. Be it known that this ruling perspective in reality is none other than just another perspective (Hudson-Weems, "Africana Womanism and the Critical Need" 79 as quoted in Yancy 163).

Flowers (An Afrocentric View of Adult Learning Theory) argues that Afrocentric theory and argumentation methods when centered within Adult Education and Learning "is more inclusive of the sociohistorical, political, race, class, and gender contributions made in the learning development of African Americans" (41). Flowers is directing the field toward an imagining of an Afrocentric view of Adult Educational Leadership preparation informed by Africana Womanism as it "is grounded in African culture and, therefore, focuses on the unique experiences, struggles, needs, and desires of Africana women" (Hudson-Weems, "Africana Womanism and the Critical Need" 158).

Africana Womanist: *Utterers of Mother Wit*

> The utterers' voice should make knowledge of the way, of heard sounds and visions seen, the voice of the utterres should make this knowledge inevitable, impossible to lose (Armah xiii).

> . . . and in her talk is the "mother wit" that is not so named for nothing: mother wit is the verbal weapon of survival that informs the experience in these works and makes them, finally, celebrations of "getting o vah," assertions of identity, proclamations of the beauty and mastery of circumstance that simply being Black and a woman can affirm (MacKethan 52).

I arrived in academia during the Fall semester of 2017, through the ability to "hit a straight lick with a crooked stick." The liminal space for Black women is typically where we experience initiatory rites. Standing in the liminal space, the threshold where it was expected that I leave at the door my varied realities of Mother wit and other cultural information—ways of knowing and sensemaking before passing through the vestibule into the academy. Here is the moment of dislocation and marginality here is where the Africana Womanist conjures mother wit or not. When I step beyond the threshold passing through the vestibule—a veil spaced, like a portal to pass through—I am cloaked with my mother wit and other cultural information as one of many armors designed for this type of veil walking. Veil walking is representative of a protective force field as I move between realities both self-defined and those that are scripted for Black women faculty. This particular armor for veil walking handed down by Black women faculty who also arrived at the Academy vestibule via the crooked stick and the lick, is the craft of "forging black skin into a spiritized 'cloak' of subterfuge and survival" (Perkinson, *Shamanism, Racism, and Hip Hop Culture*, 44) to create a ritual practice of clearing and cleansing by decolonizing, relocating, and centering what is Source.

As an Africana Womanist, junior faculty, I expose my location as African-centered, to announce that I am not dislocated and that I ritually practice "decolonizing my intellect" (Ani 2). I do so to demonstrate as the writer, my "need for self-naming, self-defining and self-identity" (Ntiri, as quoted in Hudson-Weems 2); and, that my thinking about this chapter is informed by *family-centeredness, wholeness, authenticity, flexible role-playing, and adaptability*. Therefore, I write as a commitment to family-centered and community-centered epistemologies while in political alignment with the Black man as my counterbalance, and in "*genuine sisterhood*" with Black women. As the practitioner, my charge is to forge practices that are undergirded by *strength, male compatibility, respect, recognition, respect for elders, ambition, mothering, nurturing, and spirituality*. The rendering of the following text is meant to demonstrate that I am educated in the Eurocentric system; yet, I am not of this system. To align with "Afrocentricity is the conscious process by which a person locates or relocates African phenomena within an African subject content or agency and action. It is therefore location as opposed to dislocation, centeredness as opposed to marginality" (Gray 97).

> At the heart of white supremacy and colonization is the sustained practice of cultural theft. Thus, many of the "innovative" pedagogies that white educators in the Western academy have claimed as their own such as cooperative/communal, experiential, active, student-centered, social-emotional, and service learning, as well as scholar-activism and social justice education, have been appropriated from precolonial Africa, Asia, and the Americas (Perlow et al. 5, emphasis by the authors).

Further, Perlow (2017) and the other Black female scholars in this edited canon, *Black Women's Liberatory Pedagogies: Resistance, Transformation, and Healing Within and Beyond the Academy*, aligning with Molefi Asante are quite clear in the above quote as they lay a powerful argument toward the decolonization of Adult Education. In order to (re)imagine an Afrocentric Adult Educational Leadership, I place Africana Womanism as my worldview and Afrocentric argumentation to bridge my worldview to my practice.

For us, to be Black women educators demands that we attune ourselves to the critical ways institutional structures create, shape, and manipulate our lives. We find ourselves consistently questioning what it means to be Black women educators at predominantly white institutions. Black women adult education educators are liminal space dwellers—we hang out in the margins to snatch back centeredness. We are veil walkers who leave our tools hidden in the vestibule of the liminal space. Also, it is in the liminal space where Black women are initiated in "pragmatic strategies for material social transformation" (Ladson-Billings 1998). These pragmatic strategies can be characterized as rites of passage through social environments that are "characterized by the presence of ambiguous ideas, monstrous images, sacred symbols, ordeals, humiliations, esoteric and paradoxical instructions" about the norms of racism/white supremacy when doing school or, for that matter, any other socialized organizational practice. I step beyond the threshold passing through a veil wearing one of many armors designed for veil walking, protecting Black women as they move between realities self-defined and those that are scripted. This particular armor for veil walking is handed down by Black women faculty who also arrived via the crooked stick. You see some situations call for pulling back the veil, some call for making the veil translucent, like a portal to pass through. Still, there are other situations that demand the ripping and removal of a veil all together. As Black educators, we

> . . . situate ourselves at the intersection of race, gender, and pedagogy . . . our pedagogy was inherited, consciously and unconsciously, as we watched our mothers, grandmothers, and great grandmothers, educate in unfathomable circumstances. In being with these maternal caretakers, we learned the importance of presence, being in relationship, being with ourselves, and being engaged with the past. From them we learned that to be a Black woman was to teach, to embody the political in word and deed. They taught us how and when to "read the world" [REPEAT—and to "read the word] . . ." (Roseboro and Ross 19).

The Africana Womanist adult educator has historically been considered a griot historian defined by Omolade (*The Rising Song*) as "a symbolic conveyor of African oral and spiritual traditions of the entire community . . . a scholar in any discipline who connects, uses, and understands the methods and insights of both Western and African world-views and historical perspectives" (284). As Africana Womanist adult educationists, we are tasked with initiating individuals to lead on both sides of the veil "of subverting oppressive intuitions and building liberating ones, of articulating possibilities for imprisoned souls and nurturing healthy fighting ones, of speaking as truthfully as possible about the War of the Spirit" (Gordon quoted in James xvi). To lead on both sides of the veil in this current moment of racial retrenchment is to work both hands to balance the individual experience with the communal experience not sacrificing one over the other—this is community-centered leadership. When we "veil walk we are carrying messages and possibilities back and forth between individuals and histories" (Sakho 13). However, enacting community-centered leadership through liminality and "moving that veil aside requires, therefore, certain things" (Morrison 111). The certain things here are Sankofan Approach, Nommoic Creativity, and Maatic Argumentation as core learning tasks. These learning tasks can assist Afrocentric Adult Education Leadership preparation to (1) facilitate problem thinking that centers the Black community as the primary knowing agent; (2) generate a belief that community has agency to name instances/issues/problems; and (3) discover creative and constructive ways of responding. These learning tasks represent an acquired mindset, more specific practices to be implemented, and/or core strategies for preparation programs.

Toward Afrocentric Adult Education Leadership Preparation: Three Initiation Journeys

> The Afrocentric practitioner wants ultimately to cultivate and grow Afrocentric practice within people and communities to the point that every action is a constructive Afrocentric action . . . (Gray 107).

> "Initiation processes prepare young individuals to be incorporated into the world" (Mtshali 185)

> The current moment in education and Black life in general should be understood as a moment of retrenchment along with a deepening politic of disposability. Despite rhetoric of post-raciality, the aforementioned moments of state-sanctioned violence, combined with the perpetual disinvestment in public education [and learning], should be understood as a moment when particular racialized populations have been deemed disposable by the state (Stovall 51).

> For the Negro, the one word "race," with all its mental associations, is a tragically magic charm that instantly evokes dead serious thought (Locke 352).

Since public education Prek-20 has continued to fortify corporate interests in education, it feels appropriate to utilize a business definition to take up Stovall's warning of retrenchment. In business leadership studies, the act of retrenchment involves reassessing all the ways the company is in market and to then go about reducing product production. It is a process that calls for a business to begin a strategic withdrawal from the market as an act of preservation. In a praxis sense, it is a process of formally assessing ways to exit markets that no longer serve the best interest of the whole company. Stovall ("Out of Adolescence and into Adulthood") similarly is warning of the renewed reduction in the interest of educating Black folks as well as the renewed interest in the disposability of the Black body. Taking this notion as true, then we are at a political moment one that is shining a light on James' "afrarealism" a moment made clear for Black adult educators to acknowledge the magic charm of race public Prk-20 education in America as coexisting within two realities: "democracy as a boundary defining freedom through captivity, and maroon philosophy at the borders reimagining freedom through flight" (124). Then, Black Adult Educationist are tasked with snatching back the center from Eurocentric thought and praxis in CAE by taking a much needed "dead serious" stand for Afrocentric thought and praxis. Placing Afrocentric epistemology and praxis at the center when reimagining adult learning tasks reframes the theory of action mentioned above to *if* African American adult learners engage in Afrocentric Adult Education Leadership praxis as communal self-directed learners who actionize Sankofan, Maatic, and Nommoic learning tasks as critical reflection *and* experiential knowledge; *then*, they will enact transformative learning for themselves and broader community. By reimagining the theory of action of CAE then the premise becomes "to cultivate and grow Afrocentric practice within people and communities to the point that every action is a constructive Afrocentric action" (Gray 107). The reframed theory of action calls on the capacity of Black adult educationist, who are far removed from African centers, to stretch beyond normative ideological practices and politics of respectability. In this reawakened moment of the nation's strategic withdrawal from the interest of Black folks writ large and adult education specifically, we are picking up Black adult leadership preparation with "Dubois' revision of the talented tenth" into a theory of the "guiding hundredth, which stresses struggle, sacrifice, and service, group leadership, and African historical and cultural grounding, provides Africana philosophy of education" (Rabaka 399). What prepares the Black adult educationist to lead in the reawakening of violence and inequity?

Sankofan Learning Task

"return to the source; go and get it and bring it here"

> Sankofan argumentation considers the African past, gleans its most instructive and constructive information, refines that information if necessary, then utilizes the information to achieve pro-African purposes in contemporary contexts. Asante argues repeatedly it is imperative that African people reconstruct sanity in the present, by studying, recalling, and recounting the works of sanity product by Africans of the past and present (Gray 28–29).

> We must properly historicize and contextualize our epistemological claims. This awareness places in critical relief the assumption that thinking takes place sub specie aeternitatis (Yancy 156).
>
> The Sankofan Approach is deliberate and conscious . . . includes drawing on the past functionally, anchoring efforts in that past—gleaning the most instructive and constructive information from the African past, refining that information as necessary and then utilizing the information along with one's particular personal desires to achieve pro-African purposes in the present and future.

Locke modeled the Sankofan approach as his dedicated practice of adult development, so much so, it is described clearly by the editor of the AAAE journal where Locke's first article to this journal appeared:

> The Association was founded in 1926 . . . President Locke does not only look backward, however, he analyzes the present situation, taking stock of the organization's actual and potential resources. He outlines for the future, in a spirit of complete confidence, the responsibilities and opportunities both of the Association and the Movement it represents (Hayden and DuBois 295).
>
> Locke firmly believed that any emphasis on adult education for and about Black people had to be associated with the Afro-American's past, his culture, and his place in the America of the post-World War I period. He related this to one of the principal characteristics of adult education, i.e., learning must be meaningful and turned into the exact readiness of the adult learner (Hayden and DuBois 1977).

Sankofan approach is how to decenter CAE learning tasks in order to repurposes the learning tasks as communal acts and the mechanism by which Black adult educationist can become an Afrocentric practitioner. Returning to the past for the specific purpose of understanding how to prepare Afrocentric Adult Education leaders to be communal and to operationalize "group-leadership, not simply educated and self-sacrificing, but with a clear vision of present world conditions and dangers, and conducting American Negroes to alliance with culture groups in Europe, America, Asia and Africa, and looking toward a new world culture" (Dubois 168 quoted in Rabaka 417).

To engage this time travel is to again think differently about Dubois' metaphoric veil reflected in his seminal work, *The Souls of Black Folks*. He spoke intensely about the discomfort of this ethereal type space, which he named "double consciousness." The functional message of the veil is about separating the socially constructed white world from the Black world that "operates at the personal or intrapsychic and at the institutional or structural level of social interaction" (Winant 2004). Similarly, Perkinson (*Shamanism, Racism, and Hip Hop Culture*) argues to take note of the hint embedded in Dubois' notion of double consciousness to view the veil as a liminal space, a "second site . . . a shamanic gift" (43). During Dubois' lifework, the functional task of the second-sight is Sankofan. It is learning to veil walk to embrace and re-member African-centered consciousness and both learn the Eurocentric views. The caution learned was to pass through the veil whole, intact, not leaving any parts of the African "self" in the void. To remain in the void of the veil without being anchored to the historicity of the communal African self would result in the split psyche—the sterilizing of the Soul, a "compulsory abandonment of blackness and black identity" (Winant 3). Then, the Sankofan approach as a critical learning task is navigating between veils to learn and transport knowledge from the margins to the center and back again to the margins—hence veil walking. This process requires an intense seeing and requires the entire body to see the history of the system and how that system is informed by and nested within structural and historical systems. Zora Neale Hurston (1935) tells the following story in *Mules and Men* to illustrate what happens if our Black talent remains in the void without activating second-sight. In this story that follows, Hurston is speaking to the notion of the daughters of the community—returning from higher education to the soil that cultivated them as strategic nation builders—abandoning the gifts they left with and instead, returning less fortified to "guide the hundredths":

> Ah know another man wid a daughter.
> The man sent his daughter off to school for seven years, den she come home all finished up. So he said to her, "Daughter, git yo' things and write me a letter to my brother!" So she did.
> He says, "Head it up," and she done so.
> "Now tell'im, 'Dear Brother, our chile is done come home from school and all finished up and we is very proud of her."
> Then he ast de girl "Is you got dat?"
> She tole 'im "yeah."
> "Now tell him some mo'. 'Our mule is dead but Ah got another mule and when Ah say (clucking sound of tongue and teeth) he moved from de word." "Is you got dat?" he askt de girl.
> "Naw suh," she tole 'im
> He waited a while and he ast her again, "You got dat down yet?"
> "Naw suh, Ah ain't got it yet."
> "How come you ain't got it?"
> "Cause Ah can't spell (clucking sound)."
> "You mean to tell me you been off to school seven years and can't spell (clucking sound)? Why Ah could spell dat myself and Ah ain't been to school a day in mah life. Well jes'say (clucking sound) he'll know what you' mean and go on wid de letter" (43–44).

Hurston (1995) also argued that by studying the folklore of African Americans, we can learn a significant amount of information about the "undreamed geniuses" who lived and died during the Ma'afa, the Holocaust of Enslavement (905, quoted in Ogunleye 436).

Implicit in this story is an expectation to go off, and get what you can and return the talent back to the community, without leaving nor losing your homegrown wisdom. This is the application of the Sankofan approach—the praxis. Examining the self historically in proximity to the collective and to the systems and structure continuously actively situates and resituates ourselves in critical self-work with the community, which is a new pathway and mindset can emerge. The notion of who and what we are is not to be easily dissected, nor set aside from how we engage the work. Learning to translate what we are learning during the time travel of the Sankofan approach to Afrocentric adult education leadership preparation is actualizing a process of naming, translating language, and creating new knowledge pathways or Nommoic Creativity, which is the outer manifestation.

Nommoic Creativity Learning Task

> Nommoic Argumentation can be understood as argumentation that employs definitional and semantic precision and sophistication. It introduces new words, new phrases, new concepts: and it re-introduces familiar concepts in fresh, creative-innovative ways. Nommoic argumentation invites and challenges African people-and ultimately all people –to think, perceive, conceive, create, speak, and finally to behave in new and more human ways (Gray 30).

> [P]erformance and behaviors become stronger and are maintained longer when people have new words and vitalized concepts imprinted in their psyche (Gray 107).

Hudson-Weems is adamant about the importance of "proper naming or nommo" (Hudson-Weems 208). The African concept of nommo an "interconnecting phenomenon" is representative of merging our individual and community knowledge and integrating this with historical knowing—what we do with and how we name our Sankofan experiences. When we "give name to a particular thing, [we] simultaneously give it meaning" (Hudson-Weems 449). For example, in the practice of Africana Womanism's tenet of self-naming, I am a Black woman, mother, adult educationist. I occupy this space as resistance and liberation for myself, for the Black man as my counterbalance, for my children and thus by extension, the Black community. Through Nommoic Creativity, a decolonizing act of translating discourse, I am at all times and in all ways "distinguishing between the language of centeredness and the less precise language of decenteredness in relation to culture" (Asante 98). Therefore, Nommoic Creativity as practices can be thought of in the way Thomas et al. ("Toward the Development") describes the tenets of Africana Womanism as "incorporating neutral and liberal gender roles and expectations, Afrocentric values of collective survival, emotional vitality, African-centric spiritualism, oral tradition, role sharing, nurturing relationships both within and extended from the family, and a being orientation to time" (427).

Asante ("Intellectual Dislocation") explains that to (re)language embodies the communicative power of the Nommoic learning task,

> In communication this means that our paths are complicated often by the unwieldy use of concepts, symbols, arguments, and opinions that hound our intellectual discussions. It is as if Jews were left with only the

> concepts and ideas of Nazi Germany for their own explanations of self and community. The limitation of such language imprisonment is profoundly demonstrated when we are unable to break through to our own cultural realities (98).

In other words, the key is to remain grounded as to not get lost while veil walking unable to hold nor transport a voice of African centeredness results in taking on whichever voice is dominant. Asante also offers as a Nommoic learning strategy to remain grounded and resistant to becoming fragmented, which is to embrace "close community language as well as the religious [, spiritual] allusions"; other various "cultural information" (Asante 2). The son, MK Asante, in his brilliant memoir titled *Buck: A memoir* (2013), describes operationalizing language for communal liberation to master retrieving, returning, and infusing the Sankofan learning as "laying in the cut like peroxide . . . growing eyes that hear and ears that see" (179). The father, Molefi Asante ("Locating a Text") describes the wielding language Nommoically below.

> More fundamentally, the reader must know from what center of experience the writer writes. But to really come from an African-centered perspective in literature, the writer must immerse herself or himself in the culture of the people. The value of this immersion is that one becomes more authentically a voice of the culture, speaking (9).

Gumbo ya ya is strategy to operationalize Nommoic Creativity while veil walking. Luisah Teish (1985) in *Jambalaya: The Natural Woman's Book of Personal Charms and Practical Rituals* defines *Gumbo ya ya* as a southern creole term meaning, "everybody talks at once" (140), a type of cultural information embodying Nommoic Creativity. I describe Gumbo ya ya as a sense making tool to listen to multiple conversations simultaneously and follow those various conversations around to create a communal story ". . . *all the while, calling out history*" (Sakho 6) by "layering multiple and asymmetrical stories" (Brown 307). Historian, Dr. Elsa Barkley Brown ("What Has Happened Here") defines *Gumbo ya ya* as creating a communal dialogue by synthesizing one's personal journey "in concert with the group" (297). She argues for this practice as a wholistic practice of telling and making sense of history, a form of resiliency, a tie that binds individual histories into communal histories and those into political, economic, and social histories. Sheared ("An Africentric Feminist Perspective") likens Gumbo ya ya to a Nommoic gift of Black folks to polyrhythmic, "multiple perspectives intersect simultaneously and help us interpret the word and the world. It is the multiple rhythms that flow and course through one's being. It ultimately induces a sense of self understanding and self worth which is reflected in one's words and thoughts" (5).

The process of returning to the past to retrieve information, ideology, practice, behaviors thoughts to make new meaning is the to locate purpose and center cultural knowledge of Black leadership and a justice imperative for Afrocentric Adult Education Leadership preparation. This means that the Sankofan Approach to commandeer, the social and cultural borders, gaps, margins, and liminal spaces weaponizes the veil with Nommoic Creativity to not only transport and translate knowledge from the dominant world back to these uneven and inequitable spaces but also to carry that rich thick counter-knowledge across systems of power for liberating new knowledge.

Locke speaks clearly from the past, as we are reckoning with, at this moment, a reawakening of racialized violence against Black bodies and the sociocultural illiteracy about the Afrocentric epistemologies and praxis: Do we need to recall the mass irrationalities . . . particularly if as average reactions show, its current standards are as puerile, irresponsible, and reactionary as they seem. In fact, as far as the mass media are concerned, it begins to appear that instead of accepting their fair share of the effort to make adults adult-minded, many aspects of their public offerings are in collusion either to keep them in a state of arrested adolescence or even to reduce them to a sub-normal moronic level (Locke 110).

The Learning Task of Maatic Argumentation

> Maat is a constant goal of Afrocentric practitioners. Afrocentric practitioners *apply* the Afrocentric perspective, so that Maat—justice—is more than a word. Afrocentric practitioners work so that African people experience and can continually secure justice. They practice and train others in the practice of the Afrocentric perspective, so that justice becomes an experiential norm, a regular reality. Indeed, a central point of praxis is that praxis leads to justice! Praxis—that is, thoughtful reflection combined with constructive practice, behavior, and action—results in Maat/justice. Maatic Argumentation consists of the articulation of justice, the demonstration of justice, the securing of justice and the training of others in the articulation-demonstration-and-securing of justice (Gray 109).

Dubois (1934) spoke directly in the *Nation within a Nation* speech about the wrongheadedness or "futile logic" of "Scatter, Suppress, Wait, Escape" that in present times continues to interrupt our striving for Maatic "[p]raxis—that is, *thoughtful reflection combined with constructive practice, behavior, and action*—results in Maat/justice" (Gray 109 emphasis by author). "We must have unselfish, far-seeing leadership or we fail" (Dubois 173, quoted in Rabaka 416). Karenga is firm, Maat insists on a holistic view of the moral ideal, one that gives rightful and adequate attention to self, society, and the world as component parts of an interrelated order of rightness (Karenga 408).

To accept that Maatic praxis is justice and begins with accepting that each of us as Black adult educators are communal care-givers. Ubuntuism, the African philosophy of care-giving spoken of as Hunhuism or Ubuntuism, is a "code of behavior" for being in right relationship with "others and life" (Samkange and Samkange 1980). These care-giving dispositions are the precepts and foundational behaviors that include; "kindness, courtesy, consideration and friendliness" (Samkange and Samkange 1980), and create complete acceptance of connectedness to the other that are "unselfish, far-seeing leadership." To seek justice then, we must be at home with Afrocentric strategic planning that is guided by racial fortuity. DuBois (1996) is demanding that we, Afrocentric adult educators be unapologetic and "teach that which [we] have learned in no American school" (420, quoted in Rabaka, 414).

> [DuBois'] philosophy of education did not ask but demand Africana educators to go above and beyond their training in Western European and European American history, culture, religion, politics, arts, and so forth and re-root themselves and their constituencies in African history and culture and African thought, belief, and value systems and traditions (Dubois 1996, quoted in Rabaka 415).

In *Silent Covenants: Brown v. Board of Education and the Unfulfilled Hopes for Racial Reform,* Derrick Bell's last published work before his transition to high Ancestor, leaves behind a Maatic call to develop tools, strategies, and processes to prepare the community for the next opportunity when interests converge. I argue we are here now, when it appears in the time of a global pandemic, racial violence against Black bodies—men, women, and youth—that the interests of Black folks might converge with sociocultural change. The foundation of the interest convergence thesis, as understood by critical race theorists, rests in understanding that "Black rights are recognized and protected when and only so long as policymakers perceive that such advances will further interests that are their primary concern" (Bell 49). Social and legal events unfolding around racial and economic equity place the potentiality of an interest convergence opportunity on the horizon. The sociopolitical and sociocultural atmosphere in 2020, demonstrates what might be discussed as a convergence of legal, educational, and policy interests. It is not the purpose of this chapter to expand nor debate the scholarship of interest convergence as a theoretical framework and major tenant of critical race theory. It is in the scope of this work to be interested in and bring into conversation the practical application of Maatic argumentation of Derrick Bell's suggestions for a racial fortuity plan. If, indeed, the mobilization of federal, local, and grassroots interests meet the tenets of an interest convergence, then how might Afrocentric Adult Education Leadership preparation capitalize on the momentum of the moment and be a catalyst in forging racial fortuity as Maatic praxis—justice? A rhetorical question, indeed. We simply put it into practice via creating and utilizing authentic Africana tools for our victory.

Africana Womanism is doing just that, as we insist upon the interconnectedness of

> . . . the myriad of issues encountered by our communities. "Race," class and gender, and the prioritization therein, have always been key issues for comprehending "*Africana Womanism.*" This by no means weakens the analysis of empowerment for Africana Women, for it actually strengthens the analysis from dividing Africana women from their men, whether it be spouses, brothers, nephews, cousins, uncles, fathers, and so on. . . . The Africana world is under tremendous assault. We need to take firm responsibility, and that means individual and collective, men and women (Christian 131).

In conclusion, I am, thus, positing the reoccurrence of "race-conscious education policies that fail to account for race and racism . . . still advantag[ing] the dominant group and continue to disadvantage the group that such remedies [are] designed to serve" (Horsford 294). However, to effectively and equitably converge the interests of Afrocentric Adult Education leadership preparation for our future leaders, with the current social, legal, and political interests, Africana Womanist adult educators must insist upon innovative and systematic ways to "forge racial fortuity" (Bell 189). Bell chose a mighty counter discourse in "forge" with origins meaning to make way—to move ahead and from the Latin "fabricari" (Online Etymology Dictionary 2012) to frame, construct, build through steady planning, a critical resistance to dominant discourse. Here, Bell eloquently describes this act as "providing insulation against the frustration of rejection" when the chance to converge interests occurs (189). This is a wisdom and our chance is now. Designing, implementing, and developing Afrocentric learning task toward Afrocentric Adult Education Leadership preparation require program plans that (1) develop resistance to dominant epistemologies as Maatic Argumentation; (2) frame an understanding of the situatedness Black Prek-20 education—operating in three interlocking realms: agent, situation, and context by applying a Sankofan Approach to inquiry; (3) create counter-knowledge that disrupts all dimensions of dominate narratives, a language capable of both engaging and negotiating a consensus of interests across boundaries and disciplines by applying Nommoic Creativity; and (4) develop Afrocentric Adult Education Leadership preparation networks, in the practice of Hudson-Weems' Africana Womanism, that set goals for improvement initially and eventually toward sustainable transformative change.

Bibliography

Alfred, Mary V. "The Politics of Knowledge and Theory Construction in Adult Education: A Critical Analysis from an Africentric Feminist Perspective." *TITLE AERC 2000: An International Conference. Proceedings of the Annual Adult Education Research Conference, 41st, Vancouver,* 2000.

Ani, Marimba. *Yurugu: An African-Centered Critique of European Cultural Thought and Behavior,* vol. 213, Africa World Press, 1994.

Armah, Ayi Kwei. *Two Thousand Seasons.* Heinemann, 1979.

Asante, Molefi Kete. "Intellectual Dislocation: Applying Analytic Afrocentricity to Narratives of Identity." *Howard Journal of Communication,* vol. 13, no. 1, 2002, pp. 97–110.

Asante, Molefi Kete. "Locating a Text: Implications of Afrocentric Theory." *The Afrocentric Paradigm,* 2003, pp. 235–244.

Asante, Molefi K. *Buck: A Memoir.* Spiegel & Grau, 2013.

Bell, Derrick. *Silent Covenants: Brown v. Board of Education and the Unfulfilled Hopes for Racial Reform.* Oxford University Press, 2004

Brigham, Susan. "Our Hopes and Dreams Enrich its Every Corner: Adult Education with an Africentric Focus." *Learning in Community. Joint International Conference of the Adult Education Research Conference (AERC) 48th National Conference and the Canadian Association for the Study of Adult Education (CASAE) 26th National Conference, Halifax, Nova Scotia,* 2007.

Brookfield, Stephen. "Self-Directed Learning, Political Clarity, and the Critical Practice of Adult Education." *Adult Education Quarterly,* vol. 43, no. 4, 1993, pp. 227–242.

Brookfield, Stephen D. *The Power of Critical Theory: Liberating Adult Learning and Teaching*. Jossey-Bass, An Imprint of Wiley, 2004.

Brookfield, Stephen D. *Becoming a Critically Reflective Teacher*. John Wiley & Sons, 2017.

Brown, Elsa Barkley. "'What Has Happened Here': The Politics of Difference in Women's History and Feminist Politics." *Feminist Studies*, vol. 18, no. 2, 1992, pp. 295–312.

Christian, Mark. Afterword in *Africana Womanism: Reclaiming Ourselves,* 5th ed., London and New York: Routledge, 2019, p. 131.

Colin III, Scipio A. J. "The Universal Negro Improvement Association and the Education of African American Adults." 1988. *Northern Illinois University, Department of Adult Education, Unpublished doctoral dissertation.*

Colin III, Scipio A. J. "Adult and Continuing Education Graduate Programs: Prescription for the Future." *New Directions for Adult and Continuing Education*, vol. 61, 1994, pp. 53–62.

Colin III, Scipio A. J. "Marcus Garvey: Africentric Adult Education for Self Ethnic Reliance," *Freedom Road: Adult Education of African Americans*, 1996, pp. 41–66.

Colin III, Scipio A. J., and Guy, Talmadge C. "An Africentric Interpretive Model of Curriculum Orientations for Course Development in Graduate Programs in Adult Education." *PAACE Journal of Lifelong Learning*, vol. 7, 1998, pp. 43–55.

Dillard, Cynthia B. "Leading with Her Life: An African American Feminist (Re)Interpretation of Leadership for an Urban High School Principal." *Educational Administration Quarterly*, vol. 31, no. 4, 1995, pp. 539–563.

Etymonline.com. 2017. Online Etymology Dictionary. [online] Available at: <http://etymonline.com/index.php?allowed_in_frame=0&search=tornado> [Accessed 2017].

Flowers, D. "An Afrocentric View of Adult Learning Theory." *Adult Learning Theory: A Primer*, Spiegel & Grau, 2003, pp. 1–4.

Gooden, Mark A., and O'Doherty, Ann. "Do You See What I See? Fostering Aspiring Leaders' Racial Awareness." *Urban Education*, vol. 50, no. 2, 2015, pp. 225–255.

Gray, Cecil Conteen. *Afrocentric Thought and Praxis an Intellectual History*. Africa World Press, 2001.

Guy, Talmadge C. "Prophecy from the Periphery: Main Locke's Philosophy of Cultural Pluralism and Adult Education." *AUTHOR Hyams, Melanie, Comp.; And Others TITLE Annual Adult Education Research Conference Proceedings, 35th, Knoxville, Tennessee,* 20–22 May 1993.

Haddix, Marcelle, et al. "At the Kitchen Table: Black Women English Educators Speaking Our Truths." *English Education*, vol. 48, no. 4, 2016, pp. 380.

Hayden, Robert C., and DuBois, Eugene E. "A Drum Major for Black Adult Education: Alain L. Locke." *The Western Journal of Black Studies*, vol. 1, no. 4, 1977, p. 293.

Horsford, Sonya Douglass. "Mixed Feelings About Mixed Schools: Superintendents on the Complex Legacy of School Desegregation." *Educational Administration Quarterly*, vol. 46, no. 3, 2010, pp. 287–321.

Hudson-Weems, Clenora. "Africana Womanism and the Critical Need for Africana Theory and Thought." *The Western Journal of Black Studies*, vol. 21, no. 2, 1997, pp. 79–84.

Hudson-Weems, Clenora. "Africana Womanism: An Overview." *Out of the Revolution: The Development of Africana Studies*, edited by Delores P. Aldridge, and Charlene Young, Lexington Books, 2000, pp. 205–17.

Hudson-Weems, Clenora. "Africana Womanism (1993)." *The Womanist Reader,* edited by Layli Phillips, Routledge, 2006, pp. 44–56.

Hurston, Zora Neale. "Mules and Men. 1935." New York: Harper Perennial, 1990.

James, Joy, and Farmer, Ruth. *Spirit, Space & Survival: African American Women in (White) Academe.*, London: New York: Routledge, 1993.

Johnson-Bailey, Juanita. *Sistahs in College: Making a Way Out of No Way*. Krieger Publishing Company, 2001.

Karenga, Maulana Ndabezitha. *Maat, the Moral Ideal in Ancient Egypt: A Study in Classical African Ethics.* Routledge, 2003.

Ladson-Billings, G. (1998). Just what is critical race theory and what's it doing in a nice field like education? *International journal of qualitative studies in education,* vol. 11, no. 1, pp. 7–24.

Locke, Alain. "Types of Adult Education: The Intellectual Interest of Negros." *Journal of Adult Education*, vol. 8, no. 3, 1935–36, p. 352.

Locke, Alain. "Education for Adulthood." *Adult Education Journal*, vol. 6, 1947, pp. 104–111.

MacKethan, Lucinda H. "Mother Wit: Humor in Afro-American Women's Autobiography." *Studies in American Humor*, vol. 4, no. 1/2, 1985, pp. 51–61.

Morrison, Toni. "The Site of Memory." *Inventing the Truth: The Art and Craft of Memoir*, edited by William Zinsser, Mariner Books, 1987, pp. 65–80.

Mtshali, Khondlo. "Gods, Ancestors, and Hermeneutics of Liberation in Ayi Kwei Armah's Two Thousand Seasons." *Journal of Black Studies*, vol. 40, no. 2, 2009, pp. 171–188.

Ntseane, Peggy Gabo. "Culturally Sensitive Transformational Learning: Incorporating the Afrocentric Paradigm and African Feminism." *Adult Education Quarterly*, vol. 61, no. 4, 2011, pp. 307–323.

Ogunleye, Tolagbe. "African American folklore: Its Role in Reconstructing African American History." *Journal of Black Studies*, vol. 27, no. 4, 1997, pp. 435–455.

Omolade, Barbara, and Carty, Linda. *The Rising Song of African-American Women.* Routledge, 1994.

Perkinson, James W. *Shamanism, Racism, and Hip Hop Culture: Essays on White Supremacy and Black Subversion.* Springer, 2005.

Perlow, Olivia N., et al., editors. *Black Women's Liberatory Pedagogies: Resistance, Transformation, and Healing Within and Beyond the Academy.* New York: Springer, 2017.

Rabaka, Reiland. "WEB Du Bois: From Pioneering Pan-Negroism to Revolutionary Pan-Africanism." *Routledge Handbook of Pan-Africanism*, 2020, pp. 399–449.

Richardson, Lystra M. "Making Learning Foundational in Developing School Leaders." *Procedia-Social and Behavioral Sciences*, vol. 174, 2015, pp. 2069–74.

Roseboro, Donyell L., and Ross Sabrina N. "Care-Sickness: Black Women Educators, Care Theory, and a Hermeneutic of Suspicion." *Educational Foundations*, vol. 23, 2009, pp. 19–40.

Sakho, Jacqueline Roebuck. "Black Activist Mothering: Teach Me About What Teaches You." *The Western Journal of Black Studies*, vol. 41, no. 1/2, 2017, pp. 6–19.

Samkange, Stanlake John Thompson. *Hunhuism or Ubuntuism: A Zimbabwe Indigenous Political Philosophy*. Salisbury, Rhodesia: Graham Publishing, 1980.

Sheared, Vanessa. "Giving Voice: An Inclusive Model of Instruction—A Womanist Perspective." *New Directions for Adult and Continuing Education*, vol. 61, 1994, pp. 27–37.

Sheared, Vanessa. "An Africentric Feminist Perspective on the Role of Adult Education for Diverse Communities." *International Adult & Continuing Conference*, 1996, pp. 2–11.

Sheared, Vanessa. *The Handbook of Race and Adult Education: A Resource for Dialogue on Racism*. Jossey-Bass, 2010.

Sissel, P., and Sheared, V. *Making Space*. Bergin and Garvey, 2001.

Smith, Sherwood E., and Colin III, Scipio A. J. "An Invisible Presence, Silenced Voices: African Americans in the Adult Education Professoriate." *Making Space: Merging Theory and Practice in Adult Education*, 2001, pp. 57–69.

Stovall, David. "Out of Adolescence and into Adulthood: Critical Race Theory, Retrenchment, and the Imperative of Praxis." *Urban Education*, vol. 51, no. 3, 2016, pp. 274–286.

Teish, L. (1985). Jambalaya: The natural woman's book of personal charms and practical rituals. Harper & Row.

Thomas, Anita Jones, Karen McCurtis, Witherspoon, and Speight, Suzette L. "Toward the Development of the Stereotypic Roles for Black Women Scale." *Journal of Black Psychology*, vol. 30, no. 3, 2004, pp. 426–442.

Winant, H. (2004). Dialectics of the veil. The new politics of race: Globalism, difference, justice, pp. 25–38.

Yancy, George. "Feminism and the Subtext of Whiteness: Black Women's Experiences as a Site of Identity Formation and Contestation of Whiteness." *The Western Journal of Black Studies,* vol. 24, no. 3, 2000, p. 156.

Part II
Africana Moments & Persuasions in Re-Shaping Our Lives

Few American authors have written and spoken as unreservedly, presciently—and prophetically, even—about America's diabolical, savage, and hateful treatment of African Americans, as did the incomparable James Arthur Baldwin. The celebrated, yet controversial, artivist—born in Harlem in 1924—routinely held up a mirror to American society, and never bowed, despite untold dangers, until the time of his 1assing, in Saint-Paul-de-Vence, France, at age 63. His body of work stands out in the literary canon as one of the most sublime, prolific, and imposing of the twentieth century, wherein, according to Hudson-Weems, "the Till lynching clearly establishes the fact that blacks are the most despised group and are more victimized by such heinous crimes, as tools of social control" (Hudson-Weems, *Emmett Till* 124).

(Pamela D. Reed, PhD)

Chapter 4
The Essential James Baldwin: Life and Literature, At Home and Abroad

Contributed by:
Pamela D. Reed, PhD

"Staggerlee Wonders" by James Baldwin—lines 43–44

Few American authors have written and spoken as unreservedly, presciently—and prophetically, even—about America's diabolical, savage, and hateful treatment of African Americans, as did the incomparable James Arthur Baldwin. The celebrated, yet controversial, "artivist"[1]—born in Harlem in 1924—routinely held up a mirror to the American society, and never bowed, despite untold dangers, until the time of his 1987 passing, in Saint-Paul-de-Vence, France, at age 63. His body of work stands out in the literary canon as one of the most sublime, prolific, and imposing of the twentieth century, wherein, according to Hudson-Weems, "blacks are the most despised group and are more victimized by such heinous crimes, as tools of social control" (124).

Not bound by genre, Baldwin wore numerous literary hats: novelist, essayist, poet, and playwright. From some one of his earliest and most seminal essays, to the poignant poetry volume, *Jimmy's Blues*, to his film-adapted novel, *Go Tell It on the Mountain*, to his groundbreaking play, *Blues for Mister Charlie,* as well as myriad interviews, and scholarly volumes analyzing his catalog, his works, and words are closely examined to pinpoint recurring themes and motifs that, even now, more than three decades since his passing, continue to resonate with—and inspire—generations of thinkers to study and build upon his ideas. As such, his writings have become a mainstay in the canons of both American and World Literatures.

What is more, in "A James Baldwin Book, Forgotten and Overlooked for Four Decades, Gets Another Life," the *New York Times* reports that, with the 2018 reissue of *Little Man, Little Man*, first published in 1976, "some Baldwin fans and scholars hope that, with the new edition . . . [the book] will rightfully assume its place in the canon of African-American

---

[1] Combining the words "art" and "activist," "artivist" is a portmanteau word.

children's literature, alongside works by Langston Hughes, Julius Lester, Walter Dean Myers and John Steptoe" (Alter par. 6).

This study seeks to mine the former child preacher's canonical belles lettres, both fiction and nonfiction, to gain insights into the philosophies espoused therein. His works and words are closely examined to pinpoint several recurring storylines and motifs found throughout his prolific catalogue. Of course, for Jimmy Baldwin, in this regard, White racial hatred toward Black people trumped all.

Beyond this seemingly never-ending, life-and-death problem, the Harlemite writer's prose reveals a preoccupation with the following literary cornerstones: religion, fire, birthing, love, carnality, time, police brutality, the prison-industrial complex, powerlessness, the Black family, and Black music, particularly gospel and the Blues. To be sure, this is not an exhaustive Baldwin thematic map, but the aforementioned subject-matter are the primary foci of the present treatment.

The "Negro Problem"

Baldwin "Staggerlee Wonders" 48

In his *New York Times* bestselling opus, "Begin Again: James Baldwin's America and Its Urgent Lessons for Our Own," Princeton scholar Eddie S. Glaude, Jr. points to the impassioned homily presented in the former child preacher's "The Uses of the Blues" essay to crystallize Baldwin's—and most Black people's—understanding, even if only subliminally, of the existential reality of the so-called "Negro Problem," the sense of powerlessness that grips Black parents in America when confronted with "the force of the world that is out to tell your child that he [or she] has no right to be alive" (qtd. in Glaude 450).

> In every generation, ever since Negroes have been here, every Negro mother and father has had to face that child and try to create in that child some way of surviving this particular world, some way to make the child who will be despised not despise himself. I don't know what "the Negro Problem" means to [W]hite people, but this is what it means to Negroes. (qtd. in Glaude 450–452)

"The looming danger," reasons Glaude, based on Baldwin's articulation to a group of students at Howard University, in 1963, "involved believing what the country said about them—that they would take the lies as truth and let them fester in their spirits" (449). Baldwin also spoke to this belief in "Everybody's Protest Novel," writing that it is the "peculiar triumph of society—and its loss—that it is able to convince those people to whom it has given inferior status [African Americans] of the reality of this decree; it has the force and the weapons to translate its dictum into fact, so that the allegedly inferior are actually made so, insofar as the societal realities are concerned" (2383).

Moreover, Glaude explains that, in the minds of racist White Americans, the "Negro Problem" really boils down to this: "the Negro *is* the problem" and, by extension, to this most relevant issue slash question: "What *more* does the Negro want?" (449; emphasis added). Baldwin, however, reframed this issue with the release in 1963 of, arguably, his best-known essay collection, *The Fire Next Time*.

> "The problem wasn't [B]lack people or simply reconciling our practices with our creed. The problem was [W]hite people. For Baldwin, there was no such thing as 'the Negro problem' . . . [He] maintained that navigating this contradiction was the *true* 'Negro problem'—not a problem *of* [B]lack people, but a problem *for* [B]lack people presented by the problem *with* [W]hite people" (Glaude 449–453).

Baldwin's Critics

All of this notwithstanding, in spite of Baldwin's life-long record of decrying racism and discrimination, both historical and contemporary, and using the weight of his name—and his deeds—to fight it, tooth-and-nail, not everyone found his work pleasing. On the one hand, he was beloved and hailed as a leader of the Civil Rights Movement, on the other, he was accused of being obsessed with Whites, and the openly gay activist was said, by some in the Black Power Movement of the 1960s, to be lacking in masculinity.

Black Panther leader Eldridge Cleaver was his most vociferous critic, beginning, most notably with his *Ramparts* essay, "Notes on a Native Son," later included in his acclaimed memoir and essay collection, *Soul on Ice*.

> He perceived Baldwin as a homosexual who projected his perverse love of [W]hite men onto the [B]lack freedom struggle. He seized upon Baldwin's nuance as a kind of failure of nerve in the revolutionary moment. Jimmy's desire "not to create enemies," his insistence on love, and ultimately, his version of a new kind of humanism shorn of constraining categories like race and sexuality rested upon, for Cleaver, a deep-seated self-hatred . . . For him, [W]hite supremacy emasculated [B]lack men . . . Thus, politics became [B]lack men fighting for their place among [W]hite men. Baldwin's words, his life really, called all of that into question (Glaude 224–225).

"There is in James Baldwin the most grueling, agonizing, total hatred of the [B]lacks, particularly of himself, and the most shameful, fanatical, fawning, sycophantic love of the [W]hites that one can find in any [B]lack American writer of note in our time," railed Cleaver (qtd. in Glaude 225). Baldwin was very aware of his extremely vocal detractors within the upper ranks of the Black Power and Black Arts Movements of the 1960s, even meeting with them in an effort to diffuse the tensions; however, Cleaver remained staunchly opposed. Baldwin, in *Paris Review*, addresses his relationship, or lack thereof, with the 1960s icon.

> I never had a relationship with Cleaver. I was in difficulties because of Cleaver, which I didn't want to talk about then, and don't wish to discuss now. My real difficulty with Cleaver, sadly, was visited on me by the kids who were following him, while he was calling me a faggot and

> the rest of it. I would come to a town to speak, Cleveland, let's say, and he would've been standing on the very same stage a couple of days earlier. I had to try to undo the damage I considered he was doing. I was handicapped with *Soul on Ice*, because what I might have said in those years about Eldridge would have been taken as an answer to his attack on me. So, I never answered it, and I'm not answering it now. Cleaver reminded me of an old Baptist minister I used to work with when I was in the pulpit. I never trusted him at all. As for Baraka, he and I have had a stormy time too, but we're very good friends now ("James Baldwin, the Art" par. 159).

"Baldwin's critics couldn't make up their minds if he was not [B]lack enough or too [B]lack. 'On one side of town I was an Uncle Tom,' Baldwin said in a 1984 interview, 'and on the other the Angry Young Man.'" (Dyson 194).

> It is never entirely true that you don't give a shit what others say about you, but you must throw it out of your mind. I went through a very trying period . . . It could make one's head spin, the number of labels that have been attached to me. And it was inevitably painful, and surprising, and indeed, bewildering. "I *do* care what certain people think about me" ("James Baldwin, the Art" par. 173).

His "Angry Young Man" comment, stated above, brings to mind the *Invisible Man* author, Ralph Ellison—himself, also labeled an "Uncle Tom"—who, outside of his fiction, remained mute on American race relations, and who, apparently, thought Jimmy should do likewise. Baldwin was aware that Ellison frowned upon his outspoken activism, leading to their estrangement, as revealed in that wide-ranging *Paris Review* interview, just a few years before his passing.

> No. I gather Ralph did not like what he considered I was doing to myself on the civil-rights road. And so, we haven't seen each other.
>
> I'd love to meet him for lunch tomorrow, and share a bottle of bourbon, and probably talk about the last twenty years we haven't seen each other. I have nothing against him in any case. And I love his great book. We disagreed about tactics, I suppose. But I had to go through the civil-rights movement, and I don't regret it at all. And those people trusted me. There was something very beautiful about that period, something life-giving for me to be there, to march, to be a part of a sit-in, to see it through my own eyes ("James Baldwin, the Art" par. 167–169).

Moreover, Baldwin explained, "Once I was in the civil-rights milieu, once I'd met Martin Luther King Jr. and Malcolm X and Medgar Evers and all those other people, the role I had to play was confirmed." As well, he notes, "I didn't think of myself as a public speaker, or as a spokesman, but I knew I could get a story past the editor's desk. And once you realize that you can do something, it would be difficult to live with yourself if you didn't do it ("James Baldwin, the Art" par. 52).

In keeping with this belief, the playwright also dramatized, in *Blues for Mister Charlie*, the story of the brutal murder of 14-year-old Emmett Till in Money, Mississippi, in the year 1955. As noted by the Africanist Womanist theorist and preeminent Emmett Till Scholar, Clenora Hudson-Weems, in *Emmett Till: The Sacrificial Lamb of the Civil Rights Movement*,

> James Baldwin ... makes obvious use of the Till story. In his "Notes for *Blues*" (*for Mr. Charlie*), he announces that the play was based on the Till murder case. He establishes his intention in writing the play, which is to "draw a vivid portrait of the murderer." ... products of the American racist society.
>
> The fact that the dominant culture would frequently, without reservation, inflict the cruelest forms of violence on an oppressed people, as in the case of the Till lynching, clearly establishes the fact that blacks are the most despised group and are more victimized by such heinous crimes, as tools of social control. ... The intent of the dominant culture is to control the African American and hold him or her in a subordinate position (Hudson-Weems 124).

Demonstrating, perhaps, his assertion made, in April 1980, to the legendary Nigerian writer Chinua Achebe, that "the poet is produced by the people because the people need him," Baldwin, in *Staggerlee Wonders*, using the voice of his alter ego—or, alternatively, the metaphorical voice for the African American collective, a perennially dispossessed people—the poet addressed the criticism of his alleged focus on White people, another criticism levied against the embattled author ("James Baldwin and Chinua Achebe" par. 21).

Baldwin "*Staggerlee Wonders*" 33

My former professor, mentor, and dissertation director, Temple University scholar and thought leader, Molefi Kete Asante, in a *New York Times* interview, proffers a perspective germane to this supposition that Black people, in their fight against White supremacy, should ignore White people.[2] "When one asks about the elimination of racism," insists Asante, "then the concentration cannot be on African people, but [rather], on the perpetrators of racism. Who acculturates racists? What does a [W]hite child learn about privilege?" (Yancy and Asante par. 5).

Still, Baldwin understood that when it comes to trying to collaborate with White people, there *are* limits, that too much White involvement, or perceived deference to them, was to risk stymying the movement, as he made clear in a 1964 interview.

---

[2] Asante, a historical figure in his own right, is the longtime Professor and Chair of Temple University's famed Department of Africology and African American Studies, home of the world's first doctoral program in the discipline.

> For the first time in the history of this struggle, the poor Negro has hit the streets, really. And it has changed the nature of the struggle completely. Pressure is being brought to bear by the people in the streets, especially by the poor and by the young, so that movement leaders are always in a position of having to assess, very carefully, their tactics. If the people feel betrayed, you've lowered their morale and then opened the door on a holocaust. I think that the Negro in America has reached a point of despair and disaffection. People talk about certain techniques being used that are destroying the goodwill of white people. But nobody gives a damn any longer about the goodwill of people who have never done anything to help you or to save you. Their ill will can hardly do more harm than their goodwill. And this is a very significant despair (qtd. in Warren par. 26).

When asked about the timing of his decision to have an all-White cast of characters in *Giovanni's Room*, his groundbreaking 1956 novel about same-sex and bisexual relations, he answered, "I don't quite know when it came, though it broke off from what later turned into *Another Country*" ("James Baldwin, the Art" pars. 46–47).

> I certainly could not possibly have—not at that point in my life—handled the other great weight, the "Negro problem." The sexual-moral light was a hard thing to deal with. I could not handle both propositions in the same book. There was no room for it. I might do it differently today, but then, to have a [B]lack presence in the book at that moment, and in Paris, would have been quite beyond my powers. ("James Baldwin, the Art" pars. 46–47)

Life and Literature, At Home and Abroad

When it came to American racism, increasingly, Baldwin knew, first-hand, of whence he wrote. The proverbial noose was tightening around his neck in the American northeast. Things came to a head when he and a friend were refused service at two restaurants one night in Trenton, New Jersey, prompting the incensed writer to famously throw a glass of water in the face of a White waitress. He escaped the scene, mercifully, with his life, but only after fleeing the horde of angry White men who quickly surrounded him. Two years earlier, his best friend reportedly jumped to his death from the George Washington Bridge. That was the final straw. He felt that "[his] luck was running out." (Guedj par. 2; "James Baldwin, the Art" par. 5).

Baldwin decided to leave, ultimately, seeking refuge across the pond, saying later, "I knew what was going to happen to me, I'd kill or be killed . . . I left because I didn't think I could survive the race problems." After weighing his options, the 24-year-old cipher chose Paris, where his friend and mentor, the great Richard Wright, and his family, had been living a relatively peaceful existence, then, for two years (Guedj par. 2).

Fed up with what he called the "sunlit prison of the American dream," and feeling "chewed up by the city," and "by the impossibility of being Black in the city," and, as well, convinced that "all of society [had] decided to transform [him] into nothing," Baldwin made the fateful decision to board a transatlantic flight to the storied City of Lights, on November 11, 1948, with $40 to his name, and "no grasp whatever of the French language" ("Everybody's Protest" 2063; "Equal in Paris"; "Perspective" pars. 3–4).

> It developed, shortly, that I had no grasp of the French character either. I considered the French an ancient, intelligent, and cultured race, which indeed they are. I did not know, however, that ancient glories imply, at least in the middle of the present century, present fatigue and, quite probably, paranoia; that there is a limit to the role of the intelligence in human affairs; and that no people come into possession of a culture without having paid a heavy price for it. (Baldwin "Equal in Paris" par. 3)

After having lived there just a little over a year, Baldwin would, on December 1, in 1949, pay a heavy price for his naivete, in what would prove to be the nadir of his time in France: eight days spent in a Parisian prison. This, following a strange incident at the Grand Hôtel du Bac, on the rue du Bac, near the Bon Marché department store. He faced "results which were not less dire for being also comic-opera," he writes in his essay, "Equal in Paris: An Autobiographical Story," in *Commentary Magazine*. Detailing "the machine in which [he had] become entangled," the piece was billed as "the story of the encounter of a young American with the institutions of French justice" (pars. 1–16).

> It was in this hotel that Baldwin received a young American man, [who] placed him in a delicate situation. The American . . . a guest in a neighboring hotel . . . presented Baldwin with a set of stolen sheets. Falsely accused of theft, Baldwin was imprisoned for a week, and was only released thanks to the fact he was an American citizen. But upon returning to the hotel, he was greeted with an incredibly expensive check. Unable to cope, he attempted to kill himself. Changing his mind at the last minute, he fled to Switzerland with his friend and lover, the painter Lucien Happersberger ("Equal in Paris"; Guedj par. 11).

In the end, things worked out, and the literary icon's historic sojourn in France would become the stuff of legends, but those 192 hours of Gallic incarceration, during that moment in time, made Baldwin second guess his decision to leave America.

> And it must have seemed to me that my flight from home was the cruelest trick I had ever played on myself, since it had led me here, down to a lower point than any I could ever in my life have imagined—lower, far, than anything I had seen in that Harlem which I had so hated and so loved, the escape from which had soon become the greatest direction of my life ("Equal in Paris" par. 14).

Of course, young Baldwin would bounce back from what must have been a devastating and humbling setback—and he was able to, eventually, find the humor in this chapter of his life that he refers to as his Great Adventure: that first year in Paris, moving from hotel to hotel—having come to the realization that, as he writes, "in some deep, black, stony, and liberating way, my life, in my own eyes, *began* during that first year in Paris, when it was borne in on me that . . . laughter is universal and never can be stilled" ("Equal in Paris" par. 30; emphasis added).

To be sure, his was a rocky start in Paris. "I went through this period where I was very much alone, and wanted to be," he reflected. "I wasn't part of any community until I later became the Angry Young Man in New York" ("James Baldwin, the Art" par. 6). Escaping the drab, dismal hotel rooms in which he resided, young Baldwin spent many hours in bars and cafes, particularly the Café de Flore, he recounts in the *Paris Review* interview.

> A lot of *Go Tell It on the Mountain* had to be written there, between there and the Hotel Verneuil, where I stayed for a lot of the time I was in Paris. After ten years of carrying that book around, I finally finished it in Switzerland in three months. I remember playing Bessie Smith all the time while I was in the mountains, and playing her till I fell asleep. The book was very hard to write because I was too young when I started, seventeen; it was really about me and my father. There were things I couldn't deal with technically at first. Most of all, I couldn't deal with *me* ("James Baldwin, the Art" par. 43).

Thereafter, off-and-on, for the remainder of his life, Baldwin would reside in France, where "he wrote his most famous works, such as *Notes of a Native Son* (1955), *Giovanni's Room* (1956), and *Just Above My Head* (1979), and where he was able to gain the heightened perspective he needed to fight against racial inequalities in the United States" (Guedj par. 1).[3]

The American writer boiled it down to this in a 1984 *Paris Review* interview: "The French gave me what I could not get in America, which was a sense of 'If I *can* do it, I *may* do it.' I won't generalize, but in the years I grew up in the U.S., I could not do that. I'd already been defined" ("James Baldwin, the Art" 28; emphasis added).

There, particularly in Paris, he spent many hours with immigrant African students, particularly Algerians, affording him the opportunity to expand his view of the world, and to better understand his place *in* it—to self-define—as one descended from Africa. Baldwin

---

[3] Baldwin's novel *Just Above My Head* was translated in French, titled *Harlem Quartet*, and released on January 1, 1987, less than a year before his passing, on December 1, that same year. A stage adaption of the French-language book, produced and directed by Élise Vigier, in collaboration with Kevin Keiss, and with original music by Saul William, premiered in November 2017, outside Paris, at the Maison des Arts de Creteil. The production ran for three nights, after which it toured France, through March 2018. It was staged at Princeton University's Whitman College Theatre, performed in French—with English subtitles—for two nights in September 2018 (Bloom; Parenteau; "Harlem Quartet").

volunteered, in his 1984 *Paris Review* interview, just three years before his passing, when he was 60 years old, that if he were 24 again, instead of France, he might have chosen some part of Africa in which to reside ("James Baldwin, the Art" par. 103).

Still, "as an exiled man, [he] never forgot his native land. [Chalk it up to] the 'lucidity of distance,' he thought." (qtd. in Guedj par. 16). "Baldwin insisted that it was outside of the United States that he came to understand the country more fully" (Glaude 31).

> While he never returned definitively, Baldwin spent an increasing amount of time in the United States. From 1960 onwards he also became a major player in the civil rights movement. Fighting alongside [Dr.] Martin Luther King, he often gave speeches and offered social commentary on the struggle in the press. While at the American Church of Paris in August 1963, he launched a petition for the release of . . . King [from a Birmingham jail], which was signed by several celebrities, including actor Anthony Quinn (Guedj par. 14).

Baldwin and a group of American expatriates had planned a "sympathy march" for the same day as the historic March on Washington led by Martin Luther King. Ultimately, bogged down in red tape involving the French authorities, the Americans in Paris abandoned that idea and, "instead, eighty to one hundred people 'walked' alone or in small groups from the American church to the Embassy at about the same time on August 21, a week before the actual March. Others showed up separately at the Embassy, so that by the end of the day, over 550 petitions had been delivered" (Dudziak pars. 16–20).

The culmination of the "walk" occurred when Baldwin and the group of expatriate leaders, headed by actor, William Marshall, reached the Embassy. The delegation included actress, Hazel Scott, blues pianist and singer, Memphis Slim, jazz clarinetist, Mezz Mezroe, and blues singer, Mae Mercer. They delivered "a scroll of signatures" to American career diplomat, Cecil B. Lyon, as "approximately one hundred and fifty others waited in the Embassy's main hall" (Dudziak par. 20).

> James Baldwin [then] returned to the States, and on August 28, 1963, marched with over 200,000 people to the Lincoln Memorial. The news of support from Americans overseas was conveyed to the crowd as the actor Burt Lancaster read the Paris petition to the crowd. When Martin Luther King, Jr. gave the final speech of this historic day, his words echoed across continents, as well as across time. (Barber 170–171; Washington 217–220)

Baldwin's activism did not end there. He was consumed with the fight for Black justice in America for the duration of his life.

> During the 1970s, Baldwin and French novelist Jean Genet helped to organize a group in support of the Soledad Brothers, who had been accused of killing a [W]hite prison guard. Baldwin also discussed the actions and positions taken by the Black Panther Party during numerous debates (Guedj par. 14).

Between his return visits to the United States, "[f]aced with the turmoil that accompanied his political activism," Baldwin sought more tranquility than that afforded in his beloved, yet sometimes violent, Paris. Upon the urging of friends, he eventually rented a remote, modest *poutres*-and-stone villa, outside Nice, near the Mediterranean Sea, in Saint-Paul-de-Vence, France, where he lived intermittently, from that point forward. There, at peace, he wrote his novel *Just Above My Head*, and he hosted and entertained many visiting American luminaries. "Baldwin's prestigious guest list grew ever longer, including Miles Davis, Toni Morrison, Bill Cosby, Nina Simone, Sidney Poitier, and Ray Charles. The farmhouse was modestly decorated, but everything was linked to America, such as photos and paintings of Harlem" (Guedj pars. 15–16).

While being an American expatriate, in many ways, freed him from the constant pressure of having the White man's proverbial foot on his neck in the States, he understood that France was also a notoriously racist, White supremacist nation. "I would probably have lost morale if I had made the mistake of thinking Paris was the most civilized city in the world," he said (Baldwin qtd. in Guedj par. 8).

> Baldwin also understood, through his interactions with people from colonized countries, that racism was very present in France. He discovered the demands and expectations of Africans in France, and logically compared his own condition with theirs. He wrote: "Africans have not been alienated from their own people and their past. Africans' mothers never sang 'Sometimes I Feel Like a Motherless Child'" (a traditional [N]egro spiritual composed in the United States before the abolition of slavery). Faced with this deformed reflection of himself, Baldwin asserted his own identity as a Black, American man, and decided to take back his history (Guedj par. 9).

Given all this, "one can perhaps see why James Baldwin [and] Richard Wright . . . are not given greater prominence in the literary curricula of this nation. Neither attempted to shed [their] Blackness," Asante writes, in his very important essay, "Locating a Text: Implications of Afrocentric Theory" (par. 15). Along these same lines, writers Maya Angelou and Amiri Baraka both, in their funerary remarks for their dearly departed friend, "asserted briefly but forcefully that Mr. Baldwin's novels and plays had been unjustly condemned or slighted" (Daniels par. 15).

Conclusion

Baldwin "Amen" 111

After battling cancer at his home in the South of France, Baldwin succumbed, at the age of 63, on December 1, 1987.[4] He was funeralized at the glorious Cathedral of Saint John the

---

[4] Cause of death is listed, variably, as stomach or esophageal cancer (Daniels par 5; Guedj par. 16).

Divine on the Upper West Side of Manhattan, Jimmy Baldwin's beloved Harlem. The *New York Times* report, "Friends Gather to Celebrate Baldwin's Gifts," written by filmmaker Lee Daniels, details his homegoing, one befitting a literary and cultural icon of his stature.

To name just a few, the following heavyweights of the literary and political arenas were in attendance, entering the stained-glass-adorned sanctuary in a grand processional, marching to the beat of the internationally renowned master African drummers of the Babatunde Olatunji Ensemble: filmmaker slash photographer Gordon Parks, poet, playwright, and Black Arts Movement architect Amiri Baraka (formerly LeRoi Jones), famed poet and autobiographer Maya Angelou, political activist Kwame Ture (the former Stokely Carmichael), biographer Arnold Rampersad, and Civil Rights Attorney William M. Kunstler (Daniels).

Kunstler penned an undated poem *James Baldwin*, written at an unspecified time after the celebrated writer's death, referencing Baldwin's activism during the time of the Atlanta child murders of 1979–1981, his book-length essay about which was published as *The Evidence of Things Not Seen*. Kunstler's reverent ode—now a part of the James Baldwin Archive at the Smithsonian National Museum of African American History and Culture.

The full range of the African American music canon was on full display, as numerous icons from various genres were on hand to pay musical tribute to the man who, at every turn, embedded this uniquely American art form into his writings.

> The folk singer Odetta, in a soaring voice that brought tears to the eyes of many assembled, sang passages from several songs, including "Motherless Child," "The Battle Hymn of the Republic," and "Let Us Break Bread Together." The trio of Hugh Masekela on trumpet, Jimmy Owens on flugelhorn and Danny Mixon on piano honored Mr. Baldwin with an extended salute that was by turns sorrowful and rollicking. Mr. Baldwin's own voice, a strong yet whispery baritone, was heard on a recording he made of the spiritual "Precious Lord" (Daniels par. 21).

Rampersad, the Sara Hart Kimball Professor in the Humanities, Emeritus, Stanford University, and biographer to, among others, W. E. B. DuBois, Langston Hughes, Ralph Ellison, Arthur Ashe, and Jackie Robinson, called Mr. Baldwin "an absolutely towering figure, certainly one of the greatest ever to interpret Afro-American life" (qtd. in Daniels par. 18).

The great scholar, music historian, and former Poet Laureate of the State of New Jersey, Amiri Baraka, born LeRoi Jones, once an outspoken Baldwin critic, proclaimed that his "friend and older brother," Jimmy Baldwin, "this glorious, elegant griot," was "not only a writer [and] an international literary figure, [more] he was a *man* . . . . This man traveled the earth like its [historian] and its biographer. He reported, criticized, made beautiful, analyzed, cajoled, lyricized, attacked, sang, made us think, made us better, made us consciously human" (Daniels pars. 6–17).

In his powerful, rousing eulogy to the fallen son of Harlem, as shown in the documentary, *James Baldwin: The Price of the Ticket*, Baraka, speaking in sermonic cadence, over constant applause, preached of Baldwin's greatness, his consistency, and his dedication, making clear the magnitude of what the Black World had lost with Baldwin's ascension to the ancestral realm:

> He lived his life as witness. He wrote until the end . . . Jimmy *produced*. He spoke. He sang. No matter the odds, he remained man and spirit, in voice, ever-expanding, and ever more conscious. Let us hold him in our hearts and minds. Let us make him a part of our invincible Black souls, the intelligence of our transcendence. Let our Black hearts grow big, world-absorbing eyes like his, never closed. Let us, one day, be able to celebrate him, like he *must* be celebrated if we are ever truly to be self-determining. For, Jimmy was God's Black Revolutionary mouth—if there *is* a God—and revolution His righteous, natural expression (4:29–5:26).

Maya Angelou "called upon [B]lack writers to take up Mr. Baldwin's legacy, 'to make it plain' that the task of the living is to 'try to love each other, try to hold on to each other'" (qtd. in Daniels par. 13). While wiping away her tears, she added the following, in *James Baldwin: The Price of the Ticket*:

> I first met Jim . . . [in Paris, and] we became friends, in the late 50s . . . just as Martin Luther King, Rosa Parks, and other Southerners were girding themselves for the second Civil War, in 100 years, and just when Malcolm X was giving voice to the anger in the streets and in the minds of Northern Black city-folks, in that riotous pulse of political fervor . . . James Baldwin was a brother, *incredible* (3:16–4:24).

As Toni Morrison said in her final tribute for Baldwin, his was "a life that refuses summation and invites contemplation instead . . . [with a] tenderness and vulnerability that asked everything of us, expected everything of us" (qtd. in *NY Times* par. 3). It was "one that combined a ruthless intelligence in identifying injustice with a profound pity for the frailties of human beings, part of a two-hour service—the first funeral in the cathedral since that of Duke Ellington in 1974—that was rich with ceremony, yet elegant in its simplicity" (Daniels par. 3).

The words of the Baldwin Family tribute to their beloved Jimmy seem a fitting ending to this present attempt to somehow comprehensively capture the life and works of James Arthur Baldwin, Son of Harlem and Citizen of the World:

> The voice of James Baldwin has continually come through to sing the epic grandeur of a people: sorrowful, triumphant, biblical. That voice has raised a live song, its constant refrain: "Love is a battle. Love is war. Love is growing up" . . . What also remains is that smile, those eyes, that strong hand of our son, our brother, our uncle, our father—our Jimmy—now ancestral. As he has said, "the irreducible miracle is that we have sustained each other a very long time, and come a long, long way." (qtd. in Daniels par. 23)

Bibliography

Alter, Alexandra. "A James Baldwin Book, Forgotten and Overlooked for Four Decades, Gets Another Life." *New York Times*, 20 Aug. 2018, www.nytimes.com/2018/08/20/books/review/james-baldwin-little-man-picture-book.html. Accessed 23 May 2021.

Angelou, Maya. "Eulogy." 1987, *James Baldwin: The Price of the Ticket*. Directed by Karen Thorsen, California Newsreel, 1990.

Asante, Molefi Kete. "Locating a Text: Implications of Afrocentric Theory." *Asante*, 10 May 2009, www.asante.net/articles/10/locating-a-text-implications-of-afrocentric-theory/. Accessed 19 May 2021.

Baldwin, James. "A Lover's Question." *Jimmy's Blues and Other Poems with an Introduction by Nikky Finney*. Beacon Press, 2014, Apple Books, pp. 99–101, books.apple.com/us/book/jimmys-blues-and-other-poems/id721589877. Accessed 24 May 2020.

———. "Amen." James Baldwin and Nikky Finney. "Jimmy's Blues and Other Poems." Beacon Press, 2014, Apple Books, p. 111, books.apple.com/us/book/jimmys-blues-and-other-poems/id721589877. Accessed 24 May 2021.

———. *Another Country*. Dial Press, 1962.

———. *Blues for Mister Charlie*. Dial Press, 1964.

———. "Down at the Cross: Letter from a Region in My Mind." *The Fire Next Time*. Dial Press, 1963, Apple Books, books.apple.com/us/book/james-baldwin-collection-7-books-fire-next-time-giovannis/id1549605192. Accessed 17 May 2021.

———. "Equal in Paris: An Autobiographical Story." *Commentary*, March 1955, www.commentarymagazine.com/articles/james-baldwin/equal-in-parisan-autobiographical-story/. Accessed 21 May 2021.

———. "Everybody's Protest Novel." *Partisan Review*, vol. XVI, no. 6, 1949, pp. 578–585, *James Baldwin Collection 7 Books: The Fire Next Time, Giovanni's Room, Go Tell it on the Mountain, If Beale Street Could Talk, Another Country, Notes of a Native Son, Sonny's Blues*, Apple Books, pp. 2052–2069, books.apple.com/us/book/james-baldwin-collection-7-books-fire-next-time-giovannis/id1549605192. Accessed 15 May 2021.

———. *The Evidence of Things Not Seen*. Henry Holt and Company, 1985.

———. *The Fire Next Time*. Dial Press, 1963.

———. *Giovanni's Room*. Dial Press, 1956.

———. *Go Tell It on the Mountain*. Alfred A. Knopf, 1952.

———. *If Beale Street Could Talk*. Dial Press, 1974, Apple Books, books.apple.com/us/book/if-beale-street-could-talk/id687071717. Accessed 17 May 2020.

———. "Inventory/On Being 52." James Baldwin and Nikky Finney. "Jimmy's Blues and Other Poems." Beacon Press, 2014. Apple Books, p. 105, books.apple.com/us/book/jimmys-blues-and-other-poems/id721589877. Accessed 24 May 2021.

———. "James Baldwin, the Art of Fiction No. 78." Interview with Jordan Elgrably. *Paris Review*, Issue 91, Spring 1984, www.theparisreview.org/interviews/2994/the-art-of-fiction-no-78-james-baldwin. Accessed 21 May 2021.

———. *James Baldwin Collection 7 Books: The Fire Next Time, Giovanni's Room, Go Tell it on the Mountain, If Beale Street Could Talk, Another Country, Notes of a Native Son, Sonny's Blues,* Apple Books, books.apple.com/us/book/james-baldwin-collection-7-books-fire-next-time-giovannis/id1549605192. Accessed 17 May 2020.

———. *Jimmy's Blues: Selected Poems.* St. Martin's Press, 1990, pp. 7–23.

———. *Jimmy's Blues and Other Poems with an Introduction by Nikky Finney.* Beacon Press, 2014, Apple Books, books.apple.com/us/book/jimmys-blues-and-other-poems/id721589877. Accessed 18 May 2020.

———. *Just Above My Head,* Dial Press, 1979.

———. *Little Man, Little Man: A Story of Childhood.* Dial Press, 1976.

———. *Little Man, Little Man: A Story of Childhood.* Illustrated by Yoran Cazac, edited by Nicholas Boggs and Jennifer DeVere Brody, Duke UP, 2018.

———. *No Name in the Streets.* Vintage, 2007.

———. *Notes of a Native Son.* Beacon Press, 1955.

———. "Song (for Skip)." *Jimmy's Blues and Other Poems with an Introduction by Nikky Finney.* Beacon Press, 2014, Apple Books, p. 50, books.apple.com/us/book/jimmys-blues-and-other-poems/id721589877. Accessed 18 May 2020.

———. "Staggerlee Wonders." *Jimmy's Blues and Other Poems with an Introduction by Nikky Finney.* Beacon Press, 2014. Apple Books, pp. 31–54, books.apple.com/us/book/jimmys-blues-and-other-poems/id721589877. Accessed 18 May 2020.

———. "The Uses of the Blues." *The Cross of Redemption: Uncollected Writings*, edited by and with an Introduction by Randall Kenan, Pantheon Books, 2010.

Barber, Lucy G. *Marching on Washington: The Forging of an American Political Tradition.* U of California P, 2002.

Bloom, Nicole Birmann. "Conversation With Élise Vigier, Director of *Harlem Quartet*." *The Theatre Times*, 22 Sept. 2018, thetheatretimes.com/conversation-with-elise-vigier-director-of-harlem-quartet/. Accessed 21 May 2021.

Brown, Cecil. *Stagolee Shot Billy.* Harvard University P, 2004.

Cleaver, Eldridge. "Notes on a Native Son." *Soul on Ice.* McGraw-Hill, 1968. *Ramparts Magazine*, June 1966, pp. 51–57, revolution.berkeley.edu/notes-native-son-eldridge-cleaver/. Accessed 21 May 2021.

Daniels, Lee A. "Friends Gather to Celebrate Baldwin's Gifts." *New York Times*, 9 Dec. 1987, www.nytimes.com/1987/12/09/arts/friends-gather-to-celebrate-baldwin-s-gifts.html. Accessed 20 May 2021.

Dorman, John L. "If Beale Street Could Talk Offers a Tour of a Lost New York." *New York Times*, 3 Feb. 2019, www.nytimes.com/2019/02/03/travel/if-beale-street-could-talk-new-york-james-baldwin-barry-jenkins.html. Accessed 16 May 2021.

Du Bois, W. E. B. "Criteria of Negro Art." *The Portable Harlem Renaissance Reader*, edited by and with an Introduction by David Levering Lewis, Penguin Books, 1994, pp. 100–105.

Dudziak, Mary L. "The 1963 March on Washington: At Home and Abroad." *Revue Française d'Études Américaines*, vol. 107, no. 1, 2006, pp. 61–76, www.cairn.info/revue-francaise-d-etudes-americaines-2006-1-page-61.htm. Accessed 20 May 2001.

Dyson, Michael Eric. *What Truth Sounds Like: RFK, James Baldwin, and Our Unfinished Conversation About Race in America*. St. Martin's Press, 2018, Apple Books, books.apple.com/us/book/what-truth-sounds-like/id1303600456. Accessed 14 May 2021.

Ellison, Ralph. *Invisible Man*. Random House, 1952.

Finney, Nikky. "Playing by Ear, Praying for Rain: The Poetry of James Baldwin." *Jimmy's Blues and Other Poems with an Introduction by Nikky Finney*. Beacon Press, 2014. Apple Books, books.apple.com/us/book/jimmys-blues-and-other-poems/id721589877. Accessed 18 May 2020.

Glaude, Eddie S., Jr. *Begin Again: James Baldwin's America and Its Urgent Lessons for our Own*. Crown, 2020, Apple Books, books.apple.com/us/book/begin-again/id1462587140. Accessed 16 May 2020.

Go Tell It on the Mountain. Directed by Stan Latham, performances by Paul Winfield, Rosalind Cash, Giancarlo Esposito, Douglas Turner Ward, and Ruby Dee, New Line Cinema, 1985.

Guedj, Pauline. "Perspective Through Exile: James Baldwin in France." Interview. *France-Amérique*, 4 June 2020, france-amerique.com/en/perspective-through-exile-james-baldwin-in-france/. Accessed 20 May 2021.

"Harlem Quartet." Princeton University Humanities Council, 21 Sept. 2018, humanities.princeton.edu/event/seuls-en-scene-french-theater-festival-harlem-quartet/. Accessed 21 May 2021.

Hudson-Weems, Clenora. *Emmett Till: The Sacrificial Lamb of the Civil Rights Movement*. Bedford Publishers, 1994.

James Baldwin: The Price of the Ticket. Directed by Karen Thorsen, California Newsreel, 1990.

Kunstler, William M. "James Baldwin." n.d., *National Museum of African American History and Culture*, James Baldwin Archive, Series 7, transcription.si.edu/view/34613/NMAAHC-A2017_47_7_1_26_004. Accessed 21 May 2021.

"The Legend of 'Stagger Lee' is Born." *History*, A&E Television Networks, 1 Apr. 2010, www.history.com/this-day-in-history/the-legend-of-stagger-lee-is-born. Accessed 19 May 2001.

MacGimsey, Robert. "Jonah and the Whale." *Rock in My Shoe*, performance by Tim O'Brien, 1995, genius.com/Tim-obrien-jonah-and-the-whale-lyrics#song-info, Accessed 15 May 2021.

Meisler, Stanley. "From the Archives: James Baldwin Dies at 63; Writer Explored Black Experience." *Los Angeles Times*, 2 Dec. 1987, www.latimes.com/local/obituaries/archives/la-me-james-baldwin-19871202-story.html. Accessed 21 May 2021.

Morrison, Toni. "Eulogy." Lee A. Daniels, *New York Times*, 9 Dec. 1987, www.nytimes.com/1987/12/09/arts/friends-gather-to-celebrate-baldwin-s-gifts.html. Accessed 20 May 2021.

Parenteau, Amelia. "Baldwin's Return to France: An interview with Élise Vigier." *Howl Round Theatre Commons*, 10 Feb. 2018, translate.google.com/translate?hl=en&sl=fr&u=https://howlround.com/baldwins-back-france&prev=search&pto=aue. Accessed 21 May 2021.

Popova, Maria. "James Baldwin and Chinua Achebe's Forgotten Conversation About Beauty, Morality, and the Political Power of Art." *Brain Pickings*, 21 Sept. 2016, www.brainpickings.org/2016/09/21/james-baldwin-chinua-achebe-art/. Accessed 22 May 2021.

Smith, Stephen Drury and Catherine Ellis. *Free All Along: The Robert Penn Warren Civil Rights Interviews*. The New Press, 2019.

Taubman, Howard. "Theater: 'Blues for Mister Charlie.'" *New York Times*, 24 Apr. 1964, archive.nytimes.com/www.nytimes.com/books/98/03/29/specials/baldwin-charlie.html. Accessed 22 May 2021.

Vigier, Élise, translator. *Harlem Quartet*, STOCK, 1987. By James Baldwin, *Just Above My Head*, Dial Press, 1979.

Warren, Robert Penn. "James Baldwin: 'I Can't Accept Western Values Because They Don't Accept Me.'" An Interview with Robert Penn Warren, *Literary Hub*, 1964, lithub.com/james-baldwin-i-cant-accept-western-values-because-they-dont-accept-me/. Accessed 23 May 2021.

Washington, James M., editor. *A Testament of Hope: The Essential Writings and Speeches of Martin Luther King, Jr.* Harper Collins, 1986.

Wright, Richard. *Lawd Today*. Northeastern UP, 1986.

———. *Native Son*. Harper, 1940.

Yancy, George and Asante, Molefi Kete. "Molefi Kete Asante: Why Afrocentricity?" *The Stone. The New York Times*, 7 May 2015, opinionator.blogs.nytimes.com/2015/05/07/molefi-kete-asante-why-afrocentricity/. Accessed 16 May 2021.

Chapter 5
The African American Literary Tradition

Contributed by:
Clenora Hudson-Weems, PhD

American Slavery and Antislavery (1619–1865)

From the very beginning, with the landing of the first slave ship in Jamestown, Virginia, African Americans have been expressing their reactions to their abject conditions in many ways. Most of these responses have been preserved in what is referred today as the African American literary tradition.

Although transplanted Africans were purposely kept illiterate, illiteracy is not synonymous with ignorance. Enslaved Blacks brought with them a vibrant oral tradition that reflected African culture and languages. They verbally transmitted traditional customs, values, and history to their offspring and each other. In fact, the only Black literature that survived the early period of enslavement was of the oral tradition, which vividly and collectively expressed a cadre of Black emotions, ranging from extreme fear to acquiescence, to anger, to confusion, to hope, to defiance, and to celebration.

The earliest types of the African oral tradition were the work songs and field hollers, which Blacks used to communicate to each other while working in the fields. There was also the folktale, with stories expressing African American values, explaining the unexplainable, and identifying acceptable "and unacceptable behavior." Exemplifying this category are "How Buck Won His Freedom," "The Knee-High Man Tries to Get Sizeable," and "People Who Could Fly."

Although there are debates regarding the origins of the oral tradition, which includes also proverbs, cries, and shouts, religious (spirituals) and secular (work) songs, according to Richard Barksdale and Kenneth Kinnamon in *Black Writers of America: A Comprehensive Anthology* (1972), all these oral traditions have their origins in an African folk tradition. Folklorists most noted for collecting and expounding on the origins of the folktale in particular include Richard Dorson *(American Negro Folktales* and *African Folklore)* and Julius Lester *(Black Folktales)*. To be sure, oral literature issued forth the earliest call for the deliverance of Blacks from abject servitude. In profound ways, such as double meanings in old Negro spirituals like "Go Down, Moses" and "Swing Low, Sweet Chariot," ostensibly addressing only religious needs of Blacks, these issuing forth of freedom quests invaded American slavery, collectively enabling Blacks to forge a plan for escape.

Signaling the beginning of the African American written literary tradition was the slave narrative of the early eighteenth century. Expressing an insatiable desire for the same human needs (liberty, fraternity, and equality) expressed by many white writers and thinkers of the period, the slave narrative was a genre that presented the physical and psychological conditions of servitude. Forerunner of this literary form is Olaudah Equiano, a spokesperson for the equality of all people, carrying out the mission for Blacks in particular during the critical Revolutionary War era. His slave narrative, *The Interesting Narrative of the Life of Olaudah Equiano, or Gustavus Vassa, the African* (1789), carries us through a voyage from African freedom to American slavery in which he topsy-turveys and refutes the stereotypes of Africa as a heathen land and its people as uncivilized. This reversed movement motif was appropriate for the first slave narrative, whose protagonist himself experienced such regression from having been kidnapped from his native land and relegated to servitude. According to Wilfred D. Samuel's introduction to the 1988 two-volume Bicentennial Edition of Equiano's slave narrative, earlier Equiano critics, including Paul Edwards, see Equiano's slave narrative as Black book authors' "most remarkable [account] of the 18th century." His narrative technique was later transposed to a slavery to freedom motif by African American slave narrators whose experience started out differently. An example of these narrators and orators includes Briton Hammon in his *Narrative of the Uncommon Sufferings, and Surprising Deliverance of Briton Hammon* (1760), the first published writing by an African American. This first attempt at African American autobiography displays many affinities to later examples of the genre, such as Frederick Douglass's *Narrative of the Life of Frederick Douglass, an American Slave, Written by Himself* (1845) and Gilbert Osofsky's collection of slave narratives, *Puttin' on Ole Massa* (1969), which includes a discussion of the slave narrative tradition. Equiano makes clear the quest for learning and the difficulty involved in acquiring it in his *Interesting Narrative,* wherein he sets up the trope of the talking book. Observing his master and others moving their lips and reading aloud when examining a book, he surmised that they were "talking" to the book, which was demystified the moment Equiano became literate. His telling of early childhood slave experiences and adolescence evolved, shifting from a naive, childlike persona to that of an experienced, disenchanted adult, therein constituting the primary commitment of the entire genre of the slave narrative or autobiography.

Vernon Loggins further discusses the slave narrative in *The Negro Author: His Development in America to 1900* (1931), in which he claims that Equiano's narrative renders the "spirit and vitality and the angle of vision responsible for the most effective prose writing by Black Americans." In *Great Slave Narratives* (1969) Arna Bontemps refers to it as "the first truly notable book in the genre." And William L. Andrews's *To Tell a Free Story: The First Century of Afro-American Autobiography, 1760–1865* (1986) offers the most cumulative assessment of the African American slave narrative as an autobiographical form.

The eighteenth century also brought forth one of the most intellectually skilled and well-versed figures of all times, Benjamin Banneker, who like Equiano, voiced his position on the need for the equality for all, including African Americans. In his "Letter to Thomas Jefferson," Banneker confronts the issue of contradictions and hypocrisy in a national leader who claims to be a proponent of equality. This century also witnesses its first African

American poets—Jupiter Hammon, Lucy Terry, Phillis Wheatley, and Ann Plato—most of whom demonstrated in their verses a strong religious appeal in their quest for freedom. For example, Hammon's opening line, "Salvation comes by Christ alone," in "An Evening Thought: Salvation by Christ, with Penitential Cries," and Wheatley's closing heroic couplet, "Remember, Christians, Negroes, black as Cain. May be refin'd, and join th' angelic train," in "On Being Brought from Africa to America" both appeal strongly to Christianity. Sterling Stuckey apprises us in his *Slave Culture* that "fortunate for the slave, the retention of important features of the African culture heritage provided a means by which the new reality could be interpreted and spiritual needs at least partially met." Black poststructuralist critic Houston Baker offers both a chronological overview of Black literature and an informative discussion of social and historical trends, critical standards, and their effects on Black artists beginning with Phillis Wheatley up to LeRoi Jones (Imamu Amiri Baraka) in his anthology *Black Literature in America* (1971).

Stimulating the drive toward literary production during the embryonic stage of the African American literary tradition was the conviction of such figures as Wheatley. She, among others, believed that success in a variety of literary genres would refute conclusions by whites like Thomas Jefferson, who claimed that the absence of true literature by Blacks justified their enslavement. Hence, Black poets composed lyrics, hymns, odes, short epics, pastorals, elegies, and pastoral elegies. Wheatley, whose life, work, and example virtually dominated African American literary history until the mid-nineteenth century, wrote the most in these genres, although she was not the first Black to write or publish. Lucy Terry's "Bars Fight" (written in 1746; published until 1855) represents the first recognized writing in English by an African American. Of a different style, she, according to the head notes on the poet in Patricia Liggins Hill's *Call and Response: The Riverside Anthology of the African American Literary Tradition* (1997), offers "the first symbolic portrayal portending race relations in the United States for the next two centuries: a battle between Native-Americans and Euro-Americans as witnessed and recorded by an African-American" in "Bars Fight." Terry joined in with other protest voices of the times and together they did their share in moving us on the abolitionist movement, which dominated the first half of the nineteenth century.

Jupiter Hammon's "An Evening Thought: Salvation by Christ, with Penitential Cries," composed in common hymn stanza, the first poem published by an African American, appeared in December 1760. It contains two arresting, subversive moments: Calling Jesus "thy captive Slave," Hammon suggests that the central and most acceptable focus of the Christian son of God is Hammon himself and his fellow African American rather than white oppressors. The phrase "To set the Sinner free," especially when read within the context of "thy captive Slave," constructs a subversive "freeing" of Hammon and his fellow slaves. Literary critic Sondra O'Neale, in *Jupiter Hammon and the Biblical Beginnings of African-American Literature* (1993), and others have recently called attention to the antislavery subtext within "A Dialogue, Entitled, The Kind Master and Dutiful Servant" (1783). Other key studies of these authors include Benjamin Brawley's *Early Negro American Writers* (1935), Richard Walser's *Black Poet* (1966), Saunders Reddings's *To Make a Poet Black* (1939), and Shirley Graham's *Story of Phillis Wheatley* (1949).

African American literature during the first sixty years of the nineteenth century is best characterized as a call for resistance against slavery. This era witnessed considerable abolitionist and Black nationalist activities, including fugitive slave narratives, pamphlets, poetry, and published sermons and speeches. Among the more significant works were David Walker's *Appeal* (1829), *The Confessions of Nat Turner* (1831), Henry Highland Garnet's "An Address to the Slaves of the United States" (1843), *The Narrative of Frederick Douglass* (1845), Sojourner Truth's "And Aren't I a Woman?" (1852), Frederick Douglass's "Independence Day Speech" (1852), Martin R. Delany's *Condition, Elevation, and Destiny of the Colored People of the United States* (1852), Francis Ellen Watkins Harper's *Poems on Miscellaneous Subjects* (1854), and Harriet Jacobs's *Incidents in the Life of a Slave Girl* (1861).

The antebellum period also featured important milestones in the development of African American literature. William Wells Brown's *Escape, or Leap to Freedom* (1858) represented the first play published by an African American. Similarly, Brown's *Clotel*, published in England in 1853, has the distinction of being the first novel published in English by someone of African descent. Harriet E. Wilson's *Our Nig; or, Sketches from the Life of a Free Black* (1859), represented the first novel published in the United States by an African American.

The Civil War (1861–1865)

Many writers continued to write on the peculiar institution of slavery prior to its abolishment, such as William Wells Brown and his *Negro in the American Rebellion: His Heroism and His Fidelity* (1867) and George Washington Williams and his *History of the Negro Troops in the War of the Rebellion, 1861–1865*. Most notable, however, was Elizabeth Keckley, known for her autobiography, *Behind the Scenes* (1868), in which she depicts the interior lives of the Lincoln family and Washington during the Civil War years.

Post-Civil War, Reconstruction, and Reaction (1865–1920)

The Reconstruction era was marked by significant transitions in Black literature. Some of the writers, whose careers began before emancipation, remained active, such as Harper, who published new poetry and four novels, including her celebrated novel *lola Leroy* (1892), and Brown, who produced a postemancipation edition of *Clotel* (1867). Douglass wrote the final versions of his autobiography, *Life and Times of Frederick Douglass (1881–1892)*. With the end of slavery came new forces in Black writing, with the rapid progression of education in Black communities, thereby creating a growing middle class with strong literary interests.

Rebecca C. Barton's *Witnesses for Freedom: Negro Americans in Autobiography* (1948) provides an examination of the review of themes and perspectives in selected Black autobiographies with sociological summaries of the straggles, goals, and achievements of writers, such as Booker T. Washington's *Up from Slavery* (1901). Black women writers, such as Anna Julia Cooper, Frances Ellen Watkins Harper, Josephine D. Henderson Heard, Lucy A. Delaney, and Angelina Weld Grimke, wrote ex-slave narratives, novels, essays, poetry, and drama. Ida B. Wells, a journalist and essayist, crusaded against lynchings in newspaper articles and pamphlets such as "Southern Horrors: Lynch Law in All Its Phases" (1892).

James Weldon Johnson, author of *The Autobiography of an Ex-coloured Man* (1912), published novels and sermons in verse of the Black tradition, such as "Creation" and "Go Down, Death." This literature, however, was often ignored by white literary critics.

African American literature written between 1865 and 1920 reflects the disappointments, fears, and frustrations produced by America's failure to fulfill its promises of freedom and equality after the Civil War. Yet, the literature of the Reconstruction era manifested middle-class roots in its major characteristics. Dickson D. Bruce, Jr., in *Black American Writing from the Nadir: The Evolution of a Literary Tradition, 1877–1915* (1989), maintains that through the 1890s, Black writers participated in a genteel, sentimental tradition that dominated American middle-class culture. This integrationist-oriented literature emphasized their similarities to other educated Americans and protested their exclusion from the American mainstream. Many writers like James H. W. Howard in his novel *Bond and Free* (1886) built on the tradition of the "tragic mulatto," the cultured, virtuous young man or woman who grows up as white, and whose subsequent confrontation with racial barriers confirms the arbitrariness and injustice of racial lines.

Their Victorian conservatism should not be interpreted as African Americans' absolute rejection of their identity. Encouraged by such figures as Alexander Crummell, most made racial pride a dominant motif. They took special interest in Black history, details of which they often incorporated into their works. This interest was supported by one of the more ambitious projects in African American letters from the period, that of George Washington Williams, who published one of the first scholarly histories of African Americans. One was a two-volume *History of the Negro Race in America from 1619 to 1880* (1883), the other, *History of the Negro Troops in the War of the Rebellion, 1861–1865* (1888). In Williams's histories and elsewhere, racial pride was central, if expressed less in terms of any distinctive African American characteristics than in terms of African American accomplishments measured within the framework of the larger society.

Outside the middle class, preemancipation oral traditions, with roots in slave culture, had retained their vigor after freedom. The popular trickster tales, celebrating the power of wit in the face of oppression, remained current, as did the spirituals, with their profound understanding of suffering and freedom. Reflecting the abiding force of racism and discrimination, as well as the growing independence of such institutions as the church, these traditions had even come to play a more vital role in folk society in the Reconstruction era, helping to center identity and community ties.

Despite a reliance on stereotypes, popular entertainments, including minstrelsy, used genuine Black folk materials and, though performed by whites in Blackface as well as by Blacks, helped to diffuse those materials. Joel Williamson in *The Crucible of Race: Black-White Relations in the American South since Emancipation* (1984) states that the emergence of a white "plantation tradition" literature, while equally dominated by stereotypes romanticizing the slave society of the Old South, did the same. White Georgia journalist Joel Chandler Harris, through his stories of the obsequious "Uncle Remus," gave traditional African American trickster tales a national audience. Williamson also reveals that Hampton Institute's *Southern Workman*, though a white-edited periodical, became a treasure trove of traditional materials contributed by members of the Black student body, particularly tales, folk beliefs, and songs. In Richmond, Virginia, African American preacher John Jasper achieved celebrity status with his much-preached sermon "De Sun Do Move," providing a popular view of traditional folk religion to white as well as African American audiences.

African American writers, who hoped to explore the literary possibilities of oral traditions, attempted to build on this interest, appealing to an audience that had already shown its receptiveness. Many also wanted to rescue folk society from the stereotypes that minstrel versions and such plantation writers as Harris employed in their renditions of the African American tradition. Such efforts led directly to the success of the first African American writers to achieve a genuine national audience, Charles Waddell Chestnutt and Paul Laurence Dunbar.

Chestnutt's works written in the folk tradition appeared first. Written in the Black "dialect," his "Uncle Julius" stories appeared in such popular journals as the *Atlantic* as early as 1889. Building on the trickster figure, Chestnutt recontextualized the white plantation tradition by deromanticizing the southern setting, dramatizing its violence and exploitation, with Uncle Julius, unlike Harris's Uncle Remus, leaving no doubt about the stories' aggressive possibilities.

Dunbar, however, had the greater impact, chiefly through his "dialect poetry," which was written in the putative voice of the slaves and ex-slaves of the South. He wrote out of the plantation and minstrel traditions and was most noted for his dialect poetry, evoking pathos and pity in his presentation of a humorous and sympathetic view of African American life. Although his popularity was based upon this style of writing, which epitomizes the very plight of Black people as victimized accommodationists, he also wrote some of the most effective nondialect poetry expressing the plight of Black people in poems like "Sympathy," "We Wear the Mask," and "The Poet," the last one dramatically answering to his dilemma of forced accommodation: "But ah, the world, it turned to praise/A jingle in a broken tongue." When *Lyrics of Lowly Life* (1896), his first major volume, appeared, endorsed by the dean of American letters, William Dean Howells, Dunbar attracted national attention, becoming, perhaps, the most popular poet, white or Black, in America. Many began to write in dialect poetry, including James Edwin Campbell and James D. Corrothers. By the end of the century, virtually every African American writer had tried the form.

Neither Dunbar and Chestnutt nor their contemporaries broke entirely from the older plantation tradition. Most, with the possible exception of Campbell, used a dialect based as much on literary models as on folk speech rooted in popular writing and the oral tradition. Together they defined possibilities for a folk-based literature that few of their predecessors had thought possible.

At the same time, worsening conditions also brought a growing sense of the dilemma of being African American in a racist society, the dilemma of formulating an identity, as earlier writers had, in American terms. Here, too, Dunbar and Chestnutt were pioneers, departing from dialect to reorient genteel themes and traditional modes of protest to confront the changing times. Dunbar, who was never entirely comfortable with his success in dialect, expressed his frustration in his novel *The Uncalled* (1898). Chestnutt, in stories published as early as the late 1880s and appearing most prominently in a collection entitled *The Wife of His Youth and Other Stories of the Color Line* (1900), used the older motif of racial mixture and the "tragic mulatto" to delineate, pessimistically, relationships between racial structures and questions of identity and moral choice. In his *Conjure Woman* (1900), and *The Marrow of Tradition* (1901), he depicted more complex characters to counter the literary counterpart of the Black-faced minstrel.

Chapter 5: The African American Literary Tradition   75

Since Dunbar's death, his reputation has passed through various stages—from hero to accommodationist villain, to human. What previous scholars have not noted, and what John Keeling argues convincingly in "Paul Dunbar and the Mask of Dialect," is the presence of several layers of protest contained within even the "happiest" of Dunbar poems. Keeling's argument indicates the extent to which scholars are rehabilitating Dunbar's reputation in light of new understanding about the context, which must be considered in any assessment of both Dunbar and the dialect poetry movement. Dickson Bruce's *Black American Writing from the Nadir* makes the point that the 1890s saw the rise of a particularly virulent strain of racism and oppression in America, a tendency that necessitated the use of subtle means of protest in the African American community.

The dilemmas Dunbar and Chestnutt identified were to receive increasing attention among Black writers as the Reconstruction era drew to a close, especially as an understanding of those dilemmas was given theoretical shape by W. E. B Du Bois in "The Strivings of the Negro People" (1897). There, Du Bois described the "double-consciousness" of the African American, a problem of being simultaneously American and Black. Du Bois proposed to resolve the problem through the encouragement of distinctive African genius, pointing toward a distinctive African American culture and literature as well. According to Lawrence Levine's *Black Culture and Black Consciousness*, literary attempts to realize Du Bois's vision did not appear until after 1900, although the growing concern about "duality" rendered a profound legacy from Reconstruction to the present.

The two most visible political and literary figures during this period were Booker T. Washington and W. E. B Du Bois. The former, approximately ten years the latter's senior, had emerged from the immediate Nadir era, which was characterized by extreme fear and insecurity, an era that witnessed the emergence of an accommodationist mentality. Although dialect was not his mode of writing, Washington, too, was considered an accommodationist. His autobiography, *Up from Slavery* (1900), in which his well-known "Cast down your buckets where you are" conciliatory "Atlanta Exposition Address" appears would outline his prescription for industrial education and Black subservience as an entry level to self-help, which would dominate his political persuasion and activity up to his death. In that address to a white plantation audience, Washington's anti-Du Boisean position called for survival and progress via accommodation and compromise, advocating that "there is as much dignity in tilling a field as in writing a poem. It is at the bottom of life we must begin, and not at the top." Du Bois challenged him in Chapter 3 of *The Souls of Black Folk* (1903), in which he prophetically announced the central theme of the new century: "The problem of the twentieth century is the problem of the color line." Moreover, he expounded further on the phenomenon of "double consciousness" and called for a "better and truer" self, which required investigations of European, African, and specifically American traditions. Casting his assertive approach against Washington, Du Bois emphasized the responsibility of the "talented tenth" of Black professionals to the less-privileged members of their communities. Although Du Bois later repudiated the elitism of this position and embraced Marxism, the ideas of "double consciousness" and the "talented tenth" exerted a major influence on African American life prior to and during the Harlem Renaissance.

Du Bois, William Monroe Trotter, and other Blacks of their persuasion organized the Niagara movement in 1905 and with white liberals, the National Association for the Advancement of Colored People (NAACP) in 1909, which was concerned primarily with legally combating racism and mob violence. Du Bois founded and became the editor of its publishing organ, *The Crisis* magazine. In those publications, he would formulate the later posture of the Black Aesthetics and the Black Art's Movement of the 1960s as not "l'art pour l'art" but, rather, art for people's sake, by contending that "while we [*The Crisis*] believe in Negro art, we do not believe in art simply for art's sake." Shortly after the establishment of the NAACP, the National Urban League was formed. Also Dr. Carter G. Woodson, the father of Black historiography, organized the Association for the Study of Negro Life and History in 1915, which would document the contributions of Blacks, thus creating Black pride with the realization of the significant contributions of Blacks.

Inspired by Anna Julia Cooper, noted southern woman activist who insisted on the importance of women's contributions to "uplifting the race," and by Ida B. Wells-Barnett, antilynching crusader who focused attention on lynching while editing the Memphis *Free Speech,* women working in the club movement combined Du Bois's analytical sophistication with community-based activism. Writers affiliated with the clubs contributed frequently to church publications and journals, including *Colored American Magazine* (1900), *The Crisis* (1910), *Opportunity* (1923), and *The Messenger* (1917). Pauline E. Hopkins, besides her editorship of *Colored American Magazine,* provided a woman's perspective on double consciousness in her 1900 novel *Contending Forces.* This work shares numerous thematic concerns with Paul Laurence, Dunbar's *Sport of the Gods* (1902), Charles Waddell Chestnutt's *House behind the Cedars* (1900), and James Weldon Johnson's *Autobiography of an Ex-coloured Man* (1912).

Harlem Renaissance (1920–1930)

Beginning with the years just preceding World War I up to the subsequent Great Migration of Blacks from the South to the North in search of jobs and a better life, leadership in the Black community radically shifted from Washington to Du Bois and Marcus Garvey. During this time, we witnessed the most prolific period for African American literary activity, the Harlem Renaissance, with the spirit of the "New Negro" forcing the Black middle class to reevaluate their relationship to the Black masses. The Harlem Renaissance, a term credited to Black philosopher and writer Alain Locke, was a celebration of African American culture at a time in America's history when the restraints of the Victorian age were succumbing to the bold Roaring Twenties. It demonstrated a sense of cultural heritage and racial pride, which Patricia Liggins Hill calls in *Call and Response* "a rebirth of artistic forms, . . . a rebirth of the abolitionist spirit of self-definition." It was the first opportunity Blacks had to give birth to and celebrate the uniqueness of their culture. It was a cultural and intellectual movement or awakening of the Black intelligentsia, during which time an interest in Black publications was at an all-time high. Young, educated Blacks migrated to New York City and particularly to Harlem to establish themselves in the literary scene. It was the Mecca for what Du Bois called the talented tenth. Whereas some conservative Black critics believed that Black literature should "uplift" the race, by showing Blacks in a positive light, younger, more radical Blacks believed that a "realistic" view of Black life had to be presented.

Many young Black writers came into prominence during the Harlem Renaissance, the prime ones being Claude McKay, the master sonneteer; Jean Toomer, author of the experimental lyrical novel *Cane;* Countee Cullen, ambivalent Romantic poet; Nella Larsen, author of the celebrated *Quicksand*; and Langston Hughes, the most prolific writer of the period. Others recognized for their poetry and fiction include James Weldon Johnson, author of the national Black anthem "Lift Every Voice and Sing"; poetess Anne Spencer; Zora Neale Hurston, folklorist and author of the celebrated novel *Their Eyes Were Watching God*; poetess Helen Johnson; Dorothy West, author of 1995 novel *The Wedding*; Sterling Brown, poet and critic who, in the words of Richard Barksdale in *Black Writers of America: A Comprehensive Anthology,* wrote with "hard-hitting emphasis on social protest"; and Rudolf Fisher. Du Bois continued his work by producing books and essays on the position of Blacks in this country and on the necessary steps they needed to take to achieve equality.

Also called the "New Negro movement," the Harlem Renaissance was the first cultural movement to attain widespread recognition in and outside the Black communities. According to David Levering Lewis in *When Harlem Was in Vogue* (1981), this movement attracted poets, dramatists, fiction writers, painters, musicians, and intellectuals with its promise of an atmosphere in which Black artists could interact with each other and with their white contemporaries. Defined by the "Harlem" issue of *Survey Graphic* magazine (March 1925, edited by Locke and reprinted in expanded form as *The New Negro),* the Harlem Renaissance drew energy from activity surrounding the drama of the Great Migration and the excitement and limited opportunities experienced by oppressed rural southerners now on the urban scene. Moreover, there was the response of disillusioned Black soldiers, returning home from World War I, only to experience discrimination and second-class citizenship in housing and job opportunities. Violence, too, fueled the rich literary period, epitomized by major race riots, such as the bloody "Red Summer" during 1919 when Blacks were being slaughtered in urban America. McKay's "If We Must Die" was a response to such atrocities. All these forces and the new possibilities for dissenting voices created by the death of Washington inspired the revolutionary writings. Inspiration and energy also came from literary centers in Boston, Washington, the Midwest and West, the Caribbean, and Philadelphia, where Jessie Fauset's career began before she moved to New York to serve as editor of *The Crisis.*

Most Harlem Renaissance writers had direct contact with white patrons and modernist artists, many of whom had been inspired by African and African American visual and musical traditions. Although the financial support provided by Carl Van Vechten, author of the controversial novel *Nigger Heaven* (1926), and Charlotte Osgood Mason, who supported Hughes and Hurston, helped writers find time for their work, white patronage remains a controversial topic, as indicated in George Kent's *Blackness and the Adventure of Western Culture* (1972). Many Black intellectuals of the period condemned most white participants for their stereotypical views of Blacks, and the interracial politics of the period received a scathing denunciation in Wallace Thurman's *Infants of the Spring* (1932), the dystopian double to the romantic image advanced in McKay's *Home to Harlem* (1928).

Abby Arthur Johnson and Ronald Maberry Johnson, in *Propaganda and Aesthetics: The Literary Politics of Afro-American Magazines in the Twentieth Century* (1979), assert that in addition to meeting at social events hosted by Van Vechten and Black heiress A'Lelia Walker, Harlem Renaissance writers published their works in *The Crisis, The Opportunity,* and the short-lived periodicals *Harlem* and *Fire!!* (both edited by Thurman), as well as in anthologies such as Cullen's *Caroling Dust* (1927), Richardson's *Plays and Pageants of Negro Life* (1930), and Johnson's *Book of American Negro Poetry* (1922; expanded 1931).

Tony Martin's *Literary Garveyism: Garvey, Black Arts, and the Harlem Renaissance* (1983) suggests that although it has attracted less recognition, Garvey's *Negro World* newspaper played a unique role in Black literature. The most widely circulated Black periodical of the time, *Negro World* sponsored literary contests and published hundreds of poets and fiction writers from throughout the diaspora while advancing the Pan-Africanist agenda of Garvey's Universal Negro Improvement Association.

According to Sterling Brown's *Negro in American Fiction* (1937), the Harlem Renaissance introduced issues, both thematically and aesthetically, that dominated African American literary consciousness throughout the century. Locke in "The New Negro," Hughes in "The Negro Artist and the Racial Mountain," and Johnson in his preface to *The Book of American Negro Poetry* define concerns such as the relationship between African American expression and the American mainstream, the significance of oral and folk traditions, and the impact of modern urban society on literary forms. Similarly, Marita Bonner's essay "On Being Young—a Woman—and Colored" (*The Crisis,* 1925) and Elise Johnson McDougald's "The Task of Negro Womanhood" (*The New Negro,* 1925) connect the pioneering work of Wells-Barnett and Cooper with that of later Black women activists. Anticipating later debates over Afrocentricity, Helene Johnson's "Bottled" and Cullen's "Heritage" raise the question Cullen posed in "What Is Africa to Me?" Like McKay, who expressed his militancy in his sonnets," Cullen used highly conventional formal structures to articulate his tormented double consciousness. Clenora Hudson-Weems's "Claude McKay: Black Protest in Western Traditional Form" (*WJBS,* 1992) interprets the pitting of antithetical form and content against each other as an effective form of masking. Conversely, both Hughes and Hurston explored the literary possibilities of the blues, jazz, sermons, and folktales in experimental forms paralleling those of their white modernist associates. Exploring the ambiguities of its author's position on the margins of both white and Black worlds, Robert Bone's *Negro Novel in America* (1965), points to the fact that Toomer's multigenre epic *Cane* (1923) initiates a Black modernist tradition that includes Hurston's *Moses: Man of the Mountain* (1939), Hughes's *Montage of a Dream Deferred* (1951), Ralph Ellison's *Invisible Man* (1952), and Melvin B. Tolson's *Harlem Gallery* (1965).

The tension between the minstrel tradition, masking, and open expression, personified by the great Black actor Bert Williams's compulsory Black-face routines, haunted Black playwrights throughout the first half of the century. Brown's *Negro Poetry and Drama* (1937) elaborated upon this phenomenon. Despite Paul Robeson's emergence as a prominent Black actor who eschewed stereotypical roles during the 1920s, before the Federal Theatre Project in the 1930s, Black playwrights were forced to choose between the lucrative Broadway revues that paid well but catered to white stereotypes, and "little theatres" such as Cleveland's Karamu House, Washington's Krigwa Players, and Harlem's Lafayette Theatre. Although their audiences could not support playwrights financially, these theatres provided authors such as May Miller, Willis Richardson, and Georgia Douglas Johnson with opportunities to focus on significant social problems and explore the theatrical possibilities of folk materials. The most vital forms of Black performance, however, developed on the Theatre Owners Booking Association circuit, sphere comedians like Pigmeat Markham and blues singers like Ma Rainey manipulated minstrel conventions while tapping into the West African-based folk traditions explored at length in Hurston's *Mules and Men* (1935). The lyrics of Rainey, Ida Cox, and Bessie Smith frequently addressed women and lesbian themes with a frankness that would have been impossible for writers such as

Larsen, Marita Bonner, Fauset, and Alice Moore Dunbar-Nelson (1875–1935), wife of Paul Lawrence Dunbar, all of whom were forced to negotiate the genteel literary convention.

In the final analysis, the Harlem Renaissance writers, according to Nathaniel Irvin Huggins in *Harlem Renaissance* (1971), reflected both the "uplifting" theme of the conservative Black critics and the "realistic" artist movement of the younger, more radical Black critics. Each succeeded in showing Blacks and the world that their culture was both "beautiful" and a worthy literary topic, themes that would reemerge during the civil rights, Black power, Black Panther and Black arts movements of the searing 1960s and early 1970s.

Social Changes (Early 1930–1950)

The Great Depression began with the stock market crash in 1929. In 1932, President Franklin D. Roosevelt was elected, promising the country a New Deal, one being the Federal Writer's Project under the supervision of the Works Progress administration. Established Black writers, such as Hughes, Hurston, and Arna Bontemps, who participated in the Project, and others like Walter White, social critic and lynching investigator; Eric Walrond, avant-garde writer; Gwendolyn Bennett, poetess and painter; Thurman, fiction writer and critic; and Helene Johnson, race conscious poetess were able to earn a living with their writing. New Black literary voices emerged as well, including Richard Wright, Robert Hayden, and Frank Yerby. In the 1940s, Black writers continued to address the plight of their people, with celebrated Black modernists and urban realists Wright and Chester B. Himes portraying Blacks as victims of American racism in *Native Son* and *If He Hollows Let Him Go,* respectively. Also emerging on the scene were poet Frank Marshall Davis, Ann Petty, author of *The Street,* and Margaret Walker, who won the Yale Poetry Prize for her 1942 collection of poetry, *For My People*. Hence, the dominant theme of the last half of this era was characterized by racial unrest and organized protest.

Wright was considered the major writer during the late 1930s and the 1940s. *Native Son* (1940), in which he protested the growing violence of northern urban ghetto life for Blacks, was the most popular novel published by a Black writer. Hence, almost every Black writer of the 1940s was automatically assigned to the "School of Wright." Unfortunately, this negatively affected the reception of Petty, Bontemps, Himes, and especially Sterling Brown, who was valued more for his protest poems than for his pioneering literary histories or sophisticated modernist lyrics such as "Ma Rainey." Most crucially, Wright's dominance contributed to the invisibility of women writers such as Hurston and Dorothy West, who only initially shared his leftist politics when she edited the leftist journal *Challenge*. Hurston's *Their Eyes Were Watching God* (1937), published during the grim Depression years, is now recognized as an African American classic, though the author was initially greeted by critics with apathy or hostility because they viewed her as apolitical. The book went out of print until its rediscovery by literary descendants June Jordan and Alice Walker.

The 1930s forged links between Black writers and white contemporaries such as Theodore Dreiser, Carl Sandburg, and Michael Gold, who as literary editor of the communist newspaper the *Daily Worker* played a major role in shaping a leftist response to Wright, Hughes, McKay, and William Attaway. Leftist publications, such as *New Masses, Challenge,* and *Anvil,* published Black writers interested in Marxist approaches to the economic and political problems of the Great Depression. Wright, Ellison, Shirley Graham (who later married Du Bois), Theodore Ward, and Walker were among Black writers who joined white contemporaries such as Nelson Algren and Saul Bellow in working for the Federal Theatre or Writer's Project of the Works Progress Administration.

Recognizing the gradual shift of cultural activity away from New York, the idea of a Black "Chicago Renaissance" (not to be confused with the earlier white-dominated Chicago Renaissance) provides what many critics find the most satisfactory approach to the culturally diverse production of the period and its impact on later developments. *New Challenge* (1937) played a similar role in this new movement to that of the "New Negro" issue of *Survey Graphic* in the Renaissance. The touchstone of the issue was Wright's "Blueprint for Negro Writing," which highlights the tension between the period's leftist and folk-nationalist tendencies. Literary institutions of the period pursued various approaches to these tensions with the left attempting to appropriate the literary folk form for propagandistic purposes. Several Black writers explored proletarian aesthetics in the communist-sponsored John Reed Clubs. Walker participated in the South Side Writers group, as did many other South Side poets, including Davis, Margaret Esse Danner, and Brooks, who later won the Pulitzer Prize for poetry for her collection *Annie Allen*. They developed their poetry in workshops such as that sponsored by white socialite Inez Cunningham Stark at the South Side Community Center.

Many Blacks saw the end of World War II as a sign that they could assimilate into the dominant culture. For example, Black literary critics believed that the Black writers should merge into the mainstream of American literature, thereby denying that the African American experience in this country had any influence on their work. However, poets such as Naomi Long Madgett, Walker, and Brooks continued to write poetry that reflected their knowledge of the African American community. Those fighting for integration into mainstream literature were doing so in much the same way the fight for integration was being manifested in the political arena, such as the 1954 *Brown v. Board of Education* Supreme Court case.

Wright, who insisted upon the credibility of protest literature, fled the country for Paris because of his impatience with the legal system to grant Blacks their civil rights. Yerby and Willard Motley completely abandoned anything black in their novels, including characters and themes. Both were awarded commercial success with their focus on white life instead of Black life. Ellison, who won the National Book Award for *Invisible Man* (1952), had earlier defended a Black aesthetics position that art and politics are inseparable, only to change his position in his 1964 article "The Art of Fiction." John Oliver Killens whose first novel *Youngblood* (1954) in its title connotes a new spirit, and Paule Marshall were writers during this era who did not give up the struggle. Playwrights, too, though few in number, were ever vigilant on the question of race, like Alice Childress and her one-act play *Florence*, and Lorraine Hansberry and her award-winning play *A Raisin in the Sun*.

Nevertheless, by the 1940s, most Black writers assumed a pronouncedly integrationist posture, a Lockean posture of mainstreaming, evidenced by pivotal essays by integrationist critics and writers, including Saunders Redding's "American Negro Literature" (1949) and James Baldwin's, "Everybody's Protest Novel" (1949). Baldwin's position changed during the latter part of his life, as reflected in many of his novels and in his dramatization of the Till murder case, *Blues for Mr. Charlie*. Other writers include Hugh Gloster in "Race and the Negro Writer" (1950), Arthur P. Davis in "Integration and Race Literature" (1956), and

Sterling Brown in Rayford Logan et al.'s *The New Negro Thirty Years Afterward* (1955), who paradoxically wrote very Black conscious poetry like "Strong Men," were upholding the trend of so-called universal literature. But again, staunch Black aesthetics critics, like Nick Aaron Ford (1904–1984) in "A Blueprint for Negro Authors" (1950) and Ann Petry in "The Novel as Social Criticism" (1950 in Patricia Hill's *Call and Response*) held firm to their beliefs in the validity of racial themes in Black art. Moreover, because of the demise of McCarthyism and the change in the global political climate, the conservative integrationist posture was short-lived. Evident was the onset of the modem civil rights movement of the 1950s and 1960s, ignited by the August 28, 1955, brutal lynching of the 14-year-old Black Chicago youth Emmett Louis "Bobo" Till in Money, Mississippi, followed by the refusal of Rosa Parks' to relinquish her bus seat to a white man in Montgomery, Alabama, three months later on December 1, 1955. The year-long 1956 Montgomery bus boycott ensued. According to Hudson-Weems in *Emmett Till: The Sacrificial Lamb of the Civil Rights Movement* (1994), Till's lynching was the true catalyst of the civil rights movement, setting the stage for the bus boycott. Many writers responded to this atrocity, such as Brooks in "The Last Quatrain in the Ballad of Emmett Till." The chief concern of the Black artist became not only Black liberation at home but also global Black liberation.

Especially affecting Black writers was the emergence of free and independent African countries. Poets, like other literary writers, embraced the global Black liberation struggle, as reflected in the poetry of Melvin Tolson and his "Libretto for the Republic of Liberia" and by Robert Hayden in "Middle Passage" and "Yardbird." Other poets, like Dudley Randall, Owen Dodson, Margaret Esse Danner, Walker, Brooks, and Naomi Long Madget presented their views on race issues of the time. Needless to say, the fiction writers, the literary critics, and the poets had emerged on the scene where two distinct opposing literary positions would force their hands to a commitment. They would have to choose to concentrate their literary energy in one of two camps—the integrationist aesthetics or the Black aesthetics, the latter being, the dominate posture for the next era, the decade of the 1960s.

Wright continued to dominate as a national and international literary figure throughout the 1950s, publishing three novels—*The Outsider* (1953), *Savage Holiday* (1954), and *The Long Dream* (1958)—and four works of nonfiction—*Black Power* (1954), *The Color Curtain* (1956), *Pagan Spain* (1956), and *White Man, Listen!* (1957). *Eight Men, Lawd Today*, and *American Hunger* appeared posthumously. His mentoring of and breaks with Ellison and Baldwin are often described in critical histories of the period, for their disagreements about the relationship between art and ideology in Black writings, debates that continue to shape ideas about the function of nonwhite literatures.

In 1952, Ellison's *Invisible Man* established that Black writers could write social protest literature with stylistic and philosophical complexity. His collection of essays, *Shadow and Act* (1964), and *Going to the Territory* (1987) have contributed substantially to the world of ideas.

Baldwin was a versatile writer who frequently inspired controversy because of his own homosexuality, the place of homosexuality, the place of homosexual relationships in some of his work, and his unwillingness to adopt easy political positions. The author of major works of fiction, including *Go Tell It on the Mountain* (1953), *Giovanni's Room* (1956), *Another Country* (1962), and several plays, including *Blues for Mister Charlie* (1964), he was an especially brilliant essayist. His reputation may rest ultimately on his achievement of collections such as *Notes of a Native Son* (1955), *Nobody Knows My Name: More*

Notes on a Native Son (1961), *The Fire Next Time* (1963), and *The Devil Finds* Work (1976). Baldwin's first novel, *Go Tell It on the Mountain,* further stressed Black writers' abilities to present a uniquely Black viewpoint and universal concern for personal identity. These works and those by Black writers such as dramatist Alice Childress showed that works by African Americans did not have to fit within literary mainstream to qualify as fine literature.

Traditionally, studies of African American literary production identify Wright, Ellison, and Baldwin as the dominant authors of the period from the early 1950s through the mid-1960s, but recent critiques of canon formation have made it impossible to ignore the significance of a wider range of influential writers of the period. Ann Petry, for example, ranks among the most versatile of African American writers. *The Street* (1946) addresses the plight of a Black mother struggling against race, gender, and class oppression in Harlem during the 1940s. Her second and third novels—*Country Place* (1947) and *The Narrows* (1953)—interrogate with extraordinary subtlety the notion of community in the context of small New England villages. Additionally, Petry has published many short stories as well as several books based on Black history and folklore for children and adolescent readers.

Black Nationalism, Black Aesthetics, and The Black Arts Movement (1960s)

The 1960s was a decade of richness, an era that shifted from the integrationist posture to a position of Black cultural nationalism. Motivated by the resurgence of Pan-Africanism, the writers of the 1960s demanded a new Black aesthetics, later defined by Addison Gayle, Jr., in his edited book *The Black Aesthetic* (1971), which took the position of conscious disassociation on the part of Black people from European style and ideology. Descriptively called the era of Black Nationalism, Black Aesthetics, and the Black Arts Movement, it was an era of definition and affirmation, a period when Blacks created their own paradigms and their own criteria for their own distinct art.

"Black Is Beautiful" and "Black Power" were the slogans of the era. For the first time since the Harlem Renaissance, a movement emphasizing the beauty and uniqueness of African American culture was underway. African Americans began to openly celebrate and incorporate into their lives the songs, stories, and customs of their African ancestors.

In response to the emergent nationalist movement of the mid- to late 1960s arose its cultural or aesthetic counterpart, the Black arts movement, and the concept of Black aesthetics developed. Hoyt Fuller defined it well: The "black aesthetics [is] a system of isolating and evaluating the artistic works of black people which reflect the special character and imperatives of black experience." In *Black Fire* (1968), a classic Black nationalist anthology of the time coedited by Larry Neal and Imamu Amiri Baraka, Neal declared that the "artist and the political activist are one." Continuing the tradition of the 1920s and 1930s, Black art is seen as a political weapon.

Many of the urban ghettos erupted into riots in the mid-1960s, during which time Black poetry became a political weapon. Poets like Imamu Amiri Baraka, Lany Neal, Don L. Lee (Haki Madhubuti), Sonia Sanchez, Etheridge Knight, Kristin Hunter, Conrad Kent Rivers, Nikki Giovanni, A. B. Spellman, Mari Evans, June Jordan, Dudley Randall, Lucille

Clifton, and Gwendolyn Brooks used their poetry, not to speak for themselves as individuals, but to speak in a dramatic voice for all African Americans. The Black power movement also made an impact on African American novels, such as Margaret Walker's *Jubilee* (1966) and William Melvin Kelley's *dem* (1967), satirizing "dem white folks." Powerful autobiographies and biographies appeared, including *The Autobiography of Malcolm X* (1964), by Malcolm X and Alex Haley; *Soul on Ice* (1968), by Eldridge Cleaver; and *I Know Why the Caged Bird Sings* (1970), by Maya Angelou. Playwrights dramatized the new awareness on the stage in works such as Adrienne Kennedy's *Funnyhouse of a Negro* (1963), Baraka's *Dutchman* (1964), Douglas Turner Ward's *Day of Absence* (1965), Charles Gordon's *No Place to Be Somebody* (1967), and Alice Childress's *Wine in the Wilderness* (1969). Short stories by Paule Marshall and Ernest Gaines and books by Julius Lester expressed the feeling of Black pride.

In 1968, Baraka (earlier called LeRoi Jones) and Larry Neal published *Black Fire: An Anthology of Afro-American Writing*. In the forward, the editors claimed that a new day had arrived for Black art. This anthology served as the birth of the Black arts movement. Neal explained that this movement was opposed to any concept that separated Black artists from their community, that African American art was directly related to the quest for African American self-determination. Many African American writers and critics embraced the ideas of the Black arts movement. Other more conservative African American critics argued against it. Either way, the Black arts movement focused attention on African American literature, and more independent African American and white publishers began to seek out and publish literature by Black writers. The increased availability of African American literature allowed the number of readers, both African American and white, to grow.

The superb Black oratorical tradition as exemplified by Douglass, Truth, Washington, Du Bois, and Garvey was revitalized in the 1960s. There were civil rights orations by Martin Luther King, Jr., such as his famous "I Have a Dream" speech delivered at the 1963 March on Washington, the major civil rights protest in the United States. There were Black nationalist speeches by Malcolm X that swept the nation. There were "Black Power" slogans and writings by Stokely Carmichael demanding economic as well as social and political parity.

The prime mover of the Black arts movement, Baraka, along with his contemporary Neal, set out to define the criteria for Black art. They held that Black art must be written to and about Black people in the language of the masses. It must serve a threefold function: It must entertain, as all art must do; it must educate Black people about their predicament in America; and it must arouse Black people to political action. Baraka's landmark poem "Black Art" clearly defined Black art as concrete and functional.

These new poets, along with new Black arts dramatists like Ed Bullins and Tom Dent, critics like Stephen Henderson and Mercer Cook (*Militant Black Writers*), and Black nationalists like Maulana Karenga, joined Franz Fanon (*The Wretched of the Earth*) and Black psychologist, Nathan Hare. Other Black critics include Clarence Major, Hoyt Fuller, Carolyn Fowler, and Sarah Webster Fabio. In an effort to consolidate Black economic and cultural power, the Black arts movement gave rise to a range of journals such as *Negro Digest* (later called *Black World*), *The Journal of Black Poetry, Black Expression, Black Orpheus: A Journal of African and Afro-American Literature, Black Review, Black Scholar, College Language Association Journal,* and *Phylon,* thereby giving Black conscious writers new avenues for getting their works published without the infringement of mainstream mandates in style and content. Moreover, Black presses came forth, such as *Broadside Press, Jihad Press, Free Black Press, Black Dialogue Press,* and *Third World Press.* Indeed, the Black arts movement influenced cultural production in a variety of media: music, theatre, art, dance, and literature.

Contemporary Era (1970 to Present)

In the early and mid-1970s, the civil rights protest movement began losing strength as attention shifted from gaining equal rights for African Americans as a whole to the quest for individual rights. Blacks had made some economic and political gains through the civil rights and Black power movements, but unemployment, poverty, and discrimination still plagued African Americans across the United States. The literary text of African American writers in the middle and late 1970s reflected the shift in national focus. Writers like Nikki Giovanni and Haki Madhubuti moved from writing only Black power poetry to writing poetry about political and economic conditions of people of color throughout the world. Ishmael Reed's novels *Mumbo Jumbo* (1972) and *Flight to Canada* (1976) satirized America's culture. One theme running throughout these works is still prominent in African American literature in the 1980s and 1990s. It is important for African Americans to know their history. August Wilson's dramas *Fences* (1987), which won a Pulitzer Prize, and *Piano Lesson* (1990), along with Charles Johnson's National Book Award winner *Middle Passage* (1990), illustrate the power of historical knowledge.

Although the early 1970s continued the spirit of the 1960s, new interests divided the focus. There was an evolving interest in Black women writers in the early 1970s that continues today, following the intrusion of the white women's movement in the midst of the civil rights and Black power movements of the 1960s. During this time, a host of Black women writers found publishers among mainstream publishing houses as well as a wide reception of their works as demonstrated by the numerous awards granted to them. Toni Morrison was one of the first and most prolific and highly respected Black women writers during the early part of the era, earning her numerous awards, including both the Pulitzer Prize and the Nobel Prize for literature, the first African American woman to receive the prize. Her first novel, *The Bluest Eye,* was published in 1970, followed by *Sula* (1974), *Song of Solomon* (1977), *Tar Baby* (1981), *Dreaming Emmett* (1985), *Beloved* (1987), *Jazz* (1992), *Playing in the Dark: Whiteness and the Literary Imagination* (1992), and her edited book *Race-ing Justice, En-Gendering Power: Essays on Anita Hill, Clarence Thomas, and the Construction of Social Reality* (1992). Alice Walker, too, had her share of publications and awards. In 1970, her first novel, *The Third Life of Grange Copeland* appeared, followed by *In Love and Trouble: Stories of Black Women* (1973), *Meridian* (1976), and numerous collections of essays and poetry. Her later novel *The Color Purple* (1982) was made into a controversial movie, followed by the publication of two more novels, *Temple of My Familiar* (1989) and *Possessing the Secret of Joy* (1992). Later, novelist Terry McMillan authored four popular novels, *Mama* (1987), *Disappearing Acts* (1989), *Waiting to Exhale* (1992), and *How Stella Got Her Groove Back* (1996), the last two novels giving Walker competition in the movie industry for the film versions. She also edited an anthology entitled *Breaking Ice: An Anthology of Contemporary African-American Fiction* (1990). Other Black writers of the era include Maya Angelou, author of the autobiographical novel *I Know Why the Caged Bird Sings* (1970) and the first African American and first woman to read her poetry at a US presidential inauguration; Toni Cade Bambara and her celebrated novel *The Salt Eaters* (1980); Gloria Naylor and her novels *The Women of Brewster Place* (1982), *Linden Hills* (1985), *Mama Day* (1988), *Bailey's Cafe* (1992), and *The Men of Brewster Place* (1998); and Gayl Jones, whose most well-known works are the novels *Corregidora* (1975) and *Eva's Man* (1976). Other creative women writers of the era include Shirley Anne Williams, critic, poet, and novelist; Ntozake Shange, author of the award-winning play *for colored girls who have considered suicide when the rainbow is enuf* (1977); Jamaica Kincaid, West Indian-born author of the controversial semi-autobiographical novel *The Autobiography of My Mother* (1996); and Rita Dove, the first African American and first woman to be named poet laureate of the United States and Pulitzer Prizewinning poet for her *Thomas and Beulah* volume (1986).

There is also the much-debated question regarding the role of Black women within the constructs of the modern feminist movement. Women in all genres have attempted to address this issue in many ways, presenting their position on the subject in their works. Barbara Smith, and bell hooks became the leading advocates for Black feminism. Although contending that gender, race, and class were being simultaneously addressed, most of their energy went to gender issues as a priority. Moreover, much of their emphasis on gender reflects their complaints about their exclusion from the feminist arena, as in the case of hooks in her *Feminist Theory: From Margin to Center* (1984), who complains about the racist exclusion of Black women and their writings from feminist criticism. In addition, Smith, in "Toward a Black Feminist Criticism," addresses the problem of exclusion that she and other Black lesbians experience within the feminist arena. Needless to say, although the most frequently accepted label for Black women in academe has been that of Black feminist, most women outside and some inside academe have found the terminology problematic, since any and all brands of feminism see female empowerment as their collective priority. Alice Walker attempted to offer a solution to this dilemma with her label womanist. Unfortunately, her term and definition of womanist in the introduction to her collection of essays *In Search of Our Mother's Gardens: Womanist Prose* (1983) as "a black feminist or feminist of color.... Womanist is to feminist as purple to lavender" was insufficient. Clenora Hudson-Weems, who named and refined a new terminology and paradigm relative to the true role of Africana women within the constructs of today's women movement, introduced Africana womanism in her *Africana Womanism: Reclaiming Ourselves* (1993). This concept, which earlier in the mid-1980s she called Black womanism, was designed for all women of Africana descent. It addresses the particular needs and desires relative to Africana women's unique lives revolving around their worldview and thus is distinct from all other female-based theories because it prioritizes the triple plight—race, class, and gender—of Africana women. According to *Call and Response*, "Hudson-Weems has launched a new critical discourse in the Black Women's Literary Movement," which, unlike feminism or Black feminism, is familycentered rather than female-centered and is concerned first and foremost with race empowerment rather than female empowerment. Other Black women writers focusing with race, class, and gender issues in their works include race conscious lesbian poets and essayists, June Jordan and Audrey Lorde, and Angela Davis in *Women, Race, and Class* (1983).

Besides the rise of Black women's literature, the recent appearance of new Black structuralist and deconstructionist critics, such as Robert Stepto in his coauthored book with

Dexter Fisher, *Afro-American Literature: The Reconstruction of Instruction* (1979), Houston Baker, Jr., in his *Journey Back: Issues in Black Literature and Criticism* (1980) and *Blues Ideology and Afro-American Literature and Criticism* (1984), and Henry Louis "Skip" Gates in his *Black Literature and Literary Theory* (1984), and *The Signifying Monkey: A Theory of African-American Literary Criticism* (1988) represents an important paradigm shift in African American literature. Yet, literary critic Richard K. Barksdale in his essay "Critical Theory and Problems of Canonicity in African American Literature," which appeared in his swan song essay collection *Praisesong of Survival* (1992), lamented the growing fascination with "French-based theories of textual criticism. . . [emphasizing] ignoring history and personal experience." Such was and is the case with these new Black structuralist and deconstructionist critics, who approach black texts by applying white theory, thereby awarding them power, high visibility, and credibility in academe. Be that as it may, however, successfully countering this Eurocentric bias is Molefe Asante, author of *The Afrocentric Ideal* (1987), in which he both named and refined an African-centered paradigm, Afrocentricity. He, along with other Afrocentric scholars, served as a reminder to all that Africa must be placed at the center of all analyses related to people of African descent in much the same way that Europe is placed at the center of all other analyses. Some Black aesthetics critics, like Haki Madhubuti in his *Claiming Earth: Race, Rage, Rape, Redemption* (1994), have attempted to identify, critique, and analyze the strategy of Black Eurocentric scholars, but none has been more successful than general editor Patricia Liggins Hill in the recent definitive Black aesthetics anthology *Call and Response: The Riverside Anthology of the African American Literary Tradition* (1997), who has set the record straight about the continuing struggle of Black aesthetics literature and critics.

Other male writers of the era include the following: Albert Murray, Henry Dumas, William Melvin Kelley, Michael Harper, A1 Young, Quincy Troupe, James McPherson, Askia Muhammad Toure, John Edgar Wideman, Yusef Komunyakaa, and Reginald McKnight.

Indeed, the explosion of African American writing since the 1970s has made it increasingly difficult to generalize about major themes and styles characteristic of the contemporary period. However, some of the most significant trajectories include the rise of African American women writing, the reclamation of history, the resurgence of autobiography, the rise of Black gay literature and lesbian literature, incursions into popular literary forms, and postmodernist experimentations.

As we move into a next millennium, African American writers such as J. California Cooper, Angela Jackson, Tina McElroy Ansa, Walter Mosely, Bebe Moore Campbell, and Paula Childress White have established themselves in the Black literary tradition. As the works of these and other Black writers show, African American literature continues to build on the foundation established in the eighteenth century: the structures of oral tradition and the quest for freedom and equality. This foundation has supported African Americans as they moved from the chains of slavery through war and peace, to poverty and prosperity. African American literature has recorded the defeats and the triumphs, the fears and the dreams. Its strength lies in its ability to present the truth—the good, the bad, and the ugly. To be sure, African American literature gives voice to the eternal spirit of African Americans and the legacy of Black life.

Bibliography

Anthologies

Barksdale, Richard K., and Kinnamon, Kenneth. *Black Writers of America: A Comprehensive Anthology.* Macmillan Company, 1972.

Bontemps, Arna, editor. *American Negro Poetry.* Hill and Wang, 1963.

Bullins, E. D., editor. *New Plays from the Black Theatre.* Bantam Books, 1969.

Davis, Arthur P., and Saunders Redding, editors. *Cavalcade: Negro American Writing from 1760 to the Present.* Houghton Mifflin, 1971.

Ford, Nick Aaron, editor. *Black Insights: Significant Literature by Afro-Americans, 1760 to the Present.* Ginn, 1971.

Hill, Patricia Liggins, general editor. *Call and Response: The Riverside Anthology of the African American Literary Tradition.* Houghton Mifflin, 1997.

Huggins, Nathan Irvin. *Harlem Renaissance.* Oxford UP, 1971.

Johnson, James Weldon, editor. *The Book of American Negro Poetry,* revised ed. Harcourt, Brace and Co., 1931.

Jones, LeRoi, and Neal, Larry, editors. *Black Fire: An Anthology of Afro-American Writing.* Morrow, 1968.

Richardson, Willis. *Plays and Pageants from the Life of Negro Life.* Associated Publishers, 1930.

Troupe, Quincy, editor. *Watts Poets: A Book of New Poetry and Essay.* House of Respect, 1968.

Turner, Darwin T., editor. *Black American Literature: Essays, Poetry, Fiction, Drama.* Charles E. Merrill, 1969.

Criticism

Andrews, Williams L. *To Tell a Free Story: The First Century of Afro-American Autobiography, 1760–1865.* U of Illinois P, 1986.

Asante, MolefiK. *The Afrocentric Ideal.* Temple UP, 1987.

Baker, Houston A., Jr. *Black Literature in America.* McGraw-Hill, 1971.

Barksdale, Richard K. *Praisesong of Survival.* U of Illinois P, 1992.

Barton, Rebecca C. *Witnesses for Freedom: Negro Americans in Autobiography.* Harper, 1948.

Bone, Robert A. *The Negro Novel in America.* Yale UP, 1965.

Bontemps, Arna. *Great Slave Narratives.* Beacon Press, 1969.

Brawley, Benjamin. *Early Negro American Writers.* Books for Libraries Press, 1935.

———. *The Negro in Literature and Art.* Duffield and Company, 1930.

Braxton, Joanne. *Black Women Writing Autobiography: A Tradition within a Tradition.* Temple UP, 1989.

Brown, Sterling, *The Negro in American Fiction*. Kennikat Press, 1937.

Bruce, Dickson D., Jr. *Black American Writing from the Nadir: The Evolution of a Literary Tradition, 1877–1915*. Louisiana State UP, 1989.

Christian, Barbara. *Black Feminist Criticism: Perspectives on Black Women Writers*. Pergamon, 1985.

Cook, Mercer, and Henderson, Stephen. *The Militant Black Writers in Africa and the United States*. U of Wisconsin P, 1969.

Davis, Angela. *Women, Race and Class*. Vintage, 1983.

Du Bois, W. E. B. *The Souls of Black Folk*. Fawcett, 1961.

Ellison, Ralph. *Shadow and Act*. Random, House, 1964.

Ford, Nick Aaron. *The Contemporary Negro Novel: A Study in Race Relations*. Meader Publishing, 1936.

Gates, Henry Louis. *The Signifying Monkey: A Theory of African-American Literary* v *Criticism*. Oxford UP, 1988.

Gayle, Addison, Jr., editor. *The Black Aesthetic*. Doubleday, 1971.

Giddings, Paule. *When and Where I Enter: The Impact of Black Women on Race and Sex in America*. Bantam, 1984.

Graham, Shirley Du Bois. *The Story of Phillis Wheatley*. J. Messner, 1949.

hooks, bell. *Feminist Theory: From Margin to Center*. Southend, 1984.

Howard, H. W. *Bond and Free: A Trite Tale of Slave Times*. McGrath Publishing, 1969.

Hudson-Weems, Clenora. *Africana Womanism: Reclaiming Ourselves*. Bedford, 1993.

———. *Emmett Till: The Sacrificial Lamb of the Civil Rights Movement*. Bedford, 1994.

Johnson, Abby Arthur, and Johnson, Ronald Maberry. *Propaganda and Aesthetics: The Literary Politics of Afro-American Magazines in the Twentieth Century*. U of Massachusetts P, 1979.

Jones, LeRoi, and Neal, Larry, editors. *Black Fire*. William Morrow, 1968.

Kent, George. *Blackness and the Adventure of Western Culture*. Third World Press, 1972.

Levine, Lawrence W. *Black Culture and Black Consciousness: Afro-American Folk Thought from Slavery to Freedom*. Oxford UP, 1977.

Lewis, David Levering. *When Harlem Was in Vogue*. Knopf, 1981.

Locke, Alain, editor. *The New Negro: An Interpretation*. Alfred and Charles Boni, 1925.

Logan, Rayford W., et al., editors. *The New Negro Thirty Years Afterward*. Howard UP, 1955.

Loggins, Vernon. *The Negro Author: His Development in America to 1900*. Columbia UP, 1931.

Martin, Tony. *Literary Garveyism: Garvey, Black Arts, and the Harlem Renaissance*. Majority Press, 1983.

Mbalia, Doreatha Drummond. *Toni Morrison's Developing Class Consciousness*. Susquehanna UP, 1991.

———. *John Wideman: Reclaiming the African Personality*. Susquehanna UP, 1995.

Mitchell, Loften. *Black Drama: The Story of the American Negro in the Theater*. Hawthorn, 1967.

Mootry, Maria, editor. *Gwendolyn Brooks: A Life Distilled*. U of Illinois P, 1987.

O'Neal, Sondra. *Jupiter Hammon and the Biblical Beginnings of African-American Literature*. Scarecrow Press, 1993.

Osofsky, Gilbert, editor. *Puttin' on Ole Massa*. Harper and Row, 1969.

Redding, J. Saunders. *To Make a Poet Black*. U of North Carolina P, 1939.

Samuels, Wilfred D., and Clenora Hudson-Weems. *Toni Morrison*. Prentice-Hall/ Twayne, 1990.

Walser, Richard. *The Black Poet*. Philosophical Library, 1966.

Williams, George Washington. *History of the Negro Race in America from 1619–1880*. New York, G. P. Putnam, 1883.

———. *History of the Negro Troops in the War of the Rebellion, 1861–1865*. Kraus, 1888. Reprinted in 1969.

Williamson, Joel. *The Crucible of Race: Black-White Relations in the American South since Emancipation*. Oxford UP, 1984.

Folk Tradition

Dance, Daryl C., editor. *Shuckin' and Jivin': Folklore from Contemporary Black Americans*. Indiana UP, 1978.

Dorson, Richard M. *African Folklore*. Doubleday, 1972.

———. *American Negro Folktales*. Fawcett, 1967.

Lester, Julius. *Black Folktales*. Grove Press, 1969.

Selected Works of Selected Novelists, Poets, and Playwrights

Angelou, Maya. *I Know Why the Caged Bird Sings*. Random House, 1970.

———. *All God's Children Need Traveling Shoes*. Random House, 1986.

———. *Just Give Me a Cool Drink of Water 'For I Die*. Random House, 1971.

Baldwin, James. *Go Tell It on the Mountain*. Knopf, 1953.

———. *The Amen Corner*. Dial, 1968.

———. *Another Country*. Dial, 1962.

———. *Blues for Mister Charlie*. Dial, 1964.

———. *The Fire Next Time*. Dial, 1963.

———. *Giovanni's Room*. Dial, 1956.

———. *Going to Meet the Man*. Dial, 1965.

———. *If Beale Street Could Talk*. Dial, 1974.

———. *Just above My Head*. Dial, 1979.

———. *Nobody Knows My Name: More Notes of a Native Son*. Dial, 1961.

———. *Notes of a Native Son*. Beacon Press, 1955.

———. *The Price of the Ticket: Collected Nonfiction, 1948–1985*. St. Martin/Marek, 1985.

Bambara, Toni Cade. *Tales and Stories for Black Folks*. Doubleday, 1971.

———. *The Salt Eaters*. Random House, 1980.

Baraka, Imamu Amiri (LeRoi Jones). *Preface to a Twenty Volume Suicide Note*. Totem Press and Corinth Books, 1961.

———. *Black Magic: Sabotage: Target Study: Black Art: Collected Poetry, 1961–1967*. Bobbs-Merrill, 1969.

———. *It's Nation Time*. Third World Press, 1970.

Brooks, Gwendolyn. *A Street in Bronzeville*. Harper, 1945.

———. *Annie Allen*. Harper, 1949.

———. *The Bean Eaters*. Harper, 1960.

———. *Riot*. Broadside Press, 1969.

Brown, Sterling. *Southern Road*. Harcourt, 1932.

Brown, William Wells. *The Escape, Or a Leap to Freedom: A Drama in Five Acts.*, R. F. Walcutt, 1858. Reprinted in 1969.

Bullins, editor. *Five Plays by Ed Bullins*. Bobbs-Merrill, 1969.

———. *The Theme Is Blackness: "The Comer" and Other Plays*. William Morrow, 1972.

Campbell, James Edwin. *Echoes from the Cabin and Elsewhere.*, Donahue and Henneberry, 1895.

Chestnut, Charles W. *The Conjure Woman*. Houghton Mifflin, 1900.

———. *The House behind the Cedars*. Houghton Mifflin, 1900.

———. *The Marrow of Tradition*. Houghton Mifflin, 1901.

———. *The Wife of His Youth and Other Stories of the Color Line*. Houghton, Mifflin, 1900.

Childress, Alice. *Wedding Band: A Love/Hate Story in Black and White*. Samuel French, 1973.

Corrothers, James D. *In Spite of the Handicap*. George H. Doran, 1916.

Cullen, Countee. *Color*. Harper, 1925.

———. *The Black Christ and Other Poems*. Harper, 1929.

———. *On These I Stand: An Anthology of the Best Poems of Countee Cullen, Selected by Himself and Including Six New Poems Never Before Published*. Harper, 1947.

Dove, Rita. *The Yellow House on the Comer: Poems*. Camegie-Mellon UP, 1980.

———. *Thomas and Buelah*. Camegie-Mellon UP, 1986.

Du Bois, W. E. B. *Darkwater: Voices from within the Veil*. Harcourt, Brace, and Howe, 1920. Reprinted in 1969.

Dunbar, Paul Laurence. *Oak and Ivy.*, United Brethren Publishing House, 1893.

———. *The Complete Poems of Paul Laurence Dunbar*. Dodd, Mead, 1913.

———. *Lyrics of Lowly Life.* New York, Dodd Mead, 1896. Reprinted in 1968.

———. *Lyrics of Sunshine and Shadow.* Dodd, Mead, 1905. Reprinted in 1970, 1972.

———. *Lyrics of the Hearthside.* New York, Dodd Mead, 1899. Reprinted in 1970, 1972.

———. *The Sport of the Gods.* Dodd Mead, 1902.

Elder HI, Lonne. *Ceremonies in Dark Old Men.* Farrar, Straus, and Giroux, 1969.

Ellison, Ralph. *Invisible Man.* Random House, 1952.

———. *Going to the Territory.* Random House, 1986.

———. *Shadow and Act.* Random House, 1964.

Equiano, Olaudah. *The Interesting Narrative of the Life of Olaudah Equiano, or Gustavus Vassa.* Self-published, 1789.

Evans, Mari. *I Am a Black Woman.* Morrow, 1970.

Gaines, Ernest J. *The Autobiography of Miss Jane Pittman.* Dial Press, 1971.

———. *Bloodline.* W. W. Norton, 1976.

———. *A Gathering of Old Men.* Vintage, 1983.

Giovanni, Nikki. *Black Feeling, Black Talk, Black Judgement.* Morrow, 1970.

———. *Ego-Tripping and Other Poems for Young People.* Lawrence Hill, 1973.

———. *My House.* Morrow, 1972.

———. *The Women and the Men.* Morrow, 1975.

Gordone, Charles. *No Place to Be Somebody: A Black Black Comedy in Three Acts.* Bobbs-Merrill, 1969.

Hammon, Jupiter. *An Evening Thought: Salvation by Christ, with Penitential Cries.* Self-published, 1760.

Hansberry, Lorraine. *A Raisin in the Sun.* Random House, 1959.

Harper, Frances Ellen Watkins. *Poems on Miscellaneous Subjects.* Boston, J. B. Yerrington and Son, 1854. Reprinted in 1974.

———. *Iola LeRoy or Shadows Uplifted.* Philadelphia, Garrigues Bros., 1893.

———. *Sketches of Southern Life.* Philadelphia, Merrihew and Son, 1872.

Hayden, Robert. *Heart Shape in the Dust.* Falcon Press, 1940.

———. *Angle of Ascent: New and Selected Poems.* Liveright, 1975.

———. *Selected Poems.* October House, 1966.

Howard, James H. W. *Bond and Free.* Harrisburg, PA, E. K. Meyers, printer, 1886.

Hughes, Langston. *The Weary Blues.* Knopf, 1926.

———. *Ask Your Mama: 12 Moods for Jazz.* Knopf, 1961.

———. *The Langston Hughes Reader.* George Braziller, 1958.

———. *Montage of a Dream Deferred.* Henry Holt, 1951.

———. *The Negro Mother and Other Dramatic Recitations.* Golden Stair Press, 1932.

———. *The Panther and the Lash: Poems of Our Times.* Knopf, 1967.

———. *Shakespeare in Harlem.* Knopf, 1942.

Hurston, Zora Neale. *Jonah's Wine Gourd*. Lippencott, 1934.
———. *Moses: Man of the Mountain*. Lippencott, 1939.
———. *Mules and Men*. Lippincott, 1935.
———. *Seraph on the Suwanee*. Scribners, 1948.
———. *Their Eyes Were Watching God*. Lippencott, 1937.
Joans, Ted. *All of Ted Joans and No More: Poems and Collages*. Excelsior-Press, 1961.
———. *A Black Manifesto in Jazz Poetry and Prose*. Calder and Boyars, 1971.
———. *Black Pow-Wow: Jazz Poems*. Hill and Wang, 1969.
Johnson, Charles. *Middle Passage*. Macmillan, 1990.
Johnson, James Weldon. *Fifty Years and Other Poems*. Comhill, 1917.
———. *God's Trombones: Seven Negro Sermons in Verse*. Viking, 1927.
Killens, John Oliver. *Youngblood*. Dial, 1954.
———. *And Then We Heard the Thunder*. Knopf, 1963.
———. *Sippi*. Simon and Schuster, 1967.
Knight, Etheridge. *Poems from Prison*. Broadside Press, 1968.
Larsen, Nella. *Quicksand*. A. A. Knopf, 1928. Reprinted, 1969, 1971.
———. *Passing*. A. A. Knopf, 1929. Reprinted, 1969, 1971.
McKay, Claude. *Harlem Shadows*. Harcourt, Brace, 1922.
———. *Banana Bottom*. Harper and Row, 1933.
———. *Harlem Glory: A Fragment of Aframerican Life*. Charles H. Kerr, 1990, published posthumously.
———. *Home to Harlem*. Harper and Brothers, 1928.
McMillan, Terry. *Mama*. Houghton, 1987.
———. *Disappearing Acts*. Viking Press, 1989.
———. *Waiting to Exhale*. Viking Press, 1992.
Madgett, Naomi Long. *Exits and Entrances*. Lotus Press, 1978.
———. *Octavia and Other Poems*. Third World Press, 1988.
Madhubuti, Haki R. (Don L. Lee). *Think Black*. Broadside Press, 1967.
———. *Black Pride*. Broadside Press, 1968.
———. *Don't Cry, Scream*. Broadside Press, 1969.
———. *We Walk the Way of the New World*. Broadside Press, 1970.
Marshall, Paule. *Brown Girl, Brownstones*. Random House, 1959.
———. *The Chosen Place, the Timeless People*. Harcourt, 1969.
———. *Daughters*. A Plume Book, 1991.
———. *Praisesong for the Widow*. Putnam's Sons, 1983.
———. *Soul Clap Hands and Sing*. Atheneum, 1961.
Milner, Ron. *What the Wine-Sellers Buy*. Samuel French, 1974.
Morrison, Toni. *The Bluest Eye*. Holt, Rinehart and Winston, 1970.

———. *Beloved*. Knopf, 1987.

———. *Jazz*. Knopf, 1992.

———. *Paradise*. Knopf, 1998.

———. *Song of Solomon*. Knopf, 1977.

———. *Sula*. Knopf, 1974.

———. *Tar Baby*. Knopf, 1981.

Naylor, Gloria. *The Women of Brewster Place: A Novel in Seven Stories*. Viking Press, 1982.

———. *Bailey's Cafe*. Vintage Books, 1993.

———. *Linden Hills*. Ticknor and Fields, 1985.

———. *Mama Day*. Ticknor and Fields, 1988.

Neal, Larry. *Black Boogaloo (Notes on Black Liberation)*. Journal of Black Poetry Press, 1969.

———. *Hoodoo Hollerin' Bebop Ghosts*. Howard UP, 1974.

Petry, Ann. *The Street*. Houghton, 1946.

———. *The Narrows*. Houghton, 1953. Reprinted in 1988.

Randall, Dudley. *More to Remember: Poems of Four Decades*. Third World Press, 1971.

Redmond, Eugene. *River of Bones and Flesh and Blood*. Black River Writers, 1971.

———. *Songs from an Afro/Phone: New Poems*. Black River Writers, 1972.

Reed, Ishmael. *The Free-Lance Pallbearers*. Doubleday, 1967.

———. *Conjure: Selected Poems, 1963–1970*. U of Massachusetts P, 1972.

———. *Flight to Canada*. Random House, 1976.

———. *Mumbo Jumbo*. Doubleday, 1972.

———. *Reckless Eyeballing*. St. Martin's Press, 1986.

Rogers, Carolyn. *Paper Soul*. Third World Press, 1968.

Sanchez, Sonia. *We a Badddd People*. Broadside Press, 1970.

———. *A Blues Book for Black Magical Women*. Broadside Press, 1974.

———. *Homegirls and Handgrenades: A Collection of Poetry and Prose*. Thunder Mouth Press, 1984.

———. *It's A New Day (Poems for Young Brothas and Sistuhs)*. Broadside Press, 1971.

Shange, Ntozake. *For Colored Girls Who Have Considered Suicide When the Rainbow Is Enuf: Choreopoem*. Macmillan Publishing, 1977.

Thurman, Wallace. *The Blacker the Berry: A Novel of Negro Life*. Macaulay, 1929. Reprinted in 1969.

———. *Infants of the Spring*. Macaulay, 1932.

Toomer, Jean. *Cane*. Boni and Liveright, 1923.

Walker, Alice, *Meridian*. Harcourt Brace Jovanovich, 1976.

———. *The Color Purple*. Harcourt Brace Jovanovich, 1982.

———. *In Search of Our Mothers' Gardens: Womanist Prose.* Harcourt Brace Jovanovich, 1983.

———. *Possessing the Secret of Joy.* Harcourt Brace Jovanovich, 1992.

———. *The Temple of My Familiar.* Harcourt Brace Jovanovich, 1989.

Walker, Margaret. *For My People.* Yale UP, 1942.

———. *Jubilee.* Houghton, 1966.

———. *Prophets for a New Day.* Broadside Press, 1970.

———. *This Is My Country: New and Collected Poems.* University of Georgia Press, 1988.

Washington, Booker T. *Up from Slavery.* Doubleday, 1901.

Wheatley, Phyllis. *Poems on Various Subjects, Religious and Moral.* A. Bell, Bookseller, 1773.

———. *Liberty and Peace, a Poem.* Warden and Russell, 1784.

Wideman, John Edgar. *The Lynchers.* Henry Holt and Company, 1973.

———. *Brothers and Keepers.* Penguin, 1984.

———. *Hiding Place.* Vintage, 1981.

———. *Philadelphia Fire.* Henry Holt and Company, 1990.

Wright, Richard. *Uncle Tom's Children: Four Novellas.* Harper, 1938.

———. *Black Boy: A Record of Childhood and Youth.* Harper, 1945.

———. *Native Son.* Harper, 1940.

———. *The Outsider.* Harper, 1953.

———. *Savage Holiday.* Avon, 1954.

———. *White Man, Listenl.* Doubleday, 1957.

Chapter 6

The Significance of HBCUs: The Social, Academic, & Career Determining Benefits of HBCUs

Contributed by:
Sharon H. Porter, EdD

Indeed, the historically and predominantly Black institutions could become as they were in the past, a strong and viable force in the Black community and in the society on the whole, producing a whole nation of positive, strong, and functional leaders of tomorrow. We must not fail again, for "A people who does not know its history is bound to repeat its mistakes." (Clenora Hudson-Withers [Weems], 1983)

The HBCU (Historically Black College and University) experience is an experience like no other, in my opinion and the opinion of countless HBCU graduates. As a two-time graduate of HBCUs Winston-Salem State University (WSSU), 1992, and Howard University (HU), 2017, as well as a graduate of Predominantly White Institutions (PWI), I know for a fact that I am who I am due to my experiences at both HBCUs. An HBCU is a college or university that, prior to 1964, existed with a historical mission of educating Black people, while being open to all.

The Educational Effectiveness of Historically Black Colleges and Universities Briefing Report showed that minority students attending HBCUs have increased levels of engagement, more interactions with faculty, and greater involvement with faculty research projects. According to a 2015 Gallup Report, Black graduates of HBCUs report receiving significantly higher levels of support as undergraduates. They are more than twice as likely, as Black graduates of non-HBCUs, to recall experiencing having a professor who cared about them as a person, a professor who made them excited about learning, and a mentor who encouraged them to pursue their goals and dreams.

The History of HBCUs

Before the Civil War (1861–1865), public policy in the South prohibited the education of Blacks (Briefing Report, 2010). HBCUs were established in the United States with a primary purpose, which was to serve the educational needs of African Americans. Most higher education institutions at the time were predominantly White and had limited enrollment for African Americans. Most higher education institutions in the south actually prohibited all African Americans from attending their school, which is why many HBCUs were founded in the south (Office of Civil Rights).

Cheyney University, the first higher education institution for Blacks, was founded as the African Institute in 1837, but was soon renamed the Institute for Colored Youth (Cheyney. edu). Cheyney University continues as the oldest African-American school of higher education. It joined the State System of Higher Education as Cheyne University of Pennsylvania in 1983. Soon after the establishment of Cheyney in 1837, Lincoln University in Pennsylvania (1854) and Wilberforce University in Ohio (1856) were established.

Public support for higher education for Black students was reflected in the enactment of the Second Morrill Act in 1890. This Act required states with racially segregated public higher education systems to provide a land-grant institution for Black students whenever a land-grant institution was established in each of the southern and border states. Sixteen Black institutions were designated as land-grant colleges (Office of Civil Rights). The U.S. Supreme Court's 1896 decision in *Plessy v. Ferguson* established a "separate but equal" clause in public education. Ironically, this decision encouraged Black colleges to focus on teacher training to provide a cadre of instructors for segregated schools.

Congress passed the Title VI of the Civil Rights Act of 1964, a decade after the 1954 *Brown v. Topeka, Kansas Board of Education* decision. This Act provided a means for ensuring equal opportunity in federal assisted programs and activities. Title VI also protects individuals from discrimination based on race, color, or national origin in programs or activities receiving federal financial assistance. Nineteen states were operating in racially segregated higher education systems at the time Title VI was enacted. A 1977 court order established new criteria for statewide desegregation as part of a lawsuit known as the Adams case (Office for Civil Rights).

The Significance of HBCUs

HBCUs are still safe havens for many Black students. We, as a society, have progressed, but there is still much work to be done. Indisputably, Africana leadership has its roots in HBCUs dating back to its inception in the 1800s, and up to today's new Black leadership, as HBCUs continue to educate prominent and influential Black leaders. With the recent election of Vice President Kamala Harris, a graduate of HU, the work of Stacey Abrahms, a graduate of Spelman College, and the media attention of Mayor Keisha Lance Bottoms of Atlanta, Georgia, a Florida A&M University graduate, and Senator Raphael Warnock, a graduate of Morehouse College in Atlanta, Georgia, HBCUs were front and center during the 2020 presidential election. Once presidential candidate, Joe Biden, officially announced Senator Kamala Harris as his running mate on August 11, 2020, graduates of HBCUs activated, along with the nine Black Greek Letter Organizations (BGLO), many which were founded on the campuses of HBCUs.

While today's political list is laudable, one must remember such noteworthy figures who rose to prominence as civil rights activists during the Civil Rights Movement of 1950s through the 1970, indeed, the signature for the resurgence of today's Civil Rights Movement. Atty. Alvin O. Chambliss, Jr., lead counsel for the *Ayers versus Fordice* Supreme Court case, successfully won after some 20 years, and is recognized as the "Last Original Civil Rights Attorney in America." A graduate of both Jackson State U and Howard U, he went on to receive the graduate degree, LLM, in law from the U of California, Berkley Law School. Other Civil Rights icons include James Meredith, also a Jackson State U graduate, who later finished his law degree from Columbia U School of Law, after he was shot down in 1965 as the first Black student to be enrolled at the University of Mississippi (Ole Miss). Another fine HBCU alumnus is Atty. Fred Gray, a graduate of Alabama State College, who litigated such major Civil Rights cases as Browder v Gayle on the Alabama state bus segregation laws, winning that case involving the 15-year-old Claudette Covet, who refused to relinquish her bus seat in 1955, just nine months before the Rosa Parks incident. Moreover, he was the attorney for the infamous Tuskegee Syphilis Experiment; a fair atonement has yet be done for the 40-year-human experimentation on Black men, conducted by the United States Public Health Services (USPHS), drastically affecting their families (their wives and off-springs).

The HBCU Experience

I have interviewed hundreds of graduates from HBCUs across the nation. These graduates share their experiences on their respective campuses. Three common themes that are identified from graduates as positive experiences on the campus of their HBCU are: Support of Faculty, an Extended Network, and an Appreciation of the Black culture. Many HBCU graduates interviewed about their HBCU Experiences shared that they had no real prior knowledge about their intuition of choice or HBCUs in general. While others were proud legacy graduates of their institution, as siblings, parents, and other extended family members were also graduates of that particular HBCU. There were graduates who claimed that an HBCU was not their first choice, but after their experience, it was noted that it was the best choice they could have made.

    Rictor Craig, a graduate of North Carolina Agricultural and Technical State University (NCAT) and co-founder and Founding Director of Statesmen College Preparatory for Boys, was a first-generation college student who wrote that "stepping foot on A&T's campus for the first time as a student was one of the best days of my life." He further states, "No one told me that I would meet future business owners, entertainers, lawyers, designers, and global leaders as I walked through the yard of A&T . . ." (Porter, *North Carolina A&T State University Edition*).

    Fred Whitaker, known as Fred Whit, well-known for his business strategies and negotiation savvy, behind the scenes of the entertainment industry, also a NCAT graduate, contends that HBCUs attend to the needs of their students, uniquely to each of them . . . . He discovered this first-hand when his best friend and roommate was deployed to Iraq three months into his second semester, leaving him with a monthly rent payment he couldn't afford on his own (Porter, *North Carolina A&T State University Edition*).

    Shanikka Wagner, a 2000 graduate of HU, reflects on the Howard Homecoming experience. She writes "As students and alum, a true Bison would always be quick to let you know that there is no homecoming like a Howard Homecoming." Her memorable homecoming was 1998 when Outkast performed their hit song "Rosa Parks.". Shanikka ends her reflection sharing that the love she has for HU has never ended. She continues to be active in the Howard University Alumni Club of Atlanta, raising money for scholarships for current and incoming students of Howard University (Porter, 2020).

Desmond Williams, President and Founder of Nylinka School Solutions, LLC, and 1999 graduate of HU, speaks about the overwhelming feeling of brotherhood felt at HU. He names the individuals who assisted him during his time at HU: an individual who tutored him in Spanish during his freshman year as he struggled to keep pace in his Spanish class, cut his hair for free when he couldn't afford it, and a fellow Bison who taught him to navigate the landscape of the university. Williams wrote "The Mecca taught me to determine where I want to be, and how I express myself in various places" (Porter et al., *Alumni Stories from the Mecca*).

Naomi Pleasant Barkley, a 1951 graduate of Kentucky State University (KSU), was a KSU graduate legacy. Her mother attended KSU and graduated in 1936 and her father was a 1932 KSU graduate. She would later marry the late William Barkley, KSU Class of 1950. Her first memory of Kentucky State was at the age of 4, when her mother would take her and her sister on campus to the Model School where they attended while her mother, a teacher, would attend classes on the campus. Barkley reflects getting an acceptance letter from KSU at the age of 15. The letter was dated April 30, 1947. She was required to request a room reservation, send her official transcripts, and pay $6.50.

A 2015 Gallup-USA Funds Minority College Graduates Report shows that "HBCUs provide black graduates with a better college experience than they would get at non-HBCUs." The study found that Black HBCU graduates were more prepared for life. All of the HBCU graduates who shared their reflections and experiences felt that they were more prepared for life after college because of attending an HBCU.

Jacynda P. Williams, a 1990 graduate, majoring in Mass Communication, from St. Augustine College (St. Aug), recalls her fondest memory was her mother, also a St. Aug graduate, escorting her around campus and identifying the dorms she lived in while on campus between 1965 and 1969. She writes, "The best thing about St. Aug. is that the people there really mean they will look out for and take care of you. It is truly your home away from home" (Porter, 2021).

Brian Hurd, St. Aug Class of 1992 and originally from Virginia Beach, Virgina, recalls spending the summers in Raleigh, North Carolina, while in high school. He and his uncle would go to St. Aug to watch the summer basketball league. This experience had a lasting impression on him. He made the decision to attend St. Aug in the fall of 1988. His most memorable experience was pledging Alpha Phi Alpha Fraternity, Inc through the Gamma Psi Chapter at St. Aug.

Dr. Joelle Davis Carter, a 1995 WSSU graduate, is part of four generations of Rams. Carter credits her experiences and relationships with her peers, faculty, staff, and the "essence" of the campus itself in shaping her development as a professional. She would later marry a WSSU graduate. They have shared more than twenty years of marriage and friendship.

Joy Green, a first-generation college graduate desired to attend college to "unlock opportunities, become more independent, and invest in herself." She did not initially want to attend an HBCU. Her sights were set on graduating from The Ohio State University with an International Business degree. In fact, she attended a PWI during her freshman and sophomore years. She wanted to meet and be a part of a large diverse student body. Originally from Washington, DC, her community was predominantly African American at the time. During the two years of attending a PWI, she felt she was just a number with the large number of students in a classroom. She didn't feel included and began to fall behind in her classes (Porter, *Winston-Salem State University Edition*). She reflects, "There is a big difference between attending a university and being a part of the university. At WSSU, I felt as though I was part of the university" (Porter, *Winston-Salem State University Edition*).

Support of Faculty

The support of the faculty on the campus of HBCUs were one of the main reasons cited for graduates' positive experiences on their HBCU campus. The 2015 Gallup Report asserts that the faculties of HBCUs more closely reflect the student bodies. Graduates were able to name specific professors and other faculty members who took a vested interest in their well-being while a student, such as faculty members making sure students had the financial resources to continue their education and graduate. Many provided opportunities for students beyond the academic needs. There is an emphasis placed on servicing the student, the whole student. Thus, there are high-quality student-teacher interactions on the campus of many HBCUs. Many graduates spoke about the family atmosphere on their campus. Lead author in *The HBCU Experience Anthology: Alumni Stories from the Hill of Kentucky State University*, Tywauna Wilson, (Porter et al., *Alumni Stories from the Mecca*) writes "I am thankful to Dr. Bibbins who introduced me to the field of Clinical Laboratory Sciences. . . . Had it not been for him, I wouldn't be the scientist I am today." Darrius Jerome Gourdine, contributing author in *The HBCU Experience Anthology: Alumni Stories From the Mecca*, contends, Major John D. Slade, one of the commanding officers of the Army R.O.T.C,. was an influence on the campus of HU. Jay Allen, contributing author in *The HBCU Experience Anthology: The North Carolina A&T State University* Edition notes that his professors were nurturing, but also like coaches at times.

HBCUs Today

HBCUs continued to develop and thrive. By the early 1950s, over 3,000 students were enrolled in graduate programs at HBCUs. The addition of graduate programs at HBCUs reflected three Supreme Court decisions in which the "separate but equal" principle of Plessy was applied to graduate and professional education.

    St. Augustine's University in Raleigh, North Carolina was founded in 1867, but did not offer any graduate programs until recently. It was originally the St. Augustine Normal School and Collegiate Institute when it was founded in 1867. The name was changed to St. Augustine's School in 1893, then to St. Augustine Junior College in 1919. In 1927, the college became a four-year educational institution and was renamed St. Augustine's College. On August 1, 2021, the school was renamed St. Augustine's University.

    Today, there are over 100 accredited HBCUs, public and private, in 19 states, the District of Columbia, and the U.S. Virgin Islands. In 2014, HBCUs accounted for only 3 percent of public and not-for-profit private institutions receiving federal student aid, enrolled 10 percent of African American college students nationwide, accounted for 17 percent of the bachelor's degrees earned by African Americans and 24 percent of the degrees earned by African American in STEM fields.

According to the National Science Foundation, the top eight institutions where African American PhDs in science and engineering, earning their Bachelor's Degree from 2002 to 2011, were all HBCUs.

The U.S. Small Business Administration announced in January 2021, the establishment of 20 new Women's Business Centers across the country to serve rural, urban, and underserved communities. The centers offer one-on-one counseling, training, networking, technical assistance, workshops, and mentoring. Two of the 20 new Women's Business Centers are on the campus of HBCUs, Jackson State University in Mississippi and WSSU in North Carolina. Natalie Madira Coffield (HU graduate) was appointed to serve as the Assistant Administrator for the Office of Women's Business Ownership in March 2021. She oversees the expansion of the Women's Business Center network.

Morris Brown College, founded in 1881 in Atlanta, Georgia, secured "Candidate Accreditation Status" by the Transactional Association of Christian Colleges and Schools (TRACS) on April 13, 2021. This is after two years of restructuring. The college is now eligible to apply to the U.S. Department of Education to participate in financial aid programs and Title IV funding. The efforts of Dr. Kevin James, the 19th President of Morris Brown College, cannot go unnoticed. Dr. James was unanimously appointed president by Morris Brown College Board of Trustees in May 2020. He served as interim president beginning on March 1, 2019.

It is the comeback stories of HBCUs that continue to drive my motivation to highlight HBCUs across the nation. It was Bennett College's accreditation woes that caused me to begin publishing *The HBCU Experience Anthology* as a way to give back. Bennett College for Women in Greensboro, North Carolina, lost its accreditation with the Southern Associate of Schools and Colleges on February 18, 2010, despite raising almost $10 million dollars during its #StandWith Bennett campaign (Bennett.edu). It was restored by a federal court in Atlanta, Georgia, awarded Candidate Status as a Category II institution by the TRACS Accreditation Commission on October 26, 2020. Bennett College is one of only two all-women's HBCUs in the United States. Spelman College is the other.

In 2015, Dr. Michael L. Lomax, CEO and president of the UNCF, identified six reasons HBCUs are more important than ever before:

1. Outsized Impact, Low Cost = "Best Buy" in Education
2. Meeting the Needs of Low-Income, First generation Students
3. Lower Costs Narrow the Racial Wealth Gap
4. Campus Climate Fosters Success
5. Addresses the Nation's Under-and Unemployment Crisis
6. HBCUs Offer a True Value/Values Proposition

Conclusion

Student and alumni networks that exist among HBCUs provide a continuous experience for graduates of HBCUs, professionally as well as socially. HBCUs are found to be diverse in backgrounds, perspectives, experience, interests, cultures, and philosophies. The environment is one of support, with a true sense of community. HBCUs provide an enriching academic and social experience. Whether you were a part of Student Government, were initiated into a

Chapter 6: The Significance of HBCUs   101

BGLO, known as the Divine Nine, or you were simply focused on academics, the HBCU experience was and continue to be a great one, indeed, one which must be shared. In that vein, I wish to share a *partial list of notable HBCU alumni*, compiled in DEC 2012 *by* one of the contributors for this volume, *Dr. Raymond Winbush*, who is an himself an *HBCU alumnus* (Oakwood College):

Yolanda Adams, Tennessee State University, Gospel Singer
Debbie Allen, Howard Univ., Choreographer/Director
Erykah Badu, Grambling State Univ., R & B Singer
Marion Berry, Fisk University, Politician
Mary McCloud-Bethune, Barbara Scotia, HBCU Founder
Ed Bradley, Cheyney State, 60 Minutes Anchor
Harry Carson, South Carolina State Univ., Former NFL Player
W. E. B. Du Bois, Fisk University, Author, Educator
Shawn P-Diddy Combs, Howard Univ., Hip-Hop Music Executive
Common, Florida A & M University, Hip-Hop Artist
Michael Clark-Duncan, Alcorn State University, Actor
Etu Evans, South Carolina State Univ., Shoe and Accessory designer
Louis Farrakhan, Winston-Salem State Univ., Religious leader
John Hope Franklin, Fisk Univ., Historian
Nikki Giovanni, Fisk University, Author-Poet
Earl Graves, Morgan State University, Magazine Publisher
James Clyburn, South Carolina State Univ., US Congress
Alex Haley, Alcorn State University, Author
Jesse Jackson, North Carolina A & T, Politician
Randy Jackson, Southern University, American Idol Judge
Samuel Jackson, Morehouse College, Actor
Avery Johnson, Southern University, NBA Player & Coach
James Weldon Johnson, Clark Atlanta, Composer of "Lift Every Voice and Sing"
Marcus Johnson, Howard Univ., Record Company CEO
Tom Joyner, Tuskegee University, Radio Show Host
Leroy Kelly, Morgan State University, Former NFL Player
Dr. Martin Luther King, Jr., Morehouse College, Civil Rights Activist
Kwame Kilpatrick, Florida A & M University, Former Mayor of Detroit
Spike Lee, Morehouse College, Film Maker
Omarosa Manigault, Central State University, Ohio, Celebrity Actor
Rick Mahorn, Hampton University, Former NBA Player
Ronald McNair,* North Carolina A & T, Astronaut
Steve McNair, Alcorn State University, NFL Football Player

Midnight Star, Kentucky State University, 80s R & B Group
Earl Monroe, Winston Salem State Univ. Former, NBA Player
Toni Morrison, Howard University, Noble Prize Author-Poet
Kwame Nkrumah, Lincoln Univ., 1st President of Ghana
Charles Oakley, Virginia Union University, NBA Player
Pam Oliver, Florida A & M University, Sports Anchor/Reporter
Roderick Paige, Jackson State University, U.S. Secretary of Education
Rosa Parks, Alabama State University, Civil Rights Leader
Walter Payton, Jackson State University, Former NFL Player
Keisha Pullman, Spelman College, Actor
Phylicia Rashad, Howard University, Actor
Jerry Rice, Mississippi Valley State Univ., Former NFL Player
Eddie Robinson,* Grambling State University College, Football Coach
Steven A. Smith, Winston Salem University, ESPN Anchor
Shannon Sharpe, Savannah State University, Former NFL Player
Doug Stewart, South Carolina State Univ., Radio Host
Ruben Studdard, Alabama A & M University, American Idol Singer
Wanda Sykes, Hampton University, Comedian
Susan Taylor, Lincoln University, Essence Magazine
Joe Torrey, Lincoln University, Comedian
Andrew Young, Morehouse College, Civil Rights Activist
Ben Wallace, Virginia Union, NBA Player
Booker T. Washington, Hampton Institute, Founder of Tuskegee Institute
Keenan Ivory Wayans, Tuskegee University, Actor-Director
Doug Williams, Grambling State University, Former NFL Player
Lynn Whitfield, Howard University, Actor
Nancy Wilson, Central State University, Ohio, Jazz Singer
Oprah Winfrey, Tennessee State University, Talk Show Host
Andrew Young, Howard University, Former U.N. Ambassador

HBCU Alumni, who are *Contributors for this textbook*:

Molefi Kete Asante, PhD—Southwestern Christian, Professor/Author

Clenora Hudson-Weems, PhD—LeMoyne College & Atlanta U, Professor/Author

Debra Walker King, PhD—North Carolina Central, Professor/Author

Alveda King, Hon. Dr.(h.c.)—*attended* Spelman College and received a *Certificate* in Counseling, Atlanta U; Leader, *Civil Rights for the Unborn* (Author/Niece of MLK)

Bibliography

Bennett College. www.bennett.edu/. Retrieved 26 April 2021.

Gallup-USA Funds Minority College Graduates Report Gallup. 2015. www.gallup.com/services/186359/gallup-usa-funds-minority-college-graduates-report-pdf.aspx

National Research Council. *Colleges of Agriculture at the Land Grant Universities: A Profile*. The National Academies Press, 1995. doi.org/10.17226/4980.

Porter, S. H. *The HBCU Experience Anthology: North Carolina A&T State University Edition*. Perfect Time SHP, 2019.

———. *The HBCU Experience Anthology: St. Augustine University Edition*. Perfect Time SHP, 2021a.

———. *The HBCU Experience Anthology: Winston-Salem State University Edition*. Perfect Time SHP, 2021b.

Porter, S. H., and Wilson, T. *The HBCU Experience Anthology: Alumni Stories from the Hill of Kentucky State University*. Perfect Time SHP, 2020.

Porter, S. H., Dunham, D., Williams, D., Monroe, K. F., Wagner, S., Gourdine, D. J., Conyers, Q., McDonough, A., Downing, S., and Edwards, D. L. *The HBCU Experience Anthology: Alumni Stories From the Mecca*. Perfect Time SHP, 2020.

The Educational Effectiveness of Historically Black Colleges and Universities Briefing Report. *The Educational Effectiveness of Historically Black Colleges and Universities Briefing Report*. 2010. Published.

The First HBCU. Cheyney U of Pennsylvania, 25 February 2019. cheyney.edu/who-we-are/the-first-hbcu/#:~:text=On%20February%2025%2C%201837%2C%20Cheyney,College%20and%20University%20(HBCU). Retrieved 30 April 2021.

Why choose an HBCU. uncf.org/programs/hbcu-impact. Retrieved 25 April 2021.

Chapter 7
Africana Studies and Economics In Search of a New Progressive Partnership

Contributed by:
James B. Stewart, PhD

Introduction

Many Africana Studies specialists are extremely interested in increasing the degree of the integration of historical and contemporary analyses produced by professional economists within the discipline's body of knowledge. Discourse about the economic conditions of people of African descent has always constituted an important dimension of the Black intellectual tradition that Africana Studies seeks to preserve and extend. Economics/political economy is treated as a separate chapter in major Africana Studies texts, and a conventional understanding of the field is generally adopted (Anderson; Karenga). As an example, in *Introduction to Black Studies,* Maulana Karenga opines that

> Political economy . . . can be defined as the study of the interrelationship between politics and economics and the power relations they express and produce. It focuses not simply on the economic process, but also on economic policy and the race and class interests and value judgments this suggests (p. 420).

Specific topics discussed in the economics/political economy sections of Africana Studies texts mirror various issues examined in *The Review of Black Political Economy (The Review),* including income inequality, employment status, occupational distributions, wealth disparities, class structure, Black capitalism, consumer expenditures, and community development.

The Review, published quarterly on a continuous basis since 1970, would seem to be an ideal resource for Africana Studies specialists, as suggested by its mission statement, which declares,

> *The Review of Black Political Economy* examines issues related to the economic status of African-American and Third World peoples. It identifies and analyzes policy prescriptions designed to reduce racial economic inequality. The journal is devoted to appraising public and private policies for their ability to advance economic opportunities without regard to their theoretical or ideological origins.

But although *The Review's* mission statement clearly locates the journal as a potential ally of Africana Studies in promoting research and exploring policy alternatives in the interests of people of African descent, at the same time, the language "without regard to their theoretical or ideological origins" has important implications for understanding why professional economists have had limited influence on economic discourse within Africana Studies. A careful reading of Karenga's statement about political economy suggests the existence of both ideological and sociology of knowledge-related issues that may constrain the extent to which some aspects of economic thinking and research are compatible with the approach to the pursuit of knowledge and advocacy for social change associated with Africana Studies.

Ideology, the Sociology of Knowledge, and the Potential for Africana Studies—Economics Knowledge Transfers

The scope and meaning of terms like *African American Studies, Black Studies,* and *Africana Studies* have evolved continually since the field was established in schools, colleges, and universities in the late 1960s. For present purposes, Africana Studies can be conceptualized as a field of study that systematically treats the past and present experiences, characteristics, achievements, issues, and problems of people of African descent. Africana Studies specialists pursue a comprehensive approach to this project that encompasses the historical, sociological, psychological, political, economic, creative, and expressive aspects of the lives of people of African descent. The preferred strategy for synthesizing diverse types of information and styles of inquiry involves efforts to develop a unified quasi-social science mode of analysis that synthesizes perspectives from various disciplines rather than treating individual disciplinary perspectives in isolation (Stewart, "Social Science and Systematic Inquiry"). Analyses examining the extent to which the persisting impacts of historical developments condition contemporary social relations have a privileged status, and the preferred unit of analysis is groups rather than individuals. Africana Studies research has been heavily influenced by the perspectives on historical explanation advanced by Du Bois ("The Beginnings of Slavery"), who opined,

> We can only understand the present by continually referring to and studying the past, when any one of the intricate phenomena of our daily life puzzles us, when there arises religious problems, political problems, race problems, we must always remember that while their solution lies in the present, their cause and their explanation lie in the past. (p. 104)

Africana Studies' emphasis on the agency of collectives and historically dominated causation analyses conflicts with the preference within mainstream economics for theories focusing on the behavior of individuals and empirical research methods that rely heavily on cross-sectional or highly censored time series data. Another significant barrier to collaboration between economists and Africana Studies specialists is the staunch commitment of Africana Studies specialists to prioritizing applied research designed to contribute directly to improvements in well-being over theoretical explorations. Moreover, the conduct of applied research is seen as the first step in a process followed by active policy advocacy by researchers and their direct involvement in implementation activities designed to achieve desired outcomes. Allen has described these preferences as reflecting an ideology that positions Africana Studies as an instrument of cultural nationalism and an instrument for empowering communities. These operating principles are, however, diametrically opposed to the conventional wisdom that scientific research should be uncontaminated by political considerations and that theoretical research should be more richly rewarded than applied research. As a consequence of these divergent disciplinary values, some professional economists view Africana Studies as being unscientific and/or political and overlook opportunities to influence the content of economic discourse within the field.

Unrealized Opportunities to Utilize Economic Research in Africana Studies

The disconnection between economists and Africana Studies specialists has contributed to a tradition whereby most economic discourse within Africana Studies has been produced by commentators with little or no formal training in economics. As an example, in seeking information about the historical circumstances facing Black workers, Africana Studies specialists are likely to explore the writings of W. E. B. Du Bois and Carter G. Woodson rather than the work of contemporaries formally trained in economics such as Sadie Tanner Mossell Alexander, Abram Harris, and George Edmund Haynes.

Africana Studies specialists are also not likely to be familiar with the successors to the first generation of professional Black economists, including Robert Weaver and Phyllis Wallace. Wallace established the foundations for in-depth scrutiny of labor market outcomes of African American women, which was extended by Margaret Simms and Julianne Malveaux (Malveaux; Simms and Malveaux). In seeking information about the economic circumstances facing Black women, Africana Studies specialists are more likely to turn to the work of historians like Darlene Clark Hine and Jacqueline Jones (Hine; Jones).

The focus within Africana Studies on groups has fostered an emphasis on collective approaches to economic empowerment along with a deep-seated suspicion of the extent to which significant improvements in economic fortunes can be achieved within a capitalist economic system. However, despite the high priority assigned to collective economic empowerment strategies within Africana Studies, specialists have made remarkably little use of available resources generated by economists that can facilitate systematic examination of this topic. One example is *Black Economic Development,* one of the first collections with a specific focus on community economic empowerment (Haddad and Pugh). The various essays examine issues such as entrepreneurship and the potential of small businesses, the efficacy of separatist approaches to development, and the role and intentions of the federal government. A review of the mission and activities of the Black Economic Research Center (BERC) established in 1969 by Robert Browne as a type of economic laboratory where young Black economists conducted a variety of research projects could also be instructive for Africana Studies specialists. BERC was engaged in exactly the type of community engagement that Africana Studies specialists have envisioned, but this initiative is largely unknown within Africana Studies.

Various articles examining collective economic development strategies were also published in *The Review* during the 1970s, exploring a variety of relevant topics including barriers to Black participation in the U.S. economy, cash flows in ghetto communities, political and economic challenges and prospects for Black economic development, the role of educational institutions in development, and the impact of community development corporations. This body of research was complemented by several books, including Frank Davis's *The Economics of Black Community Development* and William Tabb's *The Political Economy of the Black Ghetto*. These single-author volumes were later supplemented by the important edited volume, *Black Economic Development: Analysis and Implications* (Cash and Oliver). Many of these same issues were revisited some 30 years later in *The Inner City: Urban Poverty and Economic Development in the Next Century* (Boston and Ross).

Debates among economists about alternative community development strategies were linked to the broader discussion of the feasibility of alternatives to capitalist-based development models. Although the content of these debates could enrich the type of capitalist critiques articulated by Africana Studies specialists, this resource has not been utilized systematically. The critiques of capitalist-dominated development endorsed by Africana Studies specialists are largely based on writings outside the economics profession, including, for example, the writings of sociologist Oliver Cox. In his famous treatise, *Caste, Class, and Race*, Cox argues that racial antagonisms are organically linked to class struggle between capital and labor rather than simply a manifestation of a racial caste system (Cox; Hunter). Du Bois's challenges to global capitalism have also had an important influence in some circles, specifically his commentary in the essay "Negroes and the Crisis of Capitalism" on the expansion of global capitalism in the post-World War II world in which he advised Blacks not to fall into the trap of becoming ardent capitalist supporters ("Negroes and the Crisis of Capitalism").

These useful, but general, treatments could be usefully augmented by reexamining the lively debate that occurred between Marxists and non-Marxist economists in the 1970s, some of which appeared in *The Review,* regarding the relative significance of racism and class conflict as the principal source of racial economic inequalities. Some Marxists asserted that racism exhibited by members of the White working class resulted primarily from the successful efforts of capitalists to divide the proletariat and expressed caution about analyses emphasizing race as a primary factor in explaining economic oppression. Such concerns were directed, in part, at proponents of what was termed the *internal colony model* who adapted the traditional metropolis-colony explanation of the expropriation of indigenous resources under colonialism to characterize the relationship between predominantly Black inner cities and surrounding suburban areas. Proponents of the internal colony model emphasized the need for Blacks to develop quasi-independent economic networks in predominantly Black communities.

Current Opportunities for Collaboration in Applied Research and Policy Advocacy

The dilemma of how to confront the disproportionate vulnerability of African Americans has become even more complex in the current era of capitalist-dominated globalization. A collaborative-focused effort between economists and Africana Studies specialists could conceivably lead to new intellectual insights and operational strategies for empowering urban communities. Michael Shuman laments that "nearly every state, county, city, town, and village in America is hitching its future to globe-trotting corporations" (p. 1), which includes implementation of revival strategies that mask the disastrous effects on the most vulnerable populations, including hyper-unemployment, pervasive poverty, environmental racism, and various negative consequences of the underground economy. An update of the classic Keener Commission Report thirty years after its original 1968 publication used the metaphor "locked in the poorhouse" to describe the conditions facing many inner-city residents (Harris and Curtis).

An examination of the activities and impact of the current cohort of community development corporations, many of which have flourished as a result of federal faith-based initiatives, could be a useful starting point for meaningful collaboration. This type of targeted project would revitalize the type of applied research focus that characterized BERC in the early 1970s and provide internship opportunities for students and expanded outreach potential for many Africana Studies departments and programs. Many local development efforts, however well intentioned, have involved an oasis strategy in which community development corporations and other community-based organizations have carved out areas of revitalization and relative stability "while the forces that would undo their fragile improvements crouched just outside the door" mired in pervasive poverty and social disorganization (Grogan and Proscio).

Efforts to evaluate the potential efficacy of proposed alternative development strategies could begin with an assessment of the potential benefits of initiatives proposed by environmental racism and environmental justice advocates as well as living-wage legislation (Bullard; Bullard et al.). The environmental justice movement champions redevelopment policies that are in balance with nature, honor the cultural integrity of communities, and provide fair access for all to the full range of resources. Metropolitan sprawl is treated as an anathema because it is not environmentally friendly and is fostered through inequitable policies. Existing transportation policies (highways, light-rail networks, and other suburban-friendly public transportation modes) disadvantage inner-city residents in terms of services provided and the negative health implications of the modes of transportation that are accessible. The Turner Foundation and Ford Foundation are funding a major transportation equity project in Atlanta and several other cities to explore these issues in more detail (Atlanta Transportation Equity Project Summary). The Living Wage Movement seeks to force employers to raise the pay of low-wage workers sufficiently to enable them to escape poverty.

Outside of urban areas there are also opportunities for collaboration between economists and Africana Studies specialists. Both economists and Africana Studies specialists have been largely absent in the ongoing battle by Black farmers to pursue justice. The absence of economists is especially puzzling given the important precedent established by Robert Browne. Browne's interest in the plight of Black farmers and the loss of Black-owned farmland led him to create the Emergency Land Fund (ELF) in 1971 and to publish *Only Six Million Acres: The Decline of Black-Owned Land in the Rural South*, a seminal monograph documenting the problem (Browne). In 1985, ELF merged with the Federation of Southern Cooperatives, and as the Federation of Southern Cooperatives/Land Assistance Fund, continues to assist in efforts to aid Black farmers and retain Black-owned land. Several organizations have been formed by Black farmers in an effort to stem further land loss and to challenge discriminatory practices of the U.S. Department of Agriculture in farm credit and noncredit benefit programs. These groups have used a combination of legal challenges and direct action to seek relief. Despite a 1999 consent decree, there have been continuing allegations of mismanagement of the settlement process, and congressional hearings in 2004 addressed concerns about the large number of claims from Black farmers that were summarily rejected because they arrived after the filing deadline due to inadequate notification of potential claimants. As of November 2002, of the approximately 21,000 eligible farmers, only about 13,000, or 60%, had been approved for a cash settlement and debt relief. The approved disbursements amounted to about $780 million, much less than the original $2.5 billion estimate of the value of the settlement. The high rate of denial (9,000 or 40%) has spurred additional direct action including takeovers and attempted takeovers of Farm Service Agency offices in Tennessee, Arkansas, and Louisiana in 2002. In addition, a new lawsuit was filed in September 2004 but was dismissed in 2005. Thus, it appears that congressional action is the last hope for the many Black farmers left out of the original settlement. The ongoing saga of institutional assaults on Black farmers underscores the continuing validity of the 1995 assessment made by Joyce Allen-Smith: "As we approach the twenty-first century . . . prospects to alleviate poverty and improve the well-being of rural Blacks in the near future remain dim" (pp. 15–16). However, a collaborative intervention by economists and Africana Studies specialists could help generate additional support for legislative relief for Black farmers.

Toward a Collaborative Reconceptualization of Race and Its Role in Influencing Economic Behavior

The plight of Black farmers also highlights why Africana Studies specialists are less concerned than most economists about distinctions between market and nonmarket discrimination. From the vantage point of Africana Studies, the various forms of discrimination are so tightly intertwined that efforts to disentangle them statistically are largely empty intellectual exercises. Africana Studies specialists are attempting to decipher how political and economic agents bent on reestablishing the previous racial order are developing new strategies, including masking their objectives in language touting so-called color-blind policies. New types of discriminatory behavior have emerged, including symbolic racism, so called because its practitioners are not assumed to act out of self-interest. Instead, practitioners of symbolic racism are said to act out of a feeling of resentment over the fact that Blacks willfully refuse to adhere to the traditional American values of hard work, self-reliance, and individualism. These perspectives undergird new practices such as "rational" statistical discrimination and racial profiling, as well as screening ethnic-sounding names in making hiring decisions. At the same time, both overt and subtle racial harassment and erection of barriers to upward mobility in the workplace have intensified.

Efforts by Africana Studies specialists to understand these dynamics could be enhanced through collaboration with those economists attempting to develop the subfield of stratification economics. Within stratification economics, special attention is directed to the role of racial and caste distinctions and similar group affiliations in producing and perpetuating income and wealth inequality (Darity). Group identities are treated as produced forms of individual and collective property with both income and wealth-generating characteristics and whose supply and demand are responsive to changes in production costs and budget constraints. Cooperative economic and noneconomic behaviors are treated as normal outcomes of individuals' propensity to engage in own-group altruism and other-group antagonism. Stratification economists argue, for example, that intergroup conflict in both economic and noneconomic settings is an endogenous characteristic of the social space rather than an exogenous contaminant of market allocation processes and individual decision-making. These models predict that reductions in intergroup income and wealth differentials will not automatically lead to the erosion of traditional patterns of collective identification as long as investments in group identity generate unequal returns for different identities and also that movement toward more egalitarian intergroup distributions of wealth must be a major element in any earnest attempt to reduce intergroup conflict because inequities are institutionalized through processes that enable the transfer of material resources across generations (Darity et al.; Stewart, "NEA Presidential Address"; Stewart and Coleman). This approach to examining the interplay between racial identity production conflicts and economic conflicts is very compatible with how many Africana Studies scholars approach issues of race and culture. In addition, it allows a more systematic approach to examining long-term trends in race relations and economic well-being that is consistent with the Africana Studies emphasis on the criticality of examining the historical foundations of contemporary developments.

Conclusion

Africana Studies specialists and many progressive economists have a shared interest in developing the intellectual tools and information necessary to combat all forms of racism. But, as George Santayana so aptly observed, "The same battle in the clouds will be known to the deaf only as lightning and to the blind only as thunder." Until both progressive economists and Africana Studies specialists are willing to admit that they are victims of the ideological and theoretical blinders created by their disciplines and are largely unable to hear arguments framed in terms used by other intellectual and activist traditions, the degree of collaboration necessary for success in confronting a common enemy is not likely to materialize.

Bibliography

Allen, R. "Politics of the Attack on Black Studies." *The Black Scholar*, vol. 6, no. 1, 1974, pp. 2–7.

Allen-Smith, J. Introduction. *Blacks in Rural America*, edited by J. Stewart and J. Allen-Smith, Transaction Publishers, 1995, pp. 15–16.

Anderson, T. *Introduction to Black Studies*. Kendall-Hunt, 1993.

"Atlanta Transportation Equity Project Summary." *Environmental Justice Resource Center*, 15 July 2005, www.ejrc.cau.edu/atepannouncement.htm

Boston, T., editor. *A Different Vision: African American Economic Thought*, vol. 1, Routledge, 1997.

Boston, T., and Ross, C. *The Inner City: Urban Poverty and Economic Development in the Next Century*. Transaction Books, 1998.

Browne, R. S. *Only Six Million Acres: The Decline of Black Owned Land in the Rural South*. Black Economic Research Center, 1973.

Bullard, R. *Dumping in Dixie: Race, Class, and Environmental Quality*. Westview, 1990.

Bullard, R., Johnson, G., and Torres A., editors. *Sprawl City: Race, Politics, and Planning in Atlanta*. Island Press, 2000.

Cash, W., and Oliver, L., editors. *Black Economic Development: Analysis and Implications*. University of Michigan Graduate School of Business Administration, 1975.

Cox, O. *Caste, Class, and Race: A Study in Social Dynamics*. Doubleday, 1948.

Darity, W. "Stratification Economics: The Role of Intergroup Inequality." *Journal of Economics and Finance*, vol. 29, no. 2, 2005, 144–153.

Darity, W., Mason, P., and Stewart, J. "The Economics of Identity: The Origin and Persistence of Racial Identity Norms." *Journal of Economic and Behavioral Organization*, vol. 60, 2006, 283–305.

Davis, F. *The Economics of Black Community Development*. Markham, 1972.

Du Bois. "Negroes and the Crisis of Capitalism." *Monthly Review*, vol. 4, 1953, 478–485.

———. "The Beginnings of Slavery." *Voice of the Negro*, vol. 2, 1905, 104–106.

———, editor. *The Negro Artisan: Report of a Social Study Made Under the Direction of Atlanta University; Together with the Proceedings of the Seventh Conference for the Study of Negro Problems, held at Atlanta University, 27 May 1902*, Atlanta UP, 1902.

Greene, L., and Woodson, C. G. *The Negro Wage Earner*. Associated Publishers, 1930.

Grogan, P., and Proscio, T. *Comeback Cities: A Blueprint for Urban Neighborhood Revival*. Westview, 2000.

Haddad, W., and Pugh, G., editors. *Black Economic Development*. Prentice-Hall, 1969.

Harris, F., and Curtis, L., editors. *Locked in the Poorhouse: Cities, Race and Poverty in the United States*. Rowan & Littlefield, 1998.

Hine, D. C. *Black Women in White: Racial Conflict and Cooperation in the Nursing Profession, 1890-1950*. Indiana University Press, 1989.

Hunter, H. The Political Economic Thought of Oliver C. Cox. *A Different Vision: African American Economic Thought*, edited by T. Boston, vol. 1, Routledge, 1997, pp. 270–289.

Jones, J. *Labor of Love, Labor of Sorrow: Black Women, Work, and Family from Slavery to Freedom.* Basic Books, 1985.

Karenga, M. *Introduction to Black Studies,* 3rd ed., University of Sankore Press, 2002.

Malveaux, J. Tilting Against the Wind: Reflections of the Life and Work of Dr. Phyllis Ann Wallace. *A Different Vision: African American Economic Thought,* edited by T. Boston, vol. I, Routledge, 1997, pp. 270–289.

Shuman, M. *Going Local: Creating Self-Reliant Communities in a Global Age.* Routledge, 2000.

Simms, M., and Malveaux, J., editors. *Slipping Through the Cracks: The Status of Black Women.* Transaction Books, 1986.

Stewart, J. NEA Presidential Address, 1994: Toward Broader Involvement of Black Economists in Discussions of Race and Public Policy: A Plea for a Reconceptualization of Race and Power in Economic Theory. *African Americans and Post-Industrial Labor Markets,* edited by J. Stewart, Transaction Publishing, 1997, pp. 15–38.

———. Social Science and Systematic Inquiry in Africana Studies: Challenges for the 21st Century. *Handbook of Black Studies,* edited by M. Asante and M. Karenga. Sage, 2006, pp. 379–401.

Stewart, J., and Coleman, M. The Black Political Economy Paradigm and the Dynamics of Racial Economic Inequality. *African Americans in the U.S. Economy*, edited by C. Conrad, J. Whitehead, P. Mason, and J. Stewart, Rowman and Littlefield, 2005, pp. 118–129.

Tabb, W. *The Political Economy of the Black Ghetto.* W.W. Norton, 1970.

Notes

1. Du Bois (*The Negro Artisan*) was one of the first researchers to examine the status of Black skilled workers. Lorenzo Greene and Carter G. Woodson published one of the first comprehensive examinations of Black workers. *The Negro Wage Earner.* For information about Sadie Tanner Mossell Alexander, Abram Harris, and George Edmund Haynes, see the relevant essays in Thomas Boston's edited volume.

2. The preceding information is derived from the Web sites of several organizations, including the Land Loss Project (www.landloss.org/), the Federation of Southern Cooperatives Land Assistance Fund (www.federationsoutherncoop.com/), and the Land Loss Fund (www.federationsoutherncoop.com/).

James B. Stewart is a professor of labor studies and employment relations, African and African American Studies, and management and organization at Penn State. He previously served as vice provost for educational equity and director of the Black Studies Program. Stewart served two terms as president of the National Council for Black Studies (1997–2001). His Africana Studies monographs include *Flight in Search of Vision* (2004) and the coauthored (with Talmadge Anderson) *Introduction to African American Studies: Transdisciplinary Approaches and Implications* (2007).

Chapter 8

When Will We Learn? It's Not Their Heads, It's Their (Broken) Hearts

Contributed by:
S. Renee Mitchell, EdD

His tall and lanky body entered my high school classroom slowly, as if he thought he might trip on his own shadow. His black hair, twisted into short, ropelike locks, was tucked behind the edges of his cobalt-blue hoodie, which was tied tightly and knotted just above his chin. He told me one of his female friends had recommended he come and talk to me, the only Black teacher in the state's most diverse high school. His friend, like him, had grown up in a refugee camp in Tanzania, the largest country in East Africa. His family was "wakimbizi," which translates as runaways. He had grown accustomed to continuously struggling to survive.

He introduced himself as Japhety, a Biblical name meaning enlargement or "may he expand." Almost immediately, in my heart, he became like a son. As I am an Africana womanist practicing educator, I interact with all Black children from the perspective of a nurturer, a mother-type figure, a healer of heartbreak. According to Hudson-Weems (*Africana Womanist Literary Theory*), the natural role of a woman contently serving as a caregiver is critical to the philosophy of Africana womanism. "Lovingly and responsibly, the Africana woman is the mother of all humankind and thus, unquestionably the supreme mother nurturer" (53).

This type of interaction, though, was atypical for many Black students at my school. Like many of the Black males and females I encountered in my classroom and in the hallways, Japhety reeked with insecurity. Once he arrived in the United States as an elementary school student, not knowing any English, he had no words to process his first exposure to white adults who had the palest skin color he had ever seen. Once he learned to speak English, he endured years of methodical bullying by his white male, middle-school classmates. They teased about his endarkened skin, his lyrical Kirundi language, and any clothing he wore that represented his native land. "I got put down so much," Japhety acknowledged in his college scholarship applications, "I began to hate being African." His internalized shame showed up in his tense shoulders, his avoidance of sustained eye contact, his habit of

115

talking just a few degrees above a whisper, all tell-tale signs of an imploded self-esteem, based on his daily encounters with unchecked racism from youth and adults.

Schools—A Site of Black Suffering

For many Black students, "schools ignore their aspirations, disrespect their ability to learn, fail to access and cultivate their many talents, and impose a restrictive range of their options. Within this overwhelming, oppressive schooling context, too many Black boys simply give up-beaten by school systems that place little value on who they are and what they offer" (Davis 533). The more information Japhety shared with me, the more it became clear that he wanted to do so much more than what he was being shown was possible. He just didn't know who could point him in the right direction. So, from the very first time I met this young man, I decided, then and there, to take him under my wing, like a protective auntie unable to avoid showing favoritism to her favorite nephew. Eventually, I surmised that he had entered my life in order to expand my own spiritual understanding of my role as a Master Gardner of emotionally wounded Black children. I was not in Japhety's life to fix him, but to till the soil of his own potential by taking him on a soul-healing and critical consciousness-raising journey that would make it clearly known to him what was already inside of him. According to Dillard, "It is about being willing to be transformed and 'taught' by all we encounter and recognizing these encounters as purposeful and expansive, both in the very ways that we *think* about our relationship to others in the world, as well as how we *feel* about them" (94; italic emphasis by original author). As Black women in positions of leadership, especially in the educational or social services realm, this is our ancestral obligation. It is how we translate, in real-life terms, the meaning of the African principle of Ubuntu: *I am, therefore you are, and because you are, therefore, I am.*

Black youth, like Japhety, who are African ascendents[1], a term encouraged by Dillard, especially need these Africana womanist-based interactions as they are statistically the most likely adolescent group to experience spirit-murdering, based on racial trauma they encounter in society and in schools. As socializing institutions and places of cultural hegemony, these systems replicate damaging techniques of oppression (Benner et al.; Cronholm et al.; Dumas, "Losing an Arm"; Goldmann et al.; Love; Pincus). Williams ("Spirit-Murdering the Messenger") first used the provocative term—*spirt-murdering*—to compare the similar psychosomatic impacts on victims of sexual assault to victims of racism, in that both sets of the psychologically wounded are forced to prove that "they did not distort the circumstances, misunderstand the intent or even enjoy it" (130). The phrase "spirit-murder" has increasingly been used by scholars focused on racism within society (Jones; Williams, *The Alchemy of Race and Rights*), employment (Erskine et al.; Washington and Harris), and now, education (Erevelles and Minear; Evans-Winters and Esposito; Johnson and Bryan; Hines and Wilmot; Love).

As a majority of America's teaching staff and administrators is White, those in authority are bringing their hidden (and not-so-hidden) biases, stereotypes, and racially based

---

[1] Ascendent is a term that more optimistically describes those of African Heritage. An "Africa Rising" social movement, which began in May 2017, subscribes to a future narrative on Africa's own unconventional terms.

judgments into an environment where Black students spend half their weekday, during most weeks of the year. White teachers are more likely to underestimate the academic abilities of Black students (Tenenbaum and Ruck); and they also tend to blame Black students and their families for deficits created by 400+ years of racial oppression (Ginwright and Cammorata). These seasoned adult prejudices lead to harsher discipline. Black high school students are suspended far more often than their White counterparts and punished more severely for similar misdeeds (Duncan-Andrade). In addition, racial microaggressions and an unwelcoming atmosphere can suppress Black students' academic performance and school engagement (Cherng and Halpin; Steele). "Black youth are exiting our nation's classrooms with metaphorical broken arms and dislocated shoulders and with bruised hearts and wounded souls" (Johnson et al. 2). The vitality of anti-Blackness energy that is so pervasive within schools and in society affects the ability of Black students to learn and thrive. This persistent and assiduous unwelcoming energy can negatively affect nearly every measure of a Black child's well-being—educational, social, financial, emotional, and physical. Dumas and Nelson believe that many White teachers construe Black children as undeserving of love and compassion. This unconscious belief is a relic from America's brutal form of chattel slavery when toddlers, at the hands of White women, "were severely punished for exhibiting normal childlike behaviors. We contend that this imagination of Black children still holds" (33–34). This world view also puts Black schoolchildren at a greater risk of being subjected to continuous judgment (Dumas and Nelson) and dehumanization (Coles; Sealey-Ruiz and Green). This perception is far more dangerous than racial discrimination, according to Dumas and Nelson, because it is "a construction of the Other as not human, as less than human, and, therefore, undeserving of the emotional and moral recognition accorded to those whose shared humanity is understood" (29). Gaertner and Dovidio also maintain that even Whites who do not consider themselves to be racist, still hold anti-Black biases. So, trauma instigated because of one's skin color becomes a normative experience (Lanier et al.), when Black teens are at a critical and analytical time in their development. Hughes et al. note that "adolescence is a period during which racial knowledge becomes more intricate, due both to changes occurring within adolescents and to changes occurring in how others perceive and relate to them" (4). It is also during this stage of life when Black youths, who are trying to figure out how they fit in with their peers, start to recognize that "anti-Blackness organizes the social context of their lives" (Coles 2). And instead of spending so much of their time in a place where they feel belonging and approval, Black children are instead being precipitously and unapologetically fitted with mental shackles of inferiority, as schools, for them, serve as ripe soil for Black emotional torment and psychological suffering (Dumas, "Losing an Arm"). As most educational policies systemically ignore the prevalence of anti-Blackness, "any racial disparity in education should be assumed to be facilitated, or at least exacerbated, by disdain and disregard for the Black" students (Dumas, "Against the Dark" 17).

The Long-Lasting Mental Impact

The internalized shame instigated by America's educational system's anti-Black indoctrination begins before children can even put what they are experiencing into words. As I now often process my experiences through poetry, in 2013, I wrote a poem, titled *Invisible Me*, about one of my first memories of overt racism, when I was in the first grade. But the experience of being one of very few Black students—and, at times, the only Black student—within my K–12 classrooms in northern California, rural Ohio, and then rural Oregon, remained consistent.

at home
I am brown skinned knock knee'd sullen
coarse strands of defiant black-brown curls
escape from my rubber-banded lopsided ponytails
she looks like me
this girl in the bathroom mirror
hurriedly scraping a toothbrush across her gap-toothed smirk
I run two blocks skip every other stair
then walk slowly as to not draw ire
I sit at my desk on the front row
wiggling my hand like it is on fire
ooh oooooohhhhh I know I know
I see my teacher white haired grandmotherly
same birthday as mine
I grin even wider this day
then the dance begins
first her eyes avert past mine
then her legs shift around my yawning absence
as do the students who look like her
they repeat the same dance every day
every one of them
in the classroom
on the playground
in the lunchroom
I decide
I must check out that mirror again
just to make sure
I actually exist

The educational system's traditions of pathological conditioning perpetuate psychic trauma, fertilizes low self-esteem, and contributes to a negative self-identity for Black students (Ladson-Billings; Tatum). Even schools and school districts that enthusiastically embrace the latest "fix-the-broken-child" remedies of social-emotional learning (SEL) curriculum and trauma-informed (T-I) practices often neglect to acknowledge how anti-Black racism breeds trauma (Grinage; Legette et al.). And when Black students are not provided greater socio-political and racial context for why schools and society are so generally unwelcoming, efforts to individually soothe their encounters with racial injustice through SEL and T-I practices equates to what national SEL expert Dena Simmons calls "white supremacy with a hug" (Madda par. 10). This enigmatic challenge to address America's dirty laundry is not new. In Carter G. Woodson's seminal book, *The Mis-Education of the Negro*, he notes why the racially biased treatment of Black children by white educators is so emotionally devastating, and he chastises those who believe in freedom for their complacency in not directly acknowledging and addressing racism within schools:

> "To handicap a student by teaching him that his black face is a curse and that his struggle to change his condition is hopeless is the worst sort of lynching. It kills one's aspirations and dooms him to vagabondage and crime. It is strange, then, that the friends of the truth and the promoters of freedom have not risen up against the present propaganda in the schools and crushed it. This crusade is much more important than the anti-lynching movement, because there would be no lynching if it did not start in the schoolroom" (Woodson 3).

So, Japhety's inhibited demeanor needed no explanation. He was reflecting what I had already come to recognize within myself: Unprocessed grief and repressed rage. According to King when accumulated anger from childhood builds up, it gets "locked in our bodies and minds" and exhibits itself in six different disguises: Dominance, defiance, distraction, devotion, dependence, and depression. My particular form of hidden rage, it turned out, was presented as devotion. As a habitual martyr, I was self-sacrificing to a fault. King describes this type of behavior as unacknowledged rage because it actually is used to mask one's authentic feelings. Putting others before my own needs was a way of avoiding getting too close to anyone because internally, I felt unworthy of love. And, before King, no one had previously presented the motivations behind my behavior so achingly clear. Using the words she listed in her chart under the "devotion" category, I chose descriptions that resonated, such as "seeks significance by pleasing others," "needs to be wanted", "voiceless," "hurt," and "denial." As an artistic form of processing information, I then assembled the words and phrases into a "found" poem, which I called "(UN)pleasing":

> *i wanted to please*
> *a voiceless martyr – hurt & in denial*
> *wearing a triple woven layer of unworthiness*
> *like it was my favorite winter coat*
> *u thought i was devoted*
> *because u received all i had*
> *but what sustenance remains within emptiness*
> *what medal did I earn*
> *from ignoring my own needs*

I (over)accommodated to avoid intimacy
even with myself
until . . .
I discovered the admiration
I so desperately craved was there all along
in the loving eyes looking back
at my mirrored reflection
waiting for me to notice her

As an Africana womanist, I was determined—and, from my perspective, willingly obligated—to help other Black children from spending too much time, as I did, wandering in grief and wallowing too long in self-doubt. According to Hudson-Weems (*Africana Womanist Literary Theory*), the intention of being "mission realized" is to enable Black women "to leave a lasting legacy for future generations of Africana people so that they will not be left with a void leading down the long and tiring journey of starting from scratch for solutions" (132). So, when I first met Japhety, I was able to look past his emotionally shrunken presentation and recognize a familiar hint of something within him that was still longing to be birthed. Dillard characterized this form of resonance with other Black people's collective and deeply traumatic legacy as a strength and a practice that dates back to Africa (30). Africana-minded women tend to treat other Black children as an extension of their own family and it "is impossible for her to separate her survival from that of her family" (Hudson-Weems, *Africana Womanist Literary Theory* 53). This deep love for melanin within an Africana womanist's core may explain why Queen Hatshepsut's reign, between 1505 and 1485 BCE, was considered "one of the most outstanding in the 18th Dynasty of Egypt, proving that a woman can be a strong and effective ruler" (Clark 123). Acknowledging the legacy of African women's emotional strength and their commitment to uphold a community-focused mindset is the bridge to each individual Black person finding his or her way back to (re)embracing our collective birthright to ancestral hope, joy, and resilience, which ultimately can heal us, as a people, and revive our commitment to each other and to Mother Africa, herself. Noted Dillard, "From my view, this is a critical, sacred, and legitimate space from which the African ascendant can enact teaching and research that also affirms ourselves and our communities. (Dillard x)

The Unfolding of *I Am M.O.R.E.*

Upon our first meeting, Japhety let me know that he was a good friend of one of three youth cofounders of my then-new youth-empowerment program, called *I Am M.O.R.E.* (Making Ourselves Resilient Everyday). I founded *I Am M.O.R.E* in late November 2018 as a mentoring program, in collaboration with three Black females, then aged 18 and 19. These graduating seniors—two African immigrants and one African American—each attended the same diverse high school where I worked in a large urban city in the Pacific Northwest (Portland, Oregon). The three students were members of my Black Girl Magic Club and had received three of Portland's four $16,000 college scholarships from a statewide branch of a national educational advocacy organization. Inspired by the resiliency and courage within all three personal journeys of the scholarship winners, I intuitively designed a leadership building and arts- and performative-based program to help other Youth of Color[2] (YOC) repair the emotional harm caused by trauma, develop their creative and critical thinking skills, and inspire social-justice activism within them that would push back against racial oppression. Given the low percentages of People of Color (POC) teaching at this high school, *I Am M.O.R.E.* initially served all YOC. But the participants, mostly from word of mouth, progressively became primarily African and African American. And *I Am M.O.R.E.*'s pedagogy increasingly shifted to serve primarily Black students, considered the most prodigiously traumatized of all teen demographics.

At the time, there was little guidance on best practices to empower Black youth. So, as a former bullied and racially traumatized student who never had a Black teacher or saw Black culture positively represented within K–12 curriculum, I led from instinct. I also consulted research-based theories, such as the widely recognized Hierarchy of Human Needs framework by psychologist Maslow, which identified how to motivate individuals to reach their full potential. Based on the physiological needs identified by Maslow, I picked up hundreds of free, day-old bagels each week from a neighborhood deli and swung by the grocery store closest to the high school, where I taught journalism, to buy cream cheese, bags of cheap frozen burritos, and bunches of bananas. To meet students' psychological needs, I welcomed all students into my classroom as a hangout spot. But Maslow's framework, which is based on individualism, still wasn't meeting students' needs. Something critical was missing: Fictive kinship (Fordham and Ogbu), which involves Black people's shared identity, values, and communications styles as African Americans. Having twice visited the continent of Africa, I was inspired by the African framework of Ubuntu, which anti-apartheid activist Desmond Tutu defined as: "A person is a person through other persons" (31). This strength-based spiritual practice is characterized as "the attention one human being gives to another: the kindness, courtesy, consideration and friendliness in the relationship between people; a code of behavior, an attitude to other people and to life" (Samkange and Samkange 6).

Ubuntu has been heralded in African countries for generations. And its ways of how to be present with others has circulated through storytelling, song, and dance (Mugumbate and Chereni). "From the griots of ancient Africa to the sometimes painful lyrics of hip-hop artists, people of African descent have known that our lives and our stories must be spoken, over and over again, so that the people will know our truth" (Jackson 3). As Ubuntu focuses on interconnectedness, Black people's symbiotic ties to Africa and its collective cultural memory, those principles became the basis for how critical consciousness was incorporated into *I Am M.O.R.E.* programming. The knowing of African truths, though, requires an awakening of Black people's "amnesia, often masked as nostalgia" (Dillard 17).

---

[2] Though no term is perfect, I use Youth of Color and People of Color as political terms that refer to individuals in the United States with African, Asian/Pacific Islander, Latin American, Middle Eastern, Arab, and/or Indigenous ancestry. This recognizes race as a social construct (Cokley), and this country's racialization of groups that are politically and economically oppressed based on skin color and other traits.

This (un)remembering results from a psychological conditioning so pervasive that it requires conscious Black people to declare "we *must* be free of air, while admitting to knowing no other source of breath (Wilderson 338; italics in original).

Theoretical Grounding to Raise Hope

In order to help connect Black youth to the principles of Ubuntu, one of the first steps *I Am M.O.R.E.* takes is to raise their critical consciousness so they start to understand how structural issues breed inequities that often work against Black youth and their families. This reckoning is also a trait of Africana womanism, as she "must first address racial dominance on all fronts for the well-being of [the family]," (Hudson-Weems, *Africana Womanism* 97). Also, enabled by Black Critical Theory (BlackCrit), Black youth engage in storytelling and counter-storytelling of their narratives about surviving or resisting oppression, which then becomes a gift of wisdom for others. This activity also helps Black youth make meaning of their experiences, and deconstruct and critique complex issues (Holgate et al.). Another grounding principle, relational-cultural theory, acknowledges that we find meaning and belonging when we are engaged in interdependence, and, conversely, feelings of shame and unworthiness when we cannot wholly be ourselves without judgment or critique (Frey; Haskins and Appling; Lenz). The third theory *I Am M.O.R.E.* subscribes to is Critical Youth Empowerment (CYE), which creates a shared-power environment that helps youth take the lead where they can, as "youth workers do not empower youth as much as they create the conditions for empowerment to happen" (Greene et al. 845). Affirming students' strengths, helping them build community with their peers, and encouraging them to reflect and attach meaning to their experiences increases their capacity to learn and grow (Bogar and Hulse-Killacky). *I Am M.O.R.E.*'s practical application of these three theories, which also align with Ubuntu principles and the Africana womanist framework of community building, is a form of theory triangulation, which verifies the consistency of the positive influence on Black children.

Three Steps to Emotional Emancipation

In the short time that *I Am M.O.R.E.* has been in existence, it became the only Oregon-based, youth-development organization to receive two national SEL innovation awards from the NYC-based NoVo Foundation for our culturally specific curriculum. It also was one of only two in the country to receive funding to create an Educator Practice Community to develop a 2021–22 pilot project that would test *I Am M.O.R.E.*-inspired SEL curriculum within Portland Public Schools, Oregon's largest public school district. However the fidelity of *I Am M.O.R.E.* had never been tested in an IRB (Institutional Review Board)-approved research study. So, as part of my dissertation process at the University of Oregon, I designed a qualitative-based, critical narrative, ethnographic research study, which I completed in April 2021, in an attempt to document the effectiveness of *I Am M.O.R.E.* Like strands of braided hair, the combination of each of the three foundational steps, woven with another, demonstrates how critical consciousness, social justice activism, and arts and creativity collectively influence the potential transformation of Black youth from being spirit-murdered to emotionally emancipated. Each of the three processes will be followed by a direct quote from Japhety[3] that indicates his personal assessment.

1. *Inside-Out* begins the journey of critical consciousness by providing Black teens with skills to adopt an internal gaze in order to become analytical researchers of their own complex and often traumatic lives (Gillespie et al.). This process, which centralizes individual healing, helps them reframe negative experiences as wisdom-laden signposts to their becoming, which is an important shift away from passivity and silence. This process also helps direct youth to more deeply understand and appreciate their sense of purpose, so they can begin to walk through the world, not as victims, but as heroes of their own reimagined story.

   > I feel like *I Am MORE* is one of the very first programs to really specialize or focus on me, the individual, and as me growing. I love the way that *I Am MORE* teaches agitation so much better than schools. In schools, it was just like a textbook kind of thing that feels like I'm checking off. Like, I'm kind of just focused on grades and not really, like, internally getting that information I will need to get ahead.

2. *Outside-Up*, which is the newest of *I Am M.O.R.E.*'s three-step process, builds on youths' budding research skills, critical consciousness, and their growing confidence by providing them with guidance on how to see, name, and challenge systems of racial oppression through social-justice action. We teach youth how to analyze racial justice issues and develop a critical inquiry about systemic issues designed to privilege whiteness. This process teaches youth to question power relationships and it also has psychosocial benefits, as it helps strengthen skills, such as critical thinking, public speaking, writing, and planning. This process also supports the benefits of relational-cultural theory, which acknowledges that we find meaning and belonging when we are engaged in interdependence, (Frey; Haskins and Appling; Lenz). Noted Japhety,

   > I did a lot of research and I felt like I was learning a lot of things that I don't think I was ever learning in school. Really, just getting a hands-on experience has been a game-changer. I feel like a lot of people, especially a lot of People of Color here in the U.S. kind of go through the same trauma and having a place where they can express their feelings will be a great place. And *I Am MORE* is definitely one of those places here in Portland.

---

[3] Japhety was one of 12 youth who were individually interviewed for the *I Am M.O.R.E.* research study, which was finalized in April 2021. He gave written permission for me to use his quotes and other identifying information.

3. *Up and Beyond* allows the now emotionally emancipated Black youth to use their creative skills, such as music, spoken word, fashion, dance, and art, to share their newfound wisdom and insights with the community. This form of resistance, pushed through the filter of BlackCrit, creates cultural space for individual and collective healing that was imagined to benefit from the ancestral singing of spirituals and drumming, and, even during modern-day hip-hop rap battles.

> I was a very shy person and if I had ideas, I'd always keep it to myself and I decide, OK, this might be cool. But like, I didn't know how to act on it. I didn't know who I can go out and tell. And *I Am M.O.R.E.* kind of gave me that platform . . . . I feel, like, definitely, it's just having a place where you could continue to learn and really express your creativity without a concern. And if you have an idea, knowing that there's somebody behind you that will be able to support you and if they can't, they will find somebody that can support you.

Transformation Doesn't Take Long

Less than four months after Japhety first met me, he joined five other youth on a plane ride to Philadelphia in July 2019. This was the first time any of the youth—five Black youth and one Hmong female—had been to the east coast. The official business was three of the *I Am M.O.R.E.* youth were scheduled to speak during the opening ceremonies of a third annual trauma-informed conference of academics, educators, social workers, health-care professionals, and criminal-justice experts, on the private campus of Thomas Jefferson University. The title of the conference was "Promoting Equitable Access to High Quality Services for Vulnerable Children and Families." However, it was the first time the conference had ever invited youth to present, and the *I Am M.O.R.E.* presenters were the only young people among the 500+ attendees. I had invited another Black woman, Turiya Autry, to help chaperone the trip. Turiya is a personal friend and professional colleague, who had been working with youth as an award-winning teaching artist, performer, and thought partner for several decades. Turiya's life experience also grounded her in the African womanism "legacy of the prevalence of strong, proud, family-centered women" (Hudson-Weems, *Africana Womanist Literary Theory* 57).

> So there's all kinds of grown folks from all over. Like not just grown folks, but like psychologists, academics, PhD, university, and then, there's the youth. As a teenager, I couldn't imagine myself being in a room at a conference because I mean, I wasn't thinking about conferences, let alone that I'm going to be on the stage. (Turiya A., personal interview, 5 Apr. 2021)

Before the youth spoke, I joined them on the raised platform to perform a breathing exercise for the whole crowd. But, in my Africana womanist mindset, I knew these youth, most of all, needed one last opportunity be given space to ground themselves before performing. Then, before a conference hall full of mostly White strangers, Japhety and two other performers shared snippets of their life journeys. Japhety started his presentation by describing his carefree, love- and creativity-filled experiences as a child growing up in a refugee camp. But when he came to America and entered our school system, he told them, he was overwhelmed by the racism he was confronted with for the very first time. His White male classmates teased him relentlessly, shoved him around like they were playing a game of push tag, and regularly—and loudly—asked humiliating questions: *"Were you a slave? Did you live in a hut? Why are you so black?"* Japhety tells the crowd that through the consistent encouragement of his mother, and the *I Am M.O.R.E.* leaders, he learned to love himself again. He ended his presentation by speaking a phrase in his native tongue of Kirundi: *Huu ni mwanzo tu*, which translates: "This is only the beginning." Turiya described the scene in her interview, as part of the research study:

> So, I know they're nervous. I could see it all upon them. And they were brilliant. Do you know what I mean? They were brilliant. Brilliant! That pride you feel is like, "Oh my baby is up there; look at them fly!" You know? They rocked it, like even in their nervousness, even in their falters, because they don't have to be perfect. So not only did they make it through what I'm sure was nerve-wracking for them to even present, they got like a standing ovation. (Turiya A., personal interview, 5 Apr. 2021)

The next day, the three performers and the other two Black youth in our entourage helped co-facilitate a standing-room-only training on T-I practices from a youth's perspective. After the Philadelphia presentations, we flew to New York City, where we took a horse-driven carriage ride around Central Park; a sightseeing ferry to Ellis Island, and shopped on Fifth Avenue. We ended the six-day trip in Washington, DC, where we visited the White House, the Capitol, and the Ronald Reagan building, and spent hours in the National Museum of African American History and Culture, which was the first time any of the youth had ever visited a museum that focused solely on the Black experience. Rose V., a Hmong female, was the only non-Black student to join the trip and was one of the three performers. She had been a part of *I Am M.O.R.E.* since almost the beginning of our programming.

> That trip was the first trip I've taken out of Oregon and my second airplane ride. So it was very new. And it was really different because I've never been in hotels before either. I've never been in a populated area . . . And that experience, it felt like we were on a tour. It was very, I don't know how to explain it. The energy there was really energetic. Everyone's happy. Everyone was excited. And we were there for more than a business type. It was for fun too. (Rose V., personal interview, 5 Mar. 2021).

On the last night of our journey, we all sat around a large firepit on the roof of a Washington, DC, apartment complex, with a stunning view of the lighted Senate building. As both Turiya and I subscribe to the nurturing characteristics of Africana womanism, we created a safe emotional space for the youth to reflect about what they've learned about themselves since they began their healing journey within *I Am M.O.R.E.* Eventually, the conversation became emotional as youth shared emotions they had never before publicly discussed. In a semi-structured interview a few months later, Japhety recalled that somber experience at the fire pit.

> It just made it seem like, you know, I was at a place where I'm safe and I can be myself. Like, I know a lot of people's emotions really came out those couple of days. Like I was telling stuff that I never thought would ever let anybody else, other than my family members. (Japhety N., personal interview, 23 Mar. 2021)

I Am M.O.R.E.'s next big public event was in January 2020, its first youth-focused, creative showcase, titled "Resiliency in Rhythm: A phantasmagoria of youth storytelling, dance, art & other creative expressions." Our racially diverse group of performers ranged from a Pacific-Islander second grader who wrote, illustrated, published, and sold her book internationally; a thirteen-year-old, Black classically trained male ballet dancer whose live painting process was inspired by the youth performances; a fourteen-year-old Black female poet, and a unique fashion storytelling segment, accompanied by live drumming, where three young people, including Japhety, Rose, and an African immigrant female, represented their individual journeys from trauma to resiliency. Japhety's words expanded on the presentation he did in Philadelphia. A fellow teacher, a thirtyish White woman, helped the three YOC design each of their three changes of outfits. She said she particularly noticed how much Japhety's confidence grew throughout the process.

> I feel like a peace within himself, just like a real binding of his cross-cultural experience. And the way that he can like really make sense of both the African and the American, rather than having it be, you know, maybe something that's expressed when you're home or when you're around people that have a similar background. And then, when you're out in the world, you are code switching, essentially. But, I feel like he found this way where he can really embrace both at all times. (Kristen M., personal interview, 28 Mar. 2021)

Using Art to Inspire Resilience

I Am M.O.R.E.'s study focused on two forms of potential transformation: participants' *personal transformation*, which includes increased confidence and a sense of well-being (Clover), and *audience transformation*, where the audience gains new insights on a particular issue (Feldman et al.). It also connected the youths' storytelling elements to African oral history traditions, such as using songs, performing arts, and cultural artifacts to share wisdom or philosophies (Ilmi). Noted Herman, "While there is no way to compensate for an atrocity, there is a way to transcend it, by making it a gift to others" (p. 149). As such, less than one year after the first Resiliency in Rhythm show, Japhety decided to create a clothing business with his eighteen-year-old cousin, who also grew up in the same refugee camp. Their company, *bproud*, is intended to use T-shirts, hoodies, and other clothing to empower other YOC to embrace what makes them unique. He also intends to invest company's profits into community-based programs that empower youth.

> Just being part (of the Resiliency in Rhythm 2020), especially the one that we did with the clothing, that kinda helped me out wanting to pursue a clothing brand—just picking out the fabric, picking out what kind of clothing. Like clothing can symbolize so many different things and could really express how a person feels, how a person looks. And that was like, wow, this will be something dope for me to, like, try out and really see. And just being part of that kind of started a passion for me to want to be able to pursue something like this. (Japhety N., personal interview, 8 Feb. 2021)

In addition, because youth are treated as experts of their own experiences, they are paid every time they get in front of an audience or a microphone. Being able to be paid was motivating and inspiring to the Black youth leaders, who started to see possibilities beyond just getting a job after college graduation. In addition, at our first summer youth internship in 2020, Japhety was one of three youth who were hired as paid co-facilitator who planned and executed their own curriculum, based on their personal interests and experiences, with guidance from an adult facilitator.

> I don't think it was like the main factor was me getting paid, but, like, it definitely helped for me to continue ongoing because I was going through a lot of things and having that stable income coming in helped me out, just like taking a lot of the load off my parents, just like helping pay bills, grocery shopping and stuff like that. I was able to help my family a little bit more. So, it was, like, I was doing something I love, but at the same time I was getting paid to do something I love. It is just such a different feeling." (Japhety N., personal interview, 8 Feb. 2021)

The White teacher who helped with the Resiliency in Rhythm event said the process of working with Japhety and other YOC and witnessing their transformation from trauma to empowered resilience gave her a new perspective.

> Before *I Am M.O.R.E.*, I, as a white person thinking about the Black experience and the Black struggle, I think the main thing that I was missing was recognizing the resiliency of Black people. And, you know, it's just been fed down to me where it's like, if I'm sympathetic to that experience, it's like, "Oh, that's just so sad. That just sucks. Like that's so hard," you know and failing to recognize the other part of people being under constant hardship in so many places of their lives. I can think about experiences that I've had that have been very adverse and very hard, and the way that they have like really disabled me, you know, from being like super functional in my life. And, then being able to see the ways that Black people still thrive and find joy and are insanely creative and are so motivated to continue fighting for change, It's just incredible. (Kristen M., personal interview, 28 Mar. 2021)

Hearts Healed, Lessons Learned

Japhety's personal journey serves as a representative witness that Black children are not broken. They have just been broken hearted by the educational system's historical and unrelenting systemic bias that works against them at every turn. But, *I Am M.O.R.E.*'s research-backed, social-psychological intervention helps Black youth transcend their traumatic experiences by reframing them as gifts of wisdom and inspiration that help shape who they are becoming. In addition, through personal storytelling, Black youth can—and should—regularly use personal storytelling to challenge society's perceptions of their potential, while manifesting possibilities beyond the ones they have ever dreamed for themselves. We like to say that *I Am M.O.R.E.* doesn't just give Black youth something to do, we help them deliver back to themselves the someone they've always wanted to become: *Self-assured, transformed,* and *emotionally emancipated*. Black joy is also essential for Black youth because it serves as a meditative practice of personalized self-care, an invitation for others to join in on this defiant act of resistance in order to counteract the sometimes wearisome reality of being Black in America.

With *I Am M.OR.E.*, Black youth are not the "other;" they are the everything. They are the embodiment of what matters most to us, as Africana women, to themselves, and to each other. Using the soul-healing, spiritual practice of Ubuntu, we remind Black youth of our interconnectedness as Africana people, and the freedom awaiting them once they (re)embrace their collective cultural memory that has been calling to them from Africa's shores since before they were born. And through our spiritual and cultural grounding as Africana women, we, as adults, corroborate the dreams of our Black youth. We smile at—and with—their silliness, and we remind them of how resilient, brilliant, and creative that Black people are. We hold up a mirror to the thick phlegm blocking their authentic voices from emerging from the back of their throats, and we create space for them to build the confidence to tell their stories in their own way, without shame, apology, or permission. We do not blame them for their failures, as we have seen the road they have traveled and it was not a path designed for their success. We also let them know that we see their "bruised hearts and wounded souls" (Johnson et al. 2), and we hold space for the possibility of their full restoration. We remind them: *I Am M.O.R.E.* cannot heal you; you must learn how to heal and soothe yourselves, Black children. There must be a reason why the world has tried so hard to block your natural light. But the whispers of your ancestors will speak that ultimate truth to you when you are ready to listen. In the meantime, you must look within to find your own potential. And the profound love you allow yourselves to ingest can become the liquid salve that will heal your inner woundedness and invite Black Joy for an extended stay.

Japhety's expansive journey from trauma to empowered resilience is a critical lesson for more Africana women to learn because any internalized trauma that is not looked at, processed and individually healed, is trauma that is unconsciously transferred from generation to generation. He is the quintessential example of *I Am M.O.R.E.*'s evidence-based theory of change: *When I am grounded in my power, I instinctively want to empower others.* Japhety is not only doing that through his *bproud* clothing line, but also through his continued leadership in reaching back and training other Black youth in *I Am M.O.R.E.*'s three-step transformational process. He concludes:

> What I'm really thinking is where we should be embedding and passing onto the next generation, the next people that we are teaching, so they can continue teaching it. I want to be able to make sure everybody, including myself, is able to always be able to bounce back from whatever you go through and not letting that define who you are. Those words are just like key messages to be able to pass back to the next generation. And once you have that embedded, you don't have to be like everybody else that you interact with. (Japhety N., personal interview, 8 Feb. 2021)

In closing, I was inspired to translate the authentic and revolutionary love within my Africana womanist heart, forever reminded of the fact that for my entire family, "I got your back, Boo," for "we're all in it together" (Hudson-Weems, *Africana Womanism* 120). This is particularly the case for Black children, into *researcher-voiced poetry* (Prendergast), also called *ethnographic poetics* (Brady, "In Defense of the Sensual," *Sage Encyclopedia*). As a self-proclaimed Creative Revolutionist™, this form of writing is a wholehearted way for me to reflect a radical love for the potential of all Black youth to heal, to thrive, and to have their natural brilliance radiate as bright as the sun. I dedicate this poem to all Black youth, now and yet unborn. I title it: *Hear/For U*:

I live at the crossroads
of act/ivism, art & academia
trying to offer melanined travelers
a soft landing a warm hug
a respite that feels like home
the welcome sign beckons
but only for eyes weary & downcast
to recognize & (re)collect
what lies within endarkened shadows
those who arrive
do not come emptyhanded
the bags they lug
are rotting & unreasonable
their burdened hearts broken
their wounded souls
fatigued & aggrieved
from ancient dreams too long deferred
come, I say, closer still
let me help u unravel the lies
I cannot save or heal u
but I will remind u

yr long ago lineages
are interpreting secrets
unearthing cultural memories
listen up as they advise:
dear ones
u already have everything u need
for yr journey ahead
so release yr shackles
from yr mind, heart, body
those constraints have led u here
now let them go leave them be
give yrself permission to fly
lean yr ear toward the wind & listen
yr ancestors are whispering
(re)member
(re)member
(re)member

Bibliography

Benner, A. D., Wang, Y., Shen, Y., Boyle, A. E., Polk, R., and Cheng, Y. P. "Racial/Ethnic Discrimination and Well-Being During Adolescence: A Meta-Analytic Review." *American Psychologist*, vol. 73, 2018, pp. 855–883.

Bogar, C. B., and Hulse, Killacky, D. "Resiliency Determinants and Resiliency Processes Among Female Adult Survivors of Childhood Sexual Abuse." *Journal of Counseling and Development*, vol. 84, no. 3, 2006, pp. 318–327.

Brady, I. Ethnopoetics. *Sage Encyclopedia of Qualitative Research Methods,* edited by L. M. Given, Sage, 2008, pp. 296–298.

———. "In Defense of the Sensual. Meaning Construction in Ethnography and Poetics." *Qualitative Inquiry,* vol. 10, 2004, pp. 622–644.

Cherng, H. Y. S., and Halpin, P. F. "The Importance of Minority Teachers: Student Perceptions of Minority Versus White Teachers." *Educational Researcher*, vol. 45, 2016, pp. 407–420.

Clark, J. D. *From Hunters to Farmers: The Causes and Consequences of Food Production in Africa*. U of California P, 1984.

Clover, D. "Successes and Challenges of Feminist Arts-based Participatory Methodologies with Homeless/Street-Involved Women in Victoria." *Action Research*, vol. 9, 2011, pp. 12–26.

Cokley, K. "Critical Issues in the Measurement of Ethnic and Racial Identity: A Referendum on the State of the Field." *Journal of Counseling Psychology*, vol. 54, 2007, p. 224.

Coles, J. A. "A BlackCrit Re/Imagining of Urban Schooling Social Education Through Black Youth Enactments of Black Storywork." *Urban Education*, 2020, pp. 1–30.

Cronholm, P. F., Forke, C. M., Wade, R., Bair-Merritt, M. H., Davis, M., Harkins-Schwarz, M., Pachter, L. M., and Fein, J. A. "Adverse Childhood Experiences: Expanding the Concept of Adversity." *American Journal of Prevention Medicine*, vol. 49, 2015, pp. 354–361.

Davis, J. E. "Early Schooling and Academic Achievement of African American Males." *Urban Education*, vol. 38, 2008, pp. 515–537.

Dillard, C. B. *Learning to (Re)member the Things We've Learned to Forget: Endarkened Feminisms, Spirituality, and the Sacred Nature of Research and Teaching. Black Studies and Critical Thinking.* Peter Lang Publishing, 2012.

Dumas, M. J. "Against the Dark: Antiblackness in Education Policy and Discourse." *Theory Into Practice*, vol. 55, 2015, pp. 11–19.

———. "'Losing an Arm': Schooling as a Site of Black Suffering." *Race Ethnicity and Education*, vol. 17, 2014, pp. 1–29.

Dumas, M. J., and Nelson, J. D. "(Re)imagining Black Boyhood: Toward a Critical Framework for Educational Research." *Harvard Educational Review*, vol. 86, 2016, pp. 27–156.

Duncan-Andrade, J. R. Note to Educators: Hope required when growing roses In concrete. *Harvard Education Review*, vol. 79, 2009, pp. 181–194.

Erevelles, N., and Minear, A. "Unspeakable Offenses: Untangling Race and Disability in Discourses of Intersectionality." *Journal of Literary and Cultural Disability Studies*, vol. 4, 2010, pp. 127–145, 215–216.

Erskine, S. E, Arcibold, E. E., and Bilimoria, D. Afro-diasporic women navigating the Black ceiling: Individual, relationship and organizational strategies. *Business Horizons*, 2020, pp. 1–14.

Evans-Winters, V. E., and Esposito, J. "Other People's Daughters: Critical Race Feminism and Black Girls' Education." *Educational Foundations*, vol. 24, 2010, pp. 11–24.

Feldman, S., Hopgood, A., and Dickins, M. "Translating Research Findings into Community Based Theatre: More than a Dead Man's Wife." *Journal of Aging Studies*, vol. 27, 2013, pp. 476–486.

Fordham, S., and Ogbu, J. U. Black Students' School Success: Coping with the "Burden of 'Acting White.'" *The Urban Review*, vol. 18, 1986, pp. 176–206.

Frey, L. L. "Relational-Cultural Therapy: Theory, Research and Application to Counseling Competencies." *Professional Psychology: Research and Practice*, vol. 44, 2012, pp. 177–185.

Gaertner, S. L., and Dovidio, J. F. "Understanding and Addressing Contemporary Racism: From Aversive Racism to the Common Ingroup." *Journal of Social Issues*, vol. 61, 2006, pp. 615–639.

Gillespie, C. F., Bradley, B., Mercer, K., Smith, A. K., Conneely, K., Gapen, M., Weiss, T. Swartz, J. F., and Ressler, K. J. "Trauma Exposure and Stress-Related Disorders in Inner City Primary Care Patients." *General Hospital Psychiatry,* vol. 31, 2009, pp. 505–514.

Ginwright, S., and Cammarota, J. "New Terrain in Youth Development: The Promise of a Social Justice Approach." *Journal of Social Justice,* vol. 29, 2002, pp. 82–95.

Goldmann, E., Aiello, A., Uddin, M., Delva, J., Koenen, K., and Gant, L. M. "Pervasive Exposure to Violence and Posttraumatic Stress Disorder in a Predominantly African American Urban Community: The Detroit Neighborhood Health Study." *Journal of Traumatic Stress,* vol. 24, 2011, pp. 747–751.

Greene, S., Burke, K. J., and McKenna, M. K. "A Review of Research Connecting Digital Storytelling, Photovoice, and Civic Engagement." *Review of Educational Research*, vol. 88, 2018, pp. 844–878.

Grinage, J. "Endless Mourning: Racial Melancholia, Black Grief, and the Transformative Possibilities for Racial Justice in Education." *Harvard Educational Review,* vol. 89, 2019, pp. 227–329.

Haskins, N. H., and Appling, B. Relational-cultural theory and reality therapy: A culturally responsive integrative framework. *Theory and Practice,* vol. 95, 2017, pp. 87–99.

Herman, J. L. "Recovery from Psychological Trauma." *Psychiatry and Clinical Neurosciences,* vol. 52, 1998, pp. 145–150.

Hines, D. E., and Wilmot, J. M. "From Spirit-Murdering to Spirit-Healing: Addressing Anti-Black Aggressions and the Inhumane Discipline of Black Children." *Multicultural Perspectives*, vol. 20, 2018, pp. 62–69.

Holgate, J., Keles, J., and Kumarappan, L. "Visualizing 'Community': An Experiment in Participatory Photography among Kurdish Diasporic Workers in London." *Sociological Review,* vol. 60, 2012, pp. 312–332.

Hudson-Weems, C. *Africana Womanist Literary Theory*. Africa World Press, 2004.

———. *Africana Womanism: Reclaiming Ourselves*, Fifth Edition. London and New York: Routledge Press, 2019.

Hughes, D., Del Toro, J., Harding, J. F., Way, N., and Rarick, J. R. D. "Trajectories of Discrimination Across Adolescence: Associations with Academic, Psychological, and Behavioral Outcomes." *Child Development,* vol. 87, 2016, pp. 1337–1351.

Ilmi, A. A. "Somali Dhaqan Philosophies and the Power of African Ancestral Wisdom." *African Identities,* vol. 13, 2015, pp. 97–110.

Jackson, V. "In Our Own Voice: African-American Stories of Oppression, Survival and Recovery in Mental Health Systems." *International Journal of Narrative Therapy and Community Work,* vol. 2, 2002, p. 11.

Johnson, L. L., and Bryan, N. Using our voices, losing our bodies: Michael Brown, Trayvon Martin, and the spirit murders of Black male professors in the academy. *Race Ethnicity and Education,* vol. 20, 2017, pp. 163–177.

Johnson, L. L., Bryan, N., and Boutte, G. "Show us the love: Revolutionary teaching in (un)critical times." *The Urban Review*, vol. 51, 2019, pp. 46–64.

Jones, M. "Empowering Victims of Racial Hatred by Outlawing Spirit-Murder." *Australian Journal of Human Rights*, vol. 1, 1994, pp. 299–326.

King, R. *Healing Rage: Women Making Inner Peace Possible*. Penguin, 2008.

Ladson-Billings, G. From Soweto to the South Bronx: African Americans and colonial education in the United States. *Sociology of Education*, edited by C. Torres and T. Mitchell, State U of New York P, 1998.

Lanier, Y., Sommers, M. S., Fletcher, J., Sutton, M. Y., and Roberts, D. D. "Examining Racial Discrimination Frequency, Racial Discrimination Stress, and Psychological Well-Being Among Black Early Adolescents." *Journal of Black Psychology*, vol. 43, 2016, pp. 219–229.

Legette, K. B., Rogers, L. O., and Warren, C. A. "Humanizing Student–Teacher Relationships for Black Children: Implications for Teachers' Social–Emotional Training." *Urban Education*, 2020.

Lenz, A. S. "Relational-Cultural Theory: Fostering the Growth of a Paradigm Through Empirical Research." *Journal of Counseling and Development*, vol. 94, 2014, pp. 415–428.

Love, B. L. *We Want to Do More Than Survive: Abolitionist Teaching and the Pursuit of Educational Freedom*. Beacon Press, 2019.

Maslow, A. H. "A Theory of Human Motivation." *Psychological Review*, vol. 50, 1943, pp. 370–396.

Mugumbate, J. R., and Chereni, A. "Editorial: Now, the Theory of Ubuntu has its Space in Social Work." *African Journal of Social Work*, vol. 10, 2020, pp. v–xvii.

Pincus, F. L. "Discrimination Comes in Many Forms: Individual, Institutional, and Structural." *American Behavioral Scientist*, vol. 40, 1996, pp. 186–194.

Prendergast, M. Introduction: The Phenomena of Poetry in Research. *Poetic Inquiry: Vibrant Voices in the Social Sciences*, edited by M. Prendergast, C. Leggo, and P. Sameshima, Sense Publishers, 2009, pp. xix–xlii.

Samkange, S. and Samkange, T. M. *Hunhuism or Ubuntuism: A Zimbabwean Indigenous Political Philosophy*. Graham Publishing, 1980.

Sealey-Ruiz, Y., and Greene, P. "Popular Visual Images and the (Mis)Reading of Black Male Youth: A Case for Racial Literacy in Urban Preservice Teacher Education." *Teaching Education*, vol. 26, 2015, pp. 55–76.

Steele, N. A. "Three Characteristics of Effective Teachers." *Update: Applications of Research in Music Education*, vol. 28, 2010, pp. 71–78.

Tatum, B. D. *"Why Are All the Black Kids Sitting Together in the Cafeteria?" and Other Conversations About Race*, Rev. ed., Basic Books, 2003.

Tenenbaum, H. R., and Ruck, M. D. "Are Teachers' Expectations Different for Racial Minority Than for European American Students? A Meta-Analysis." *Journal of Educational Psychology*, vol. 99, 2007, p. 253.

Tutu, D. *No Future Without Forgiveness*. Doubleday, 1991.

Washington, P. A., and Harris, B. J. Women of color standpoints: Introduction. *NWSA Journal,* vol. 13, 2001, pp. 80–83.

Wilderson, III, F. B. *Red, White & Black: Cinema and the Structure of US Antagonisms.* Duke University, 2010.

Williams, P. J. "Spirit-Murdering the Messenger: The Discourse of Fingerpointing as the Law's Response to Racism." *University of Miami Law Review,* vol. 42, 1987, pp. 127–157.

———. *The Alchemy of Race and Rights.* Harvard UP, 1991.

Woodson, Carter G. *The Mis-Education of the Negro.* Book Tree, 2006.

Part III
Evolutionary Movements: Beliefs, Ideas and Action

Emmett Louis Till [fourteen] lived and died. His murder and trial were a mockery of the value of African American life. This incident exemplified racial atrocities in modern history. As the people were keenly cognizant of this case then, through mass media, so should they be today through recorded history. Indeed, it so pressed upon the minds of Americans then that it ultimately exploded into the Civil Rights Movement. It is crucial for the civil rights struggles of today, yesterday, and tomorrow that the importance of Emmett Till to the Modern Civil Rights Movement be written, understood for its merit, and become a focal point for positive, consciousness-raising thought and action for all American citizens who love the ideas of trust, truth, integrity, and justice.

Clenora Hudson-Weems. *Emmett Till*, 1994

Chapter 9

Networks of Steel: How Reparations for European Enslavement of Africans Unite the African Diaspora

Contributed by:
Raymond A. Winbush, PhD

> If you are the son of a man who had a wealthy estate and you inherit your father's estate, you have to pay off the debts that your father incurred before he died. The only reason that the present generation of white Americans are in a position of economic strength . . . is because their fathers worked our fathers for over 400 years with no pay . . . We were sold from plantation to plantation like you sell a horse, or a cow, or a chicken, or a bushel of wheat . . . All that money . . . is what gives the present generation of American whites the ability to walk around the earth with their chest out . . . like they have some kind of economic ingenuity. Your father isn't here to pay. My father isn't here to collect. But I'm here to collect and you're here to pay.
>
> (Malcolm X on Reparations, November 23, 1964, Paris, France)

The struggle for reparations resulting from the European Enslavement of Africans (EEA) is history's greatest crime against humanity. Beginning in 1441 when 12 Africans were stolen from their homeland of Cabo Branco (now Mauritania) by captains Antão Gonçalves and Nuno Tristão and enslaved in Portugal,[1] and ending in 1888, when Brazil officially outlawed slavery, some 60 million Africans[2] were kidnapped, transported, raped, enslaved, hanged, maimed, sold, and burned. It is common for researchers to count the Africans transported during the Middle Passage, the horrendous two-and-a-half to three months of journey aboard ships, as the *total* number of Africans arriving in the so-called "new world." This erroneous view of the EEA produces appallingly low numbers[3] that exclude many

---

[1] ("Portugal and the African Slave Trade", 2011).

[2] (Anderson, 1994).

[3] (Gates, 2013).

137

Africans stolen from the continent. *Five stages of capture* should always be included when counting the number of Africans taken from their homelands: (1) those who died fighting the invaders of villages where Africans lived, (2) those who died on the march to the sea, which often took weeks, (3) those who died in the barracoons and castles waiting for the ships, (4) those who died during the Middle Passage, and (5) those who died in the first two years of their captivity from disease and trauma.[4] When asked how many Africans were enslaved during this period, the late historian, John Henrik Clarke, said the following:

> "The Middle Passage, Our Holocaust! It is our holocaust because this is a holocaust that started 500 years ago and it is not over. We do not start our count at six million, we start at sixty million, and we have just begun to count. Now I don't mean to negate the German and the European Holocaust. Whether the number was six or sixty million, even if it was wrong. But it was a problem started in Europe by Europeans. There is no comparison between this tragedy and our tragedy which is the greatest crime in the history of the world."[5]

What is important to note is that the reparations struggle has always been global and has involved activists throughout the African diaspora. It is the only political struggle that unites the African diaspora. In Australia, the Aborigines press for them[6]; in the Caribbean, the Caribbean Community (CARICOM) is a consortium of 15 nations in that region that have struggled for reparations for years.[7] In Europe, the movement unites Africans across that continent,[8] and on the continent itself, there have been conferences held by several nations demanding reparations from their former colonizers.[9]

What are Reparations, and How is the Struggle for Them Going in the United States?

> *Reparations: Payment for a debt owed; the act of repairing a wrong or injury; to atone for wrongdoings; to make amends; to make one whole again; the payment of damages to repair a nation; compensation in money, land, or materials for damages.*
>
> —National Coalition of Blacks for Reparations in America (N'COBRA)[10]

---

[4] (Beckles & Shepherd, 2007).
[5] (Clarke, 1992 & 1999).
[6] (Hartley, 2019).
[7] (caricomreparations.org).
[8] (Miller, 2019).
[9] (Samuehl, 2021).
[10] (N'COBRA, 1993).

The word "reparations," describing compensation plans for crimes against humanity, was not used until 1921. The French at the Paris Conference employed it to describe proposed sanctions against Germany for nations it victimized during World War I. Before this, words such as "indemnity" and "war payments" were employed to describe what some saw as punitive sanctions against aggressor states following their defeat in a war. This chapter will use the term "reparations" to describe compensatory mechanisms for and by the victims of the European chattel slavery from 1441 to the present. This reflects N'COBRA's definition of reparations cited above and Randall Robinson's argument[11] that repairing the damage wrought by enslavement is both an *external* and *internal* process involving the perpetrating nation and its victims.

The 60 million lives ripped apart by the EEA resonates through time and space in the form of the 240-year struggle for reparations. Beginning with Elizabeth Freeman, the first *documented* petitioner for reparations in the United States, there is a straight and uninterrupted historical line for compensatory justice running down to the present. Freeman asked attorney Thomas Sedgwick (fourth grandfather to actress Kyra Sedgwick) to sue for her freedom in 1780 after hearing the Massachusetts Constitution read aloud (she was illiterate) and set in motion a 240-year history of Africans in America seeking compensatory justice for their enslavement. Along with "Brom," an enslaved male who was also "owned" by John Ashley, the case of *Brom and Bett v. Ashley* was not only won by the two Africans, but the jury awarded them 30 shillings for unpaid work, the equivalent of $367 in today's currency. Given that a laborer's wages were $0.33/day in 1781, Bett and Brom were awarded the equivalent of three years of work—a tidy sum for that time.[12]

The last case, and perhaps the best known, was Belinda Royall-Sutton. In 1783, she petitioned the Massachusetts legislature for reparations from her former master, Isaac Royall, whom she claimed "had denied the enjoyment of one morsel of that immense wealth, a part whereof hath been accumulated by her own industry." Her enslaver had been loyal to the British before the American Revolution and fled to Nova Scotia in 1775 near the outbreak of the war, leaving his 63 enslaved charges behind. Eight years later, in 1783, Belinda decided to petition the legislature for the unpaid years of serving her former enslaver. Her *Petition of an African Slave*[13] to the Massachusetts legislature is an eloquent statement and captures the essence of the reparations struggle by Africans in America.

The *Petition* argues that her labor had enriched her enslaver and that she had a right to lay claim to his estate. Her appeal for her and her daughter was successful. She was granted £15, 12 shillings per year (approximately $3,700) from the wealth accumulated by the Royall family on the Ten Hills Plantation as restitution for her 40 years of enslavement. Unfortunately, this one-time sum was reneged upon by the Royall heirs in subsequent years. She continued to petition for reparations, with her final appeal made in 1793. Her death occurred sometime during 1799 when the caretaker of the Royall estate claimed that the last of "two family servants who were left behind" were now dead. As a footnote, scholars speculate that Belinda could not have written the actual petition because of her illiteracy, since all of them were signed with an "X." Either Black poet Phillis Wheatley or

---

[11] (Robinson, 2001).
[12] (*Mass.gov*, 2019).
[13] (Belinda, 1787).

Primus Hall, the son of Prince Hall who founded the first Black Masonic Lodge in the United States was its likely author.[14]

Reparations and the Struggle for Them in the Caribbean

While one could argue that the push for reparations in the Caribbean began with the Thirty-Fourth Regular Meeting of the Conference of Heads of Government of CARICOM (CARIbbean COMmunity) in July 2013 in Trinidad and Tobago, the struggle has its roots in Rastafarianism and its beginnings nearly ninety years ago. Furthermore, one can easily argue that the 2013 CARICOM establishment of reparations commissions in its 15-member nations resulted from the Rastafarians' long-held desire to repatriate to Africa and specifically to Ethiopia. The idea of diasporic Africans returning to Africa is a centuries-old theme wherever African people gather; when monumental events and movements such as the American Civil War, the Red Summer of 1919, Marcus Garvey, the 1950s and 1960s liberation of African nations from their colonizers or the recent "Year of Return" in Ghana occur, this discussion intensifies. While Caribbean Rastafarians are very intentional in this demand as a reparation, it is not unique to their group. It is why it is #2 in the "Ten-Point Plan of Reparatory Justice" of CARICOM.[15]

1. Full Formal Apology

The healing process for victims and the descendants of the enslaved and enslavers requires, as a precondition, the offer of a sincere formal apology by the governments of Europe. Some governments, in refusing to offer an apology, have issued in place Statements of Regrets.

Such statements do not acknowledge that crimes have been committed and represent a refusal to take responsibility for such crimes. Statements of Regrets represent, furthermore, a reprehensible response to the call for apology in that they suggest that victims and their descendants are not worthy of an apology. Only an explicit formal apology will suffice within the context of the CARICOM Reparations Justice Program (CRJP).

2. Repatriation

Over 10 million Africans were stolen from their homes and forcefully transported to the Caribbean as the enslaved chattel and property of Europeans. The transatlantic slave trade is the largest forced migration in human history and has no parallel in terms of man's inhumanity to man.

This trade in enchained bodies was a highly successful commercial business for the nations of Europe. The lives of millions of men, women, and children were destroyed in

---

[14] (*Ibid.*, 23).
[15] (caricom.org/caricom-ten-point-plan-for-reparatory-justice/).

search of profit. The descendants of these stolen people have a legal right to return to their homeland.

A repatriation program must be established and all available channels of international law and diplomacy used to resettle those persons who wish to return. A resettlement program should address such matters as citizenship and deploy available best practices in respect of community reintegration.

3. Indigenous Peoples Development Program

The governments of Europe committed genocide upon the native Caribbean population. Military commanders were given official instructions by their governments to eliminate these communities and to remove those who survive pogroms from the region.

Genocide and land appropriation went hand in hand. A community of over 3,000,000 in 1700 has been reduced to less than 30,000 in 2000. Survivors remain traumatized, landless, and are the most marginalized social group within the region.

The University of the West Indies offers an Indigenous Peoples Scholarship in a desperate effort at rehabilitation. It is woefully insufficient. A development plan is required to rehabilitate this community.

4. Cultural Institutions

European nations have invested in the development of community institutions such as museums and research centers in order to prepare their citizens for an understanding of these Crimes Against Humanity (CAH).

These facilities serve to reinforce within the consciousness of their citizens an understanding of their role in history as rulers and change agents.

There are no such institutions in the Caribbean where the CAH were committed. Caribbean schoolteachers and researchers do not have the same opportunity.

Descendants of these CAH continue to suffer the disdain of having no relevant institutional systems through which their experience can be scientifically told. This crisis must be remedies within the CJRP.

5. Public Health Crisis

The African descent population in the Caribbean has the highest incidence in the world of chronic diseases in the forms of hypertension and type 2 diabetes.

This pandemic is the direct result of the nutritional experience, physical and emotional brutality, and overall stress profiles associated with slavery, genocide, and apartheid. Over 10 million Africans were imported into the Caribbean during the 400 years of slavery.

At the end of slavery in the late nineteenth century less than 2 million remained. The chronic health condition of Caribbean Blacks now constitutes the greatest financial risk to sustainability in the region. Arresting this pandemic requires the injection of science, technology, and capital beyond the capacity of the region.

Europe has a responsibility to participate in the alleviation of this heath disaster. The CRJP addresses this issue and calls upon the governments of Europe to take responsibility for this tragic human legacy of slavery and colonization.

6. Illiteracy Eradication

At the end of the European colonial period in most parts of the Caribbean, the British in particular left the Black and indigenous communities in a general state of illiteracy. Some 70 percent of Blacks in British colonies were functionally illiterate in the 1960s when nation states began to appear.

Jamaica, was home to the largest number of such citizens. Widespread illiteracy has subverted the development efforts of these nation states and represents a drag upon social and economic advancement.

Caribbean governments allocate more than 70 percent of public expenditure to health and education in an effort to uproot the legacies of slavery and colonization. European governments have a responsibility to participate in this effort within the context of the CRJP.

7. African Knowledge Program

The forced separation of Africans from their homeland has resulted in cultural and social alienation from identity and existential belonging. Denied the right in law to life and divorced by space from the source of historic self, Africans have craved the right to return and knowledge of the route to roots.

A program of action is required to build "bridges of belonging." Such projects as school exchanges and culture tours, community artistic and performance programs, entrepreneurial and religious engagements, as well as political interaction, are required in order to neutralize the void created by slave voyages.

Such actions will serve to build knowledge networks that are necessary for community rehabilitation.

8. Psychological Rehabilitation

For over 400 years Africans and their descendants were classified in law as nonhuman, chattel, property, and real estate. They were denied recognition as members of the human family by laws derived from the parliaments and palaces of Europe. This history has inflicted massive psychological trauma upon the African descent populations. This much is evident daily in the Caribbean.

Only a reparatory justice approach to truth and educational exposure can begin the process of healing and repair. Such an engagement will call into being, for example, the need for greater Caribbean integration designed to enable the coming together of the fragmented community.

9. Technology Transfer

For 400 years the trade and production policies of Europe could be summed up in the British slogan: "not a nail is to be made in the colonies."

The Caribbean was denied participation in Europe's industrialization process, and was confined to the role of producer and exporter of raw materials. This system was designed to extract maximum value from the region and enable maximum wealth accumulation in Europe.

The effectiveness of this policy meant that the Caribbean entered its nation-building phase as a technologically and scientifically ill-equipped backward space within the postmodern world economy.

Generations of Caribbean youth, as a consequence, have been denied membership and access to the science and technology culture that is the world's youth patrimony. Technology transfer and science sharing for development must be a part of the CRJP.

Debt Cancellation

Caribbean governments that emerged from slavery and colonialism have inherited the massive crisis of community poverty and institutional unpreparedness for development. These governments still daily engage in the business of cleaning up the colonial mess to prepare for growth.

The pressure of development has driven governments to carry the burden of public employment and social policies designed to confront colonial legacies. This process has resulted in states accumulating unsustainable public debt levels that now constitute their fiscal entrapment. This debt cycle properly belongs to the imperial governments, who have made no sustained attempt to deal with debilitating colonial legacies. Support for the payment of domestic debt and cancellation of international debt are necessary reparatory actions.

The 10-point plan of CARICOM represents the core issues and demands of the global reparations movement. They summarize the damage inflicted upon African people by Europeans during the past 580+ years. Essentially, what the international African community has been doing for the past 500 years is attempting to repair the damage done by the system of White supremacy in the form of enslavement, apartheid, and genocide. The struggle reflects the work of Marcus Garvey of Jamaica; the nationalism of Kwame Ture and Eric Williams of Trinidad; the work of Elizabeth "Mum" Bett, Belinda Royall-Sutton, Callie House, and Queen Mother Moore in the United States; and the expatriatism of the Rastafari throughout the Caribbean and the commitment of continental Africans . . .

Reparations and the Struggle for Them in Africa

Ultimately, the goal of the reparations movement is for Europe and the United States to begin paying for the damage it did for half a millennium toward the people of African descent. In Africa, there was always resistance toward the European rape of the continent. It began in the raided villages on the West Coast and continued on the death march to the sea. During the European enslavement of Africans, cooperation with Whites is often discussed but rarely understood. These discussions usually accuse Africans of being responsible for their enslavement because of their minor participation in this crime against humanity. Slavery created an entirely new class of Africans who sold and traded human beings as readily as they sold and traded cocoa and groundnuts. Over the years, many Whites have asked me with feigned curiosity, "Weren't the Africans themselves responsible for slavery since they sold their own people to Europeans?" I am sure that when White people ask this question, they seek partial absolution for their ancestors' sins. What is exaggerated about African complicity in the slave "trade" is that Africans did not have much choice in the matter. This is similar to making the indigenous people of the United States who scouted for Custer responsible for the establishment of reservations in Montana years later. These questioners would have us think that the entire population of the west coast of Africa, where most Blacks in the *Maafa na Maangamizi*[16] originate, was involved with the slave trade. The fact is that very few Africans were directly involved, and the tiny minority who were could not have done it without the absolute cooperation of Europeans. The converse is not valid. Europeans had the power to get their workers with or without the collaboration of Africans. They needed laborers, and Africans were available. The deracinated west Africans collaborating in the slave trade at first found cooperation with the Europeans difficult, eventually easy, and ultimately destructive.[17]

In 1990 then President of Nigeria, Ibrahim Babangida, called for reparations for the centuries-old damage to the entire continent of Africa. He said the systematic kidnapping of Africans from the continent led to Africa's "marginalization" in the world order today.[18] His declaration, along with the First Pan-African Conference on Reparations for the Enslavement, the Colonization, and the African Neo-Colonization headed by M.K.O. Abiola, was held in Abuja, Nigeria, from April 27 to April 29, 1993. The *Abuja Proclamation* stated in part:

Serves notice on all states in Europe and the Americas which had participated in the enslavement and colonization of the African peoples, and which may still be engaged in racism and neo-colonialism, to desist from any further damage and start building bridges of conciliation, co-operation, and through reparation.

> Exhorts all African states to grant entrance as of right to all persons of African descent and right to obtain residence in those African states, if there is no disqualifying element on the African claiming the "right to return" to his ancestral home, Africa.

Urges those countries which were enriched by slavery and the slave trade to give total relief from Foreign Debt, and allow the debtor countries of the diaspora to become free for self-development and from immediate and direct economic domination.

Calls upon the countries largely characterized as profiteers from the slave trade to support proper and reasonable representation of African peoples in the political and economic areas of the highest decision-making bodies.[19]

---

[16] The *Kiswahili* word *Maafa* means *disaster* with a discrete beginning and end, usually applied to natural events like hurricanes, earthquakes, and so on. *Maangamizi*, another *Kiswahili* word, means *destruction* but a type resulting from deliberately imposed human actions, not a natural occurrence. Moreover, *Maangamizi* embraces no implication of the destruction having come to an end. Maafa has come into use as a term for the collective pan-Afrikan experience under millennia-long tyranny by non-Africans. Using both words create a more comprehensive yet still understandable descriptive expression for our contemporary use. And, since both words are from the same language, the conjunction to join them, "*na*" ("and"), should also be *Kiswahili*, thus *Maafa na Maangamizi*.

[17] (Winbush, 2018).

[18] (Noble, 1990).

[19] (N'COBRA, 1993).

Conclusion

This First Pan-African Conference on Reparations will certainly not be the last. It continues the 400+ years of Africans on the continent and the diaspora seeking compensatory justice for the greatest crime against humanity in history, the EEA. It is difficult to document a movement that is still unfolding. It is similar to writing a history of the civil rights movement immediately after the Birmingham demonstrations, hip hop culture in 2005, or an assessment of Barack Obama's presidency in 2016. Reparations are like that; it is a movement that continues to "make sense" to those who wish to understand the so-called "Black-White Wealth Gap," crime rates in African communities, "educational gaps," and "health disparities" in those same communities. Once reparations are achieved for the *global* Africana community, it will liberate them economically, psychologically, and spiritually, but will also begin the long and arduous process of liberating the descendants of Europeans from a false sense of superiority over their accomplishments, long thought to be of their ingenuity rather than their violence.

Bibliography

Anderson, Claud. *Black Labor, White Wealth: The Search for Power and Economic Justice*. Poultry Science Association, 1994.

Beckles, Hilary, and Verene Shepherd. *Trading Souls: Europe's Transatlantic Trade in Africans*. Kingston, Jamaica, Miami: Ian Randle Publishers, 2007, pp. 50–57.

Belinda, "Petition of an African Slave, to the Legislature of Massachusetts", *The American Museum; or, Repository of Ancient and Modern Fugitive Pieces & c. Prose and Poetical (1787–1788)*, vol. 1, no. 1, 1787, p. 538, 3 pgs.

Ibid., 23.

"CARICOM Ten Point Plan for Reparatory Justice." *CARICOM*, caricom.org/caricom-ten-point-plan-for-reparatory-justice/.

Henrik, Clarke John. *Christopher Columbus and the Afrikan Holocaust: Slavery and the Rise of European Capitalism*. A & B Books, 1992 & 1999.

Gates, Henry. "How Many Slaves Landed in the U.S.? | the African Americans: Many Rivers to Cross | PBS." *The African Americans: Many Rivers to Cross*, 19 Sept. 2013, www.pbs.org/wnet/african-americans-many-rivers-to-cross/history/how-many-slaves-landed-in-the-us/.

Hartley, Kaya. "A Necessary Conversation: Reparations for Indigenous Dispossession." *Independentaustralia.net*, 7 Apr. 2019, independentaustralia.net/australia/australia-display/a-necessary-conversation-reparations-for-indigenous-dispossession.

"Homepage." *Caribbean Reparations Commission*, caricomreparations.org.

"Massachusetts Constitution and the Abolition of Slavery." *Mass.gov*, 2019, www.mass.gov/guides/massachusetts-constitution-and-the-abolition-of-slavery.

Miller, Matt. "EU Parliament Calls for 'Reparations for Crimes against Humanity' to Afro-Europeans." *Dailycaller.com*, 28 Mar. 2019, dailycaller.com/2019/03/28/eu-parliament-reparations-afro-europeans/. Accessed 4 Mar. 2021.

National Coalition of Blacks for Reparations in America (N'COBRA). *The Abuja Proclamation.* 29 Apr. 1993.

Noble, Kenneth B. "Nigeria's Leader to Seek Slavery Reparations (Published 1990)." *The New York Times*, 24 Dec. 1990, www.nytimes.com/1990/12/24/world/nigeria-s-leader-to-seek-slavery-reparations.html. Accessed 10 Mar. 2021.

"Portugal and the African Slave Trade." *Nicole's Final Project*, 9 Nov. 2011, jicolerenaissance.wordpress.com/portugal-the-african-slave-trade/.

Robinson, Randall. *The Debt: What America Owes to Blacks.* Plume, 2001.

Samuehl, Fluksman. "Namibia: Genocide Reparations Negotiations and the Future of Shark Island." *AllAfrica.com*, 3 Mar. 2021, allafrica.com/stories/202103030682.html. Accessed 4 Mar. 2021.

Winbush, Raymond A. *The Warrior Method: A Parents' Guide to Rearing Healthy Black Boys.* Amistad, An Imprint of HarperCollins Publishers, 2018.

Chapter 10
"The Modern Civil Rights Movement" (1994)

Contributed by:
Clenora Hudson-Weems, PhD

Historians will talk about the good and the bad, but they don't want to deal with the ugly ... The ugliness of racism is not a white man's telling a black woman to give him her bus seat—bad as that is—but the—confident home-invasion, kidnapping and murder of a fourteen-year-old black youth and the exoneration by jury of the youth's apparent killers.

—Rayfield Mooty[1]

The subject here is the history of the Civil Rights Movement with regard to the Till murder case and how this case has been treated or ignored by traditional historians. Since the involuntary migration of Black people from Africa (the motherland for all Blacks), throughout the bloody transatlantic slave trade, to the seasoning islands of the Caribbean, to the incomprehensible atrocities of American slavery, Blacks have been struggling for human rights. During the earliest stages of American slavery (near the beginning of the seventeenth century) to its final legal period in the mid-nineteenth century (marked by the Civil War and the signing of the Emancipation Proclamation in September 1862, which went into effect on January 1, 1863), emphasis on physical freedom from human bondage characterizes the Black American struggle. Subsequent White retaliation and bitterness, resulting from the Whites' displaced ownership of Black people and their stubborn sense of White superiority, ultimately evolved into the establishment of the Jim Crow laws in the early 1880s. These laws, which according to Woodward were "the public symbols and constant reminders of his [black's] inferior position," legalized what W. E. B. DuBois metaphorically designates in *Souls of Black Folk* as the "veil," the wall or curtain of segregation.[2] Just as Blacks rose up against forms of oppression then, they continue to do so today. Extreme

---

[1] (Rayfield Mooty, 1986).
[2] (Woodward, 1957).

White opposition to the Black resistance to oppression, in the form of heinous, brutal crimes such as rape and lynchings, clearly validates the need for Black people to continue and even to intensify their struggle as a proud and historically determined people. This act of self-determination in turn would protect Blacks against a designed vulnerability to which they are assigned in this dehumanization and blatant denial of their "inalienable rights" as fellow human beings.

The 1950s mark the beginning of the era of the widely publicized struggle for the civil rights of African Americans. No longer a question of emancipation, the key issue for the early part of that decade was the notion of being "separate but equal" as a way of life. This aspiration proved to be both hypocritical and unrealistic within the American system. The Supreme Court's landmark decision in the 1954 controversial *Brown v. Topeka Board of Education* established: the unconstitutionality of the "separate but equal" public school systems. Thus, desegregation in the public schools was officially ordered. Blacks, like any other people, desired to have a share in all the benefits American society had to offer—educational, political, economic, as well as social rights. However, the resolution to demand boldly their civil rights did not come without a high price. As in the past, Blacks were severely dehumanized; but they were to be now alarmed into consciousness of the urgent need to remedy the powerlessness and insignificance of their lives as perceived by the dominant White culture. Such was the case in the infamous murder and mock trials of the Emmett Till.

From 1877 to 1965

The Till murder case has been vastly underappreciated as a main stimulus for the Modern Civil Rights Movement, despite the fact that it was one of the most important events that occurred in African American, and even American, culture in the 1950s. It embodies the ugliness of American racism, affecting the most vicious form of violence to be bestowed upon a human being. Lynching is an atrocity that finds its victims both powerless and, more important, too often guiltless. After reflecting upon the nuances of the scores of atrocities heaped upon African Americans between the years 1877 and 1965, marking the beginning to the end of the Till scenario, it appears that symbolically the stage for the Till slaying was set by Rutherford Birchard Hayes's infamous 1877 Compromise. The 19th president of the United States, Hayes won by only one electoral vote. As a strategy to win the presidential election, he agreed to a "laissez-faire" policy on the matter of the laws and practices of the southern conservative states. One of the ramifications of the Hayes Compromise was that the North ignored the plight of the African American in the South, and the Till case, seventy-eight years later, forced America to take another look.

The ramifications of the Hayes Compromise would not be legally concluded until Lyndon Baines Johnson, the 36th president of the United States, signed the 1965 Voting Rights Bill, that removed the legal shackles from African Americans. Mooty has this to say:

> *I have to go back to the presidential election of 1877 . . . when all of the rights that we had (President Abraham Lincoln did give us a little relief of freedom) were taken front us by the stroke of one pen and only by one vote! One electoral vote! . . . In 1877 Rutherford B. Hayes made a compromise with the South that "if you give me your vote and make me*

president, I will pull the troops out of there." And the troops were what they called a toothache to the southerners, and he said, "I will pull that tooth out, and then you can do whatever you want to."

Just prior to the Hayes election, Whites were retaliating against the legal progress of the African Americans, directly related to Lincoln's signing of the Emancipation Proclamation. They particularly resisted the newly acquired freedom of African Americans in Reconstruction to exercise voting rights, so they used terrorist tactics at the polls.

During the mid-twentieth century, Till became part of that historical continuum, although voting was not the issue with him. The climate was much the same just before his lynching, when voting registration drives in Mississippi were posing a threat to the White power system. As in the 1870s, Whites used lynching as a means of intimidation and of discouraging African American participation in the voting processes. The Thirteenth, Fourteenth, and Fifteenth Amendments provided constitutional rights and protections for African Americans; however, the established institution of Black servitude and White supremacy was a way of life, and one that Whites were not willing to surrender peacefully.

The Jim Crow Laws

Another critical event in the history of the Modern Civil Rights Movement was the emergence of the Jim Crow laws of the 1880s. These were various laws that sprang up in different states, culminated by the *Plessy v. Ferguson* case in 1896, which was decided by the Supreme Court and which gave federal and constitutional sanction to "separate but equal facilities," thus making racial segregation both legal and constitutional. This legally established second-class citizenship for African Americans during the nadir of the post-Reconstruction period. These limitations on African Americans culminated in countless lynchings as terrorist political tools for social and economic control. And the lynchings continued, legally uncontested in the courts, until the Till lynching in 1955: the first of its kind to hold a trial of Whites for the lynching of an African American.

The Till lynching was a culminating experience in African Americans' feelings of powerlessness. Demonstrations erupted and continued. Ten years later, in 1965, President Lyndon B. Johnson, with the stroke of a pen, granted African Americans the voting rights that were needed to change this abject victimization. He cautioned that every African American must register and vote, for one is not truly free until then, until one can ensure oneself proper protection through proper political representation. Johnson knew that the dominant culture would stop at nothing to secure the votes of African Americans, once the latter had that privilege. And since over half of the African American population lived in northern and western states where they had voting rights already, southern Whites knew that once southern Blacks had that right too, the Whites would have trouble. Realizing that much of the power of the dominant culture as American citizens in a democratic society lies in the voting power, Johnson moved all the more on the potential of the ballot for African Americans. This represents the true meaning of the signing of the Voting Rights Bill, reflecting its significance to the plight of all African Americans, and reversing Hayes's earlier regressive act.

As for Till, his death carried that race and sex inference. His murderers had the security that the law would not be implemented against them. The point of the trial following Till's lynching is that African Americans did not and could not become jurors in Mississippi, and Whites would not convict any other White for murdering any African American. According to John Popham of *The New York Times,* race was a key issue with John C. Whitten, one of the defense attorneys, who established his confidence in the all-White jury: "Every last Anglo-Saxon one of you has the courage to free these men in the point that several people who handled the dead body testifies they thought it had been too decomposed to be identified."[3] That was just what happened: the jury unanimously found the defendants not guilty.

The Fear Beneath

There is something beneath the surface in the meaning of Till's murder. It has always been said that opposites attract—men are attracted to women, women are attracted to men, and in some cases White men are attracted to Black women, and Black men are attracted to White women. According to Calvin Hemton, "Out of his [white man's] guilt [because of his relationships with black women] grew fear—if he found it difficult to stay away from the 'animal' attraction of black women/was it not possible that his wife felt that same attraction to the black 'bucks'? Something had to be done."[4] Given the time period, the location, and the state of race relations during the pre-Civil Rights era in the south, the attraction between the different races (particularly of African American men to White women) was not only illegal and unacceptable, but abhorred and dangerous. This was true because the fear that Hemton analyzes on the part of White men is that, given the freedom of choice their women may demonstrate a mutual attraction to the African American men. Wells explored this concept earlier with the following conclusions:

> *I also found that what the white man of the South practiced as all right for himself, he assumed to be unthinkable in white women. They could and did fall in love with the pretty mulatto and quadroon girls as well as black ones, but they professed an inability to imagine white women doing the same thing with Negro and mulatto men. Whenever they did so and were found out, the cry of rape was raised, and the lowest element of the white South was turned loose to wreak its fiendish cruelty on those too weak to help themselves.*[5]

Winthrop Jordan takes the fear to another level in *White Over Black,* in which he examines the White man's attitudes toward the African American man. He contends that the White man fears the African American man's sexual aggression:

> *The concept of the Negro's aggressive sexuality was reinforced by what was thought to be an anatomical peculiarity of the Negro male. He was*

---

[3] (Popham, 1955).
[4] (Hemton, 1965).
[5] (Duster 70).

> *said to possess an especially large penis . . . If a perceptible anatomical difference did in fact exist, it fortuitously coincided with the already firmly established idea of the Negro's special sexuality; it could only have served as striking confirmation of that idea, as salt in the wounds of the white man's envy.*[6]

The White, therefore, finds the need to prove to himself that he is the master.

According to William Bradford Huie, a White investigator of racial atrocities who wrote the celebrated story of Till's murderers for *Look* magazine after the trial, "They didn't take him out to kill him. They killed him because he had a white girl's picture in his pocket, and he told 'em that she was his girl. It was at the time that they thought that this sorta thing had to be stopped in order to defend the 'Southern way of life.'"[7] The thought that such an attraction might get out of hand and cause widespread miscegenation was regarded by the dominant culture as a critical problem, and hence was treated with utmost urgency and drastic measures. The scenario surrounding the Till incident was indeed explosive.

Arnold Rose asserts in his condensed version of Gunnar Myrdal's *The American Dilemma* that "a lynching is not merely a punishment against an individual but a disciplinary device against the Negro group."[8] Although the reaction and response, of Till's murderers to such an issue was both extreme and unwarranted, it was, nonetheless, the trend. It was easy to repeat such an act, since it had happened over and over again. The difference with Till was that he was a teenager who could not have had the same ultimate intentions as a grown man. His lynching was called to the public's attention, and the ugliness of American racism became known to the world.

These insights into the socioeconomic and psychological ramifications of lynchings confirm that the motivations behind them are multifaceted, complicated, and intricate. The lynching of Till symbolizes the ultimate deterioration of race relations. His death reflects a threefold victimization: of a human being denied his life, of an African American man deprived of dignity, and of a child robbed of his future.

The Till Case and the Modern Civil Rights Movement

It appears that, for a number of reasons, there has been a conscious effort to neglect the fact that this incident is a key historical event in the record of the movement. To begin with, the victim of this incident was not a member of the upper-middle class, bourgeoisie, and his experience was more prone to happen among the lower and working classes than among the upper class. On the whole, established historians, as is the case of academicians in general, were members of the upper-middle class, the bourgeoisie, and generally tended not to focus on the particular plight of the lower or working-class African Americans, except as their plight affected the whole race. In other words, the neglect of the Till case stems from a class issue.

---

[6] (Jordan, 1968).
[7] (Quoted in Howell Raines, 1983).
[8] (Rose 185).

Then the nature of Till's "crime"—wolf-whistling at a White woman—was ambiguous. At that time, it was considered taboo behavior, particularly in the deep south. Finally, because Till was an outsider (a northern African American youth visiting in the south who did not conduct himself according to White people's expectations, according to southern etiquette), the whole Till case posed an embarrassment to the movement, both for African American leaders and Whites. The respected Black leaders and historians possibly feared that the incident would alienate them from White culture. For example, there has always been that segment of the African American population who seeks approval of and direction from the dominant culture. During slavery they were generally among the "house niggers" and later they were identified among the "Black bourgeoisie." Having been accepted by the dominant culture, this group directs its energies toward protecting that relationship to maintain the alliance, which necessitates protecting Whites through avoidance of the embarrassment of having their shortcomings exposed. Therefore, in avoiding the Till incident as a significant part of the fabric of American culture, they protect both their established relationships with Whites and the reputations of the Whites as well.

Another possible explanation for the lack of attention to the Till case is that those historians, leaders, and reporters of the Civil Rights Movement had more to gain from a "peaceful" movement. This is true because they could that way appease both Blacks and Whites: the former by articulating and spearheading their demands to end segregation in the social and educational spheres, and the latter by addressing the eradication of their acceptable chosen issues of concern. The historians in particular acted to downplay Till's lynching, to downplay the embodiment of racial violence and the ugliness of racial victimization. They chose, instead, to celebrate the refusal of Rosa Parks to relinquish her bus seat to a White man, a morally acceptable act of proclaiming one's common humanity through integration, a major issue with the National Association for the Advancement of Colored People (NAACP). Unlike Till, Parks was not the object of brutal racism. Her symbolic act was a peaceful one and a more appealing media image than the slaughtered Till. Had the Till case continued to receive maximum attention, under the leadership of organized labor (with its legacy of marshalling the demands for economic parity as well as civil rights for Blacks since the early 1940s), the direction of the then-evolving Civil Rights Movement would have probably taken on another dimension or even direction.

Ranking Till with Established Leaders

Although Till, technically, cannot be included among the martyrs who gave their lives in the pursuit of African American freedom (for instance, two Black Mississippians murdered shortly before Emmett, Rev. George W. Lee, who had just delivered a sermon giving a review of the history of Black Americans' struggle for freedom on the Sunday before he was murdered by members of the White Citizens' Council for registering to vote, and Lamar Smith, also involved in voter registration efforts), Till's untimely death, and the public's reaction to it, helped set the stage for the Civil Rights Movement. Richard Aubrey McLemore in the second volume of *A History of Mississippi* concludes that "the effect of the crime and its aftermath was to intensify an already emotional atmosphere, and the state's preoccupation with a politics of race increased."[9]

---

[9] (McLemore, 1973).

Indeed, even Rosa Parks herself acknowledges the uniqueness and importance of this case. She asserts that "it [the Till murder case] was a very tragic incident ... Many such incidents had gone unnoticed in the past."[10] Dr. King, too, referred to the Till case twice in *Stride Toward Freedom*. Discussing the impermanence of publicity and popularity, he asserted, "Today it is Emmett Till, tomorrow, it is Martin Luther King. Then in another tomorrow it will be somebody else."[11] Later he alluded to the fact that Till's murder is ever present in the minds of the oppressed who fear that there is no recourse for their victimization: "With the Emmett Till case in Mississippi still fresh in our memories, the Negroes held little hope of conviction."[12] Undoubtedly, this case bore heavy on their minds, as it did on the minds of many others.

Although Juan Williams does not postulate that the Till incident was the catalyst for the movement, in his work *Eyes on the Prize*, he does acknowledge that "the *Montgomery Advertiser* in Montgomery, Alabama, picked up the Till story and gave it prominent display. Three months later, the Black population of Montgomery began an historic boycott of their municipal bus system."[13] He investigates the motivations behind the prime movers of the boycott, such as Rosa Parks's continuous refusal to relinquish her bus seat at times dating back as early as 1944; Jo Ann Robinson's traumatic and dehumanizing experience of being forced to relinquish her bus seat during the Christmas rush in 1949; and Edgar Daniel Nixon's leadership in waiting for the "right person" and soliciting the Black ministers (one of whom was Martin Luther King, Jr., then a new minister in the town).

It should be noted here that, for a number of reasons, Till was not the "right person." The leaders of the Civil Rights Movement have always made choices. For example, according to Taylor Branch in *Parting the Waters*, approximately seven months before Rosa Parks's demonstration, there was the case of

> *a feisty high school student named Claudette Colvin, who defended her right to the seat in language that brought words of disapproval from passengers of both races ... Colvin was crying and madder than ever by the time the policemen told her she was under arrest. She struggled when they dragged her off the bus and screamed when they put on the handcuffs ... Prosecutors had thrown the book at Colvin, charging her with violating the segregation law, assault, and disorderly conduct.*

Unlike Parks, Claudette did not surrender peacefully. On May 6, Judge Eugene Carter

> *sentenced Colvin to pay a small fine—a sentence so much lighter than anticipated that it ruined her martyr status. Many Negroes who supported her case nevertheless came to believe she was lucky.*[14]

---

[10] (Rosa Parks, "Slain.").
[11] (King, 1958, 127).
[12] (King 145).
[13] Williams 57).
[14] (Branch, 1988, 120, 123).

The Black leadership did investigate the situation. However, after the discovery that the teenager was also pregnant and unmarried, they decided that she would not be the proper model to rally behind. In other words, because her character and sense of morality were questionable, she was not selected as the perfect model for a movement against institutionalized racism.

Parks, on the other hand, was another story. Nixon, a Black leader in Montgomery, went to Clifford Durr, an attorney and one of the few White liberals in the town, for consultation.

> *He asked for Durr's legal opinion: was this the case they had been waiting for? Could they use it to win a victory over segregation on appeal? ... The only flaw with the case as he saw it was that the charges would first be heard in state court rather than federal court. But there were ways to move cases. Otherwise, the circumstances were highly favorable. There were no extraneous charges to cloud the segregation issue, and Rosa Parks would make a good impression on white judges. This was enough for Nixon, who already knew instinctively that Rosa Parks was without peer as a potential symbol for Montgomery's Negroes—humble enough to be claimed by the common folk, and yet dignified enough in manner, speech, and dress to command the respect of the leading classes.*[15]

A respectable, light-skinned gentlewoman, Parks was a perfect model, both impressive and appealing.

As for Till, particularly with his bloated brutalized face, and the whole White woman/Black man sex scenario, he was not the proper model to choose. There were still those who said that Till should have known better, and who were angry with him for being mannish, and for stepping out of line. Williams' investigation in *Eyes on the Prize* (which is the most detailed account of Till in the traditional historical canon) is a demonstration of individual or personal history, reflections on the lives of the heroes or "great" people (or, as in the case of Parks and Robinson, established, respected citizens), rather than the history of the masses. His study would have been strengthened had he attempted to include an assessment of the mood of the Black masses who in fact carried out the Montgomery Bus Boycott.

It seems that since Blacks had been subjected to the segregated bus system there for sixty-five years, something more dramatic or traumatic than their "tired feet" was needed to carry them through this unyielding yearlong bus boycott. And it seems plausible and natural to suggest that a people would react in the manner they did only after a supreme insult to their race—the racially motivated murder of a Black youth, for example. Indeed, after Till's death, Blacks in large numbers bravely demonstrated and publicly confronted the racial immoralities in the American system. Even though all were moved by the Till murder case, the movement itself physically needed a Rosa Parks, the symbolic impetus for the movement.

---

[15] (Branch, 130).

Chapter 10: "The Modern Civil Rights Movement" (1994)   155

Till and Traditional History

Prior to the Till case and the Montgomery Bus Boycott, the *Brown v. Topeka Board of Education* case had in a sense established a mood of optimism. The Till case exploded approximately a year after this legal landmark and jarred people back to the realization that Black freedom would be achieved only through independent Black efforts, since the Till case made it once again obvious that the courts would not take up the fight for equal justice. Moreover, the Till case occurred about a year before the Montgomery Bus Boycott, which points to the fact that there was the need for another vehicle—mass demonstrations—by which to achieve justice and exposure for Black victims.

Until *Eyes on the Prize,* Black and White historians alike have failed to recognize the significance of the Till case and even this work does not do it justice. Even though Williams's work introduced Till, still there has been no official full-length scholarly discussion of the implications of the Till case on the future development on the Modern Civil Rights Movement, particularly from an endemic perspective. Williams implicitly corroborates the thesis of this work: that Till's contribution to the growing militancy of the Black community was significant, and worthy of a full-length scholarly examination.

Consider the historical account of the Black American struggle in the 1950s and the 1960s as documented by the foremost Black historian, John Hope Franklin. In his most recently revised edition, the 1994 seventh edition of *From Slavery to Freedom,* there is only one reference to the Till case, and it is not even indexed. Franklin wrote, in a brief catalogue of Black victims during that period: "Near Greenwood a fourteen-year-old Negro boy from Chicago was murdered for allegedly whistling at a white storekeeper's wife."[16] He failed to even identify the victim. So much for the Till murder case in this standard textbook.

Consider Kenneth G. Goode's *From Africa to the United States and Then: A Concise Afro-American History.* Nowhere is Till mentioned in the text, not even in the chronological table of events, which appears in the back of the book.

Consider Peter M. Bergman's *The Chronological History of the Negro in America.* Here Till receives minimum coverage, as he appears in the list of three victims of lynchings occurring in Mississippi in 1955: "Lynching returned to the South. Mississippi accounted for three: Rev. George W. Lee at Belzoni, Lamar Smith at Brookhaven, and Emmett Till near Money."[17] While there is some elaboration on the other two, Rev. George Lee and Lamar Smith relative to their involvement with the Mississippi voter registration drive, no additional comment on the Till case is made.

Consider coauthors Albert P. Blaustein and Robert L. Zangrando who wrote *Civil Rights and the American Negro: A Documentary History.* In the entire 671-page book on the African Americans' civil rights from 1619 until 1968, only one reference is made to Emmett Till: "Moreover, segregationist and states' rights opposition had encouraged the formation of such organized groups as the White Citizens' Councils and the initiation of such unorganized violence as the kidnap-lynching of fourteen-year-old Emmett Till at

---

[16] (Franklin, 1980).
[17] (Bergman, 1969).

Money, Mississippi, in the summer of 1955."[18] Even then, the reference does not reflect the impact Till's murder and trial had on the American people, particularly African Americans. On the contrary, it merely emphasizes intimidation of the Black community by the dominant culture.

Consider one of the greatest Black historians of the twentieth century, Benjamin Quarles and *The Negro in the Making of America*. Nowhere in his entire book is the Till murder case mentioned. In recapitulating the activities of the 1950s, he asserts that "This movement [Civil Rights Movement] started on December 1, 1955, when seamstress Rosa Parks boarded a bus in downtown Montgomery, took a seat in the section reserved for whites, and refused to surrender it to a white man who subsequently entered the bus."[19]

Consider the recently published coauthored historical account of the Black American by two highly credible Black historians, Mary Frances Berry and John Blassingame, *Long Memory: The Black Experience in America*. Again the reference to the Till murder case is limited to one sentence, and like other historians they fail to put this case in the historical perspective of the Civil Rights Movement. Hence, "Emmett Till, a fourteen-year-old boy, was kidnapped and killed in Money, Mississippi, in 1955 because he allegedly whistled at a white woman."[20] Their reference to the Till case only exemplifies the taboo of the Black man and the White woman in the long-debated issue of sex and racism.

According to Gunnar Myrdal, who devised what he called "The Rank Order of Discrimination" in *An American Dilemma,* he found that Whites contended that Blacks wanted sexual relations, and intermarriage, with White women more than other forms of equality. When he questioned Blacks, he found that they contended that, they valued the sexual attraction least.[21] Calvin Hernton discusses this issue in *Sex and Racism in America*, in which he concluded "that the race problem is inextricably connected with sex . . . The sexualization of the race problem is a reality, and we are going to have to deal with it even though most of us are, if not unwilling, definitely unprepared."[22]

Finally, consider the interpretive historian Vincent Harding in *The Other American Revolution*. Till is not mentioned at all.

Others, too, have been guilty of side-tracking or bypassing the Till case, as reflected in the records of both *The World Almanac* and the *Reader's Digest*. In recording the significant events of the month and year, *The World Almanacs* cite the Rosa Parks incident, but fail to mention Till. The *Reader's Digest,* too, mentions Parks, but not Till. Clearly, the Till murder case is a lost chapter in the history books on the Civil Rights Movement.

There is a discrepancy between the underplayed account of the Till case in history and the detailed media coverage it received. Only through reviewing the Till case as interpreted by journalists, as well as everyday people, photographers, creative writers, singers, and autobiographers, can the oversights of historians be corrected. One important publication (important because of its accuracy on the Till murder case), which documented testimonies by persons with insights on it, was one of several small pamphlets covering this atrocity.

---

[18] (Blaustein & Zangrando, 1968).
[19] (Quarles, 1969).
[20] (Berry & Blassingame, 1982).
[21] (Myrdal, 1944).
[22] (Hernton, 1965).

Published in 1956, *Time Bomb* was written by Olive Arnold Adams, editor of *Global News Syndicate*, with a foreword by Dr. T. R. M. Howard, the civil rights activist in whose home Till's mother, grandfather, and cousin Mooty resided during the murder trial. This book relates detailed information surrounding the murder. Mooty attests to the insights in this book, as he was an intricate part of the case from its inception. In all these testimonies, one crucial thing comes out: that at the outset of the Civil Rights Movement, a fourteen-year-old northern Black youth fell prey to the treachery of American racism, both in his death and in the subsequent mock trials. The unrelenting restlessness, fervor, and anger of the African American established on that day that obsequiousness, helplessness, and complacency had passed, at least for the moment.

In spite of it all, Till has yet to receive his deserved place in the historical chronicles of the African American struggle. As Simeon Booker observes, "Today, only one statue of Emmett Till exists in the entire nation. That being, in a city park in Denver. The Black mother who changed the course of history is almost forgotten—except for a three-part series on the lynching, broadcast by Chicago's WMAQ-TV station's Rich Samuels."[23] Although Till has not been properly remembered or immortalized by Americans, Congressman Gus Savage of Chicago wrote in a moving letter addressed to the fallen victim that, "A monument to serve as a shrine has been suggested in your memory; but we know the only monument not decayed by time is freedom. So we shall fight for freedom in your memory."[24]

Sacrificial Lamb

Emmett Till has been called the sacrificial lamb of the Civil Rights Movement. As Jordan asserts: "There was no way for progress to be made without someone dying . . . There had to be sacrificial lambs and that is what Emmett Till was." The editor of *Freedom*, Louis E. Burnham, said shortly after Till's death: "The fight to avenge the murder of Emmett Louis Till has become a symbol of the Negro people's bitter struggle for first-class citizenship."[25]

Although many regard the Parks incident as the beginning of the Civil Rights Movement, it is a mistake to ignore the earlier impact of the Till murder, which occurred just three months and three days before the Parks incident. Inundating the world press, the Till murder case was thoroughly covered by the news media, but it has not been adequately chronicled in history books. In a 1956 *Ebony* article, Clotye Murdock wrote:

> The state [Mississippi] has been referred to in the foreign press as the "land of the Till Murder." Racial clashes between Negroes and whites there have made headlines in a Babel of languages. In lands far distant from America, where Mississippi is only a word, a name, for a state or a city or a province—many know not which—people frown in bewilderment as they hear it, and say: "Is that not the place where the Negro boy was killed?"[26]

---

[23] (Booker 14).
[24] (Savage, 1985).
[25] (Burnham, 1955).
[26] (Murdock, 1956).

Labor Unions Take Up the Case

Since Till was neither the first nor the last Black to be lynched, one may question why this case became a big issue. First of all, the Till incident happened at the right time, just as the age of modernity with mass media technology reached an all-time high in the area of communication. Radio, newspapers, and television ushered the news of the Till lynching into the homes of countless American citizens, making a traditionally isolated incident public information. With this new technology, events that would not have reached the national public were now known to all.

Another reason is that a major national labor union organization, the AFL-CIO, had just merged in August, bridging the gap between the two most prominent Black labor leaders—A. Philip Randolph, president of the Brotherhood of Sleeping Car Porters, and William S. Townsend, president of the Former Red Caps, president of the Transportation Services Employees—who embraced this case from the outset and obtruded it upon the American society for public censure. The following memorandum, dated September 27, 1955, from labor union official Boyd L. Wilson to David J. McDonald, the president of the United Steel Workers Union, and I. W. Abel regarding the labor meeting on the Till case states that:

> *Monsignor Cornelius J. Drew, pastor, St. Charles Roman Catholic Church, before an impressive crowd of ten thousand people in New York City last Sunday, made an impassioned plea that the decent, right-thinking people of the United States rise up and make a repetition of the Till case impossible in America.*
>
> *He was joined by A. Philip Randolph, president, Brotherhood of Sleeping Car Porters; Roy Wilkins, executive director, NAACP, and City Councilman Earl Brown, before a rally sponsored by trade unions and instigated by the Brotherhood of Sleeping Car Porters, AFL . . .*
>
> *Resolutions were adopted calling upon Governor Hugh White of Mississippi, and the United States Department of justice to investigate and establish the whereabouts of two missing witnesses. Likewise, to establish, beyond the shadow of a doubt, as to the identity of the body discovered in the river, if indeed it was not that of Till.*
>
> *The Till case has been a rallying point for liberal movements and peoples within the United States in recent weeks, and it has been my considered judgement that it is to the best interests of the Steel Workers' Union to carry its share of the responsibility and to do what it can to further the case of justice of all people.*

Mooty had much to say about the labor-union involvement: "The whole labor union was involved in it [the Till case] before it [public exposure] happened."[27] A relative of Till

---

[27] (Mooty).

through his uncle Henry Spearman, Rayfield Mooty, a member of the Community Services Committee and the president of a steel labor union local in Chicago, had spent years in the labor movement and was in the position to make the necessary contact with the right people who had the influence to expose this case nationally. As Mamie Bradley-Mobley recalls, "Mr. Mooty was the one who was sort of like steering me which way to go because he was quite active in the labor movement and he knew the politicians. I didn't know a politician."[28]

He first contacted one of the most influential Blacks in the United Automobile Workers, vice-president of the Cook County Industrial Union, vice-president of the newly merged AFL-CIO, and vice-president of the NAACP (Chicago branch), Bill Townsend. Townsend, in turn, was able to bring the entire United Automobile Workers and the Cook County Industrial Council into the case. Some other influential persons who were drawn into the case included Boyd Wilson (personal representative of the United Steel Workers of America), Bill Abner (vice-president of the Cook County Industrial Union Council and vice-president of the NAACP Chicago branch), David McDonald (president of the United Steel Workers Union), Doug Anderson (former chairman of the Community Services Committee and manager of Senator Paul Douglas's office in Chicago), Senator Paul Douglass, Congressman William Dawson (of the First Congressional District of Illinois), and three executive board members of the union, Lucius Love (staff member of the United Steel Workers and executive board member of the Cook County Industrial Union Council), Charlie Hayes (Cook County Industrial Union Council), and Hugh Lewis (public school teacher with the school union). And finally the president of the International Brotherhood of Sleeping Car Porters himself, A. Philip Randolph, was brought into the case. These people had worked together for years and thus, as Mooty asserts, "It was easy to swing them into place."[29] Clearly they could together influence the entire labor movement to act.

Demonstrating the commitment of the Steel Workers' Union, it was revealed in *Steel Labor: The Voice of the United Steelworkers of America*—C.I.O. that "the brutal slaying of a 14-year-old Chicago Negro boy ... was vigorously condemned in a resolution on Civil Rights adopted by delegates at the annual conference of District 31, United Steelworkers."[30]

The following telegram to Rayfield Mooty from Theodore Brown, director of research and publicity for the Brotherhood of Sleeping Car Porters in New York, dated September 23, 1955, documents the national involvement of the labor union:

> Would appreciate deeply your acceptance of invitation of New York division of the Brotherhood of Sleeping Car Porters to attend and speak at mass meeting occasion to protest and organize New York public opinion against the brutal lynching of your nephew in Mississippi. This meeting first organized effort in New York on this unfortunate incident to take place this Sunday, September 25, at Williams Institutional C.M.E. Church located 2225 Seventh Avenue, New York City. Time is 2:30 pm. The organization's international president, Mr. A. Philip Randolph, will be chairman and speakers will include some of New York's distinguished

---

[28] (Bradley-Mobley, 1988).
[29] (Mooty).
[30] ("Steelworkers Condemn Racial Slaying of Boy," 1955).

citizens, white and colored. We would also deeply be very happy to have Mrs. Mamie Bradley. I have talked to our mutual friend Boyd Wilson, of your union. The Brotherhood of Sleeping Car Porters will be happy to pay all expenses for you and Mrs. Bradley if it is possible for you to accept this invitation. Kindly wire or telephone me collect at Monument 2-5079.

Theodore Brown, Director of Research and Publicity,
Brotherhood of Sleeping Car Porters
217 West 125th Street, Suite 301
New York 27, New York.

The involvement of the National Labor Union and particularly the Brotherhood of Sleeping Car Porters offered an interesting diffusion of sentiments and information. In the case of the porters, they talked to the passengers on the trains, which was assumed to be a part of their job. People heard about the Till case and naturally wanted to talk about it, and so, oftentimes for hours at a time, the porters, who had become themselves involved in the national movement against this murder, would share their information with the passengers.[31] This sort of activity, passing the information by word of mouth, served as an information channel from the North to the South, from the East to the West.

Communist organizations, too, expressed demands for action against the Till lynching; however, efforts to conceal their interest were undertaken, as revealed in the following memorandum from Boyd Wilson dated September 28, 1955, to Mr. Mooty:

Reliable information from New York supports the suspicion that the meeting now being arranged for that city, October 2nd, involves some questionable possibilities.

You probably noticed a number of telegrams received at last Sunday's meetings. You will recall none of them were read. The reason was some of these wires were from known communists. We could not properly read some of these telegrams and not read others without having demands made for reading all of them, hence rather than read communists demands for action, none of the wires were made public.

I am reliably informed that next Sunday's meetings will provide an opportunity for these communists' telegrams to be read, thereby furnishing an opportunity for communists to be identified with our movement. I fear this will tend to kill the support and give hundreds of liberal people an excuse to refuse to support our demand for redress in the brutal murder of an innocent boy in the State of Mississippi.

To be sure, the labor union officials knew that involvement from the communists could alienate other legitimate organizations, which considered communists as illegitimate and un-American, from continuing their involvement in the case.

---

[31] (Mooty).

Bibliography

Alfreda M., ed. *Crusade for Justice: The Autobiography of Id B. Wells*. Chicago: The University of Chicago Press, 1970.

Bergman, Peter M. *The Chronological History of the Negro in America*. The New American Library, 1969, p. 542.

Berry, Mary Frances, and John W Blassingame. *Long Memory: The Black Experience in America*. Oxford University Press, 1982, p. 124.

Blaustein, Albert P., and Robert L Zangrando. *Civil Rights and the American Negro: A Documentary History*. Washington Square Press, Inc., 1968, p. 471.

Branch, Taylor. *Parting the Waters: America in the King Years 1954-63*. Simon and Schuster, 1988, p. 120, 123.

Branch. *Parting the Waters: American in the King Years 1954–63*. New York: Simon and Schuster, 1988, p. 130.

Burnham, Louis. *Behind the Lynching of Emmett Louis Till*. Freedom Associates, Inc., 1955, p. 5.

Franklin, John Hope. *From Slavery to Freedom: A History of Negro Americans*. Alfred A. Knopf, 1980, p. 459.

Hernton, Calvin C. *Sex and Racism in America*. Doubleday & Company, Inc., 1965, pp. 4–5.

Hemton, Calvin C. *Sex and Racism in America*. Doubleday & Company, Inc., 1965, p. 16.

Jordan, David. "Slain Chicago Young Was a 'Sacrificial Lamb.'" *The Clarion-Ledger Daily News*, edited by Joe Atkins, Jackson, MS, 25 AUG. 1985: 1-2.

Jordan, Winthrop D. *White Over Black*. Penguin Books Inc., 1968, pp. 158–159.

King, Martin Luther, Jr. *Stride Toward Freedom*. Ballantine Books, 1958, p. 127.

King, p. 145.

McLemore, Richard Aubrey. *A History of Mississippi, Volume II*. Univ. & College Press of Mississippi, 1973, p. 153.

Mooty, Rayfield. Tape recorded interview with Clenora Hudson, Chicago, Illinois, April, May, July 1986.

Murdock, Clotye. "Land of the Till Murder." *Ebony*, April 1956, 91.

Myrdal, Gunnar. *An American Dilemma*. Harper & Brothers, 1944.

Popham, John N. "Mississippi Jury Frees 2 in Killing." *The New York Times*, 24 Sept. 1955, p. 38.

Quarles, Benjamin. *The Negro in the Making of America*. Collier-MacMillan Ltd., 1969, p. 250.

Quoted in Howell Raines. *My Soul Is Rested*. Viking Penguin Books, 1983, p. 393.

Rosa Parks was quoted in Howell Raines book, My Soul Is Rested.

Rose, Arnold. *The Negro in America*. Boston: The Beacon Press, 1948, 185.

Simeon. "30 Years Ago: How Emmett Till's Lynching Launched Civil

Rights Drive," *Jet* (17 June 1985), 12–13.

Tape-recorded interview with Mamie Bradley-Mobley, Chicago, IL, 6 January 1988.

Video-tape-recorded interview with Rayfield Mooty, Chicago, Illinois, April 1986.

Williams, Juan. *Eyes on the Prize: America's Civil Rights Years, 1954–1965.* New York: Viking Penguin Inc., 1987, 57.

Woodward, C. Vann. *The Strange Career of Jim Crow,* Oxford Univ. Press, 1957, p.7.

Chapter 11

End Emmett Till Continuums: Beyond George Floyd, Breonna Taylor, and Ma'Khia Bryant

Contributed by:
Ngeri Nnachi, JD, MPPL

Black intellect, Black smiles, Black joy, Black creativity, gone in moments. Trayvon Martin wanted to work with airplanes. Sandra Bland had just completed her new employee forms at her alma mater, Prairie View, to start her position as a Community Outreach Coordinator. Michael Brown was murdered senselessly and left on display for hours as his whole neighborhood experienced mounting grief. A Google search will explicitly tell you how those dreams were extinguished with these violent murders. What those searches fail to acknowledge is that these victims dreamed at all. Fathers, mothers, brothers, sisters, so violently taken from their families . . . from us, leaving voids that no measures of justice or accountability can ever fill. All we are left with is our words, and our attempts to uphold their memories. In this chapter, we honor that they dreamed, they loved, they hoped. We honor the lives of all of our Black bodies that dream to see another day in the hopes that we make this reality manifest for us all.

Emmett Till's murder sparked something in us as a country, a desire to get to the root of anti-Blackness in the hopes that we would never see a Black child's body so severely disfigured and mangled that he could not be recognized. Unfortunately, we saw this again and again. The murder of Trayvon Martin served as a catalyst for social justice, igniting a spark of desire to protect the Black youth. Thousands took to the streets protesting the unlawful killing of Black boys and girls. Unfortunately, that moment lost its steam but found resurrection in the murder of George Floyd. We find ourselves yet at another crossroads, using the despair of hopes past to fuel our energy to fight not only for ourselves but for the humanity of those yet to exist. We mourn for babies unborn, reminded that even before they arrive, they can be targeted, marked by White supremacy as unworthy. For generations, we have had our loss on display so publicly; traumatic imagery that never leaves our psyches. Constantly seeing our mortality on loop dehumanizes and psychologically wounds us. We need to protect our babies and raise them in spaces full of love, joy, and community so that the time that they are granted is spent meaningfully.

Black girls, too, are sadly failed by systems and communities daily. Many are left to fend for themselves in hostile educational settings and fractured home lives. Media also does Black girls a disservice by perpetuating negative imagery that they become conditioned to reinforcing by way of keeping up with common trends. A survey conducted by the American Advertising Federation (AAF), and others found that Black women were watching a number of shows that influenced how other women may view them as well as how seeing those images could impact their own self-image (Freeman). Freeman highlights that in many media representations "[B]lack women aren't always allowed to be completely human, flaws and all" which gets to the issue that exists in there being a representation gap when it comes to depictions of Black girlhood and Black womanhood. Black girls and Black women do not get the privilege of seeing themselves positively and diversely represented in media. Reality television especially does Black girlhood and womanhood a disservice in perpetuating constant imagery of discord and aggression, with many women resorting to fighting to settle disagreements. While many women are portrayed as aspirational and entrepreneurial, they are also portrayed as aggressive and physically violent (Adegoke). When this becomes the common imagery for Black girls and women to rely upon, it follows naturally that we would see this showing up within socialization settings, including schools.

In April 2016, sixteen-year-old Amy Joyner-Francis was beaten to death in her school bathroom by her fellow classmates. The fight allegedly started over a boy and the fight resulted in Amy's head being banged against a bathroom sink so hard that she fell unconscious (Esposito and Edwards). She walked into the bathroom in the hopes that there would be an opportunity to talk to her classmates and left on a stretcher fighting for her life (Esposito and Edwards). The altercation unfortunately left one young Black girl dead and three more Black girls facing criminal charges carrying various prison sentences (Esposito and Edwards). These unfortunate encounters not only happen within our schools but in our home life as well. For example, Ma'Khia Bryant had hopes of leaving the foster care system and being back home with her mother. Twenty-three days before her murder, Ma'Khia called 9-1-1 "I want to leave this foster home" she said twice (*New York Times*). After the police officers arrived, they told Ma'Khia that there was nothing they could do, documented in their report that she grew irate and told them that if she could not leave, "she was going to kill someone" (*New York Times*). Clearly, this was a young girl under severe distress, in an environment that did not provide the nurturing that she deserved. She had to have endured inconceivable amounts of stress that led to her expressing her frustrations to law enforcement. Some of the other young women involved in the altercation on the day that led to the murder of Ma'Khia Bryant were in their twenties, the 911 recording contained a young woman saying "we got these grown girls over here trying to fight us. Trying to stab us. Trying to put their hands on our grandma" (Amiri and Welsh-Huggins). Many people failed these young girls, systemically and communally.

These media representations also perpetuate dissonance between Black men and Black women, reinforcing stereotypes that suggest that we cannot work well together. According to Adegoke, "most series unapologetically exacerbate the worst stereotypes that plague that black community: toxic relationships, absent fathers, [and] financial irresponsibility" (p. 1). Being constantly bombarded with this negative imagery reinforces a false narrative of conflict between Black men and Black women. On that note, Sisterhood is absolutely essential to our survival. We support and complement each other, thereby making each feel safe. As one of the 18 characteristics of Africana Womanism, it commands that we engage in the bonding that cannot be broken between women—genuine sisterhood (Hudson-Weems, *Africana Womanism* 42). "They are joined emotionally, as they embody empathetic understanding of each other's shared experiences" (Hudson-Weems, *Africana Womanism* 43). bell hooks narrates for us how the spirit of womanism comes alive in the lives of her students, and in turn, her own life, as she shares in space with them supporting one another in the unfamiliar territory of academia. In *Sisters of the Yam*, she speaks about creating a support group for her Black women students and calling it "sisters of the yam." hooks spoke of the daily assaults that Black women experienced, including assaults from "institutionalized structures of domination that have as one of their central agendas undermining our capacity to experience well-being" (23). We see this relational experience being necessary within K–12 educational spaces as well. Youth participatory action research has become a safe space for sisterhood as a research process that is a valuable educational experience that can serve to combat racist and sexist school practices (Evans-Winters). Evans-Winters collaborated with youth researchers as active participants in the research process providing them with the agency to learn, while developing gender and culturally relevant ways for presenting their findings (Evans-Winters). Culturally specific educational opportunities such as Youth Participatory Action Research (YPAR) are important ways to engage Black girls, providing them learning opportunities as well as a sense of agency to positively inform their educational trajectories. YPAR as a research method embodies the spirit of Africana Womanism, in providing Black girls with the agency to tell their own stories, from their own vantage points and being equipped with the tools to properly Sisterhood is absolutely imperative for us. We have a responsibility to foster opportunities for Sisterhood to take form in its truest fashion for our Black girls to flourish. Black boys also deserve the opportunities to experience the joys of true Brotherhood.

We are stronger as a community when we work in tandem with one another and not against one another. According to Hudson-Weems (*Africana Womanism*), the true Africana Womanist "continues in concert with her male counterpart in the global struggle for racial parity" (40). She "knows that the future of her children rests in the fruition of the collective goals for Africana people" (40). In fact, "The intertwined destiny of all Africana people speaks volumes to the dependence upon the participation of the male sector in the Africana womanist's struggle" (40). Mainstreamed narratives of feminism that allegedly set out to empower women misstep by ignoring the role of the man within our communities. When men and women take on their respective roles as community members, together they sow seeds of hopefulness to aide our collective struggles. Our fight for freedom and survival is dire and requires the hands of all Africana people. We are spiritually connected and must honor that connection. Our survival depends upon stressing the importance of a strong understanding of our spirituality. hooks mentioned that she had "been raised among black women and men who were in touch with their healing powers, who had taught me how to 'draw up the powers from the deep'" (hooks 23). hooks understood the importance of us being united as one. Unfortunately, we struggle to remain in concert with one another in educational spaces, where we need to be as united a front as possible. In *Pushout*, Black girls described feelings of neglect by their teachers and not being received well when requesting assistance (Morris). In 2015, a school resource officer flipped sixteen-year-old Shakara to the floor from her desk and dragged her across the classroom all because she allegedly refused to surrender her cellphone (The Associated Press). The police officer wrapped his forearm around her neck, flipped her, and the desk backward onto the floor, tossed her toward the front of the room and handcuffed her . . . all because of a cellphone

(The Associated Press). There was a Black man in the classroom, presumably her instructor, who stood as an onlooker doing nothing to intervene. The only person to intervene on Shakara's behalf was her classmate, a fellow Black girl, Niya (Craven). As a result of stepping in to record the incident and reprimand the police officer for his brutality, Niya found herself charged with disturbing schools, which was a misdemeanor (Craven). State prosecutors eventually dropped the charges against both students (Craven). Nonetheless, this should not have happened. The ways that White supremacy has infiltrated our sense of community to where we no longer act on feeling compelled to defend one another works to our detriment as a people.

Our youth deserve a strong sense of agency to guide them in understanding that they do have authority. Counter-storytelling is an essential tenet of Critical Race Theory (CRT). Counter-storytelling is defined as a method of telling a story that aims to cast doubt on the validity of accepted premises or myths, especially ones held by the majority (Delgado and Stefancic). Counter-storytelling "changes the form and content of research and conversations about events, situations, and societal participation" (Love 232). Counter-storytelling is a commonly engaged method of having students present their own narratives which allows them a freedom of voice. Monique Morris, in her book *PUSHOUT*, highlights the power of storytelling to fully grasp what Black girls are experiencing within their educational experiences. She highlights how stories grant us the opportunity to learn the impact of how Black girls are stigmatized by identity politics that constantly misclassify or marginalize them with stereotypical behaviors (Morris 10).

It is vital that we foster spaces within our community that empower young people to speak up for themselves. They are the experts of their livelihoods and who better to tell the world what their experiences consist of but them. In this social media age, it is young people leading the charge on what we see and how quickly we see it. From TikTok to Twitter, young Black boys and girls are keeping us creatively engaged. We owe it to the many before them, robbed of this opportunity, to give them the platforms to exercise their power.

We are in a unique moment, where the advancement of technology has afforded us more reach and opportunity for connection over racial injustice than ever before. Television shows, movies, podcasts, and many more mediums of engagement have called the masses into dialogues chronicling the depths of anti-Blackness in unprecedented ways. We owe it to ourselves to capitalize on this and resound the alarm; the livelihoods of our babies depend on it. As we move forward with intentionality, it is crucial that we be in community with one another as Africana men and women so that we model liberatory ideals for our children. We have an opportunity to be hands-on in crafting what our way forward looks like with the intentional steps that we take today. I implore you, our reader, to lean into your community and actualize the change that we deserve by speaking truth to power while rejecting White supremacist ideology. As a collective, we are powerful beyond measure and we can only see that when we work together.

As we review the crimes against nature relative to the murder of young Black men and women, we witness many excuses from outsiders who try to justify why such crimes took place. Their narratives almost invariably present the victims as culprits instead, and so yet another scenario of "blaming the victim" occurs. When efforts to reverse those interpretations with counter narratives, wherein the victims are, indeed, the victims, those justifications/justifiers are ironically classified as "racist" and hence, designated to a category of race defenders solely on the basis of the race factor. It is here important that we critically engage not just the media that we are constantly taking in, but that we also understand the larger contexts of intentionality in the production of the imagery that we consume. Although the reason behind this mainstream position is not totally clear, it is nonetheless important to correct that misinterpretation. CRT, which has been lately erroneously construed and publicized in the media as a negative, it is one way to approach the issue of racial discrimination or victimization. It provides us, as it did at its inception, with the tools necessary to critically engage our realities with a holistic lens encompassing our history, and our culture. Indeed, sadly, today, we find CRT being co-opted by White supremacy as a way to deter us from seeking and speaking truth. CRT is a movement that began from a "collection of activists and scholars interested in studying and transforming the relationship among race, racism, and power" (Stefancic and Delgado). In fact, the CRT Movement, rooted in the Movement of the 1960s "considers many of the same issues that conventional civil rights and ethnic studies discourses take up, but places them in a broader perspective that includes economics, history, context, group—and self-interest, and even feelings, and the unconscious" (Stefancic and Delgado). It "contains an activist dimension" which in some educational disciplines becomes critical analysis of White studies (Stefancic and Delgado). This kind of advocacy and activism understanding is absolutely necessary to humanize the experiences of Black children right now. Therefore, it is contradictory of us as a society to make the claims that we look to our next generation to carry the mantles of justice if we are not willing to equip them with the knowledge necessary to do so.

Throughout the Civil Rights Movement, Black students demanded the opportunities to learn truth. In a 2016 article appearing in *The Diverse Issues of Higher Education*, entitled "The Benefits of Campus Activism," Hudson-Weems references the demonstrations that took place around the country on college campuses around that life-shaping era of the 1960s, demanding that Black/Africana studies be offered in course catalogs. It was the activism of Black students across the country, who remained steadfast in their demands that brought about various Africana Studies departments, dedicated to honoring our rich histories and efforts of Black people that have served to benefit us all (Hudson-Weems, "The Benefits of Campus Activism"). This spirit of activism continues today in the works of Black students across the country, fighting for their humanity and visibility on college campuses. Maxwell Little, a founding member of MU's Concerned Student 1950, committed to this work despite White supremacy's attempt to confuse him into feeling remorse for playing a seminole role in his campus' activism (Hudson-Weems, "The Benefits of Campus Activism"). The fight for educational inclusion interconnects with our collective desire to best represent ourselves as Africana people by learning our truths and teaching our fellow Africana men, women, and children. Being well equipped with paradigms to effectively do this serves our best interest. And CRT, as well as Africana Womanism, effectively allow for contextualizing our connectedness, which results from our cultural tendency to relate to one another communally.

Be that as it may, there are five (5) tenets of CRT, which offer us the opportunity to critically engagement our positioning as Black people in a White supremacist world:

1. Race and Racism are central, endemic, permanent, and fundamental in defining and explaining how the U.S. society functions.
2. CRT challenges dominant ideologies and claims of race neutrality, objectivity, meritocracy, color blindness, and equal opportunity.
3. CRT is activist in nature and propagates a commitment to social justice.

4. CRT centers the experiences and voices of the marginalized and oppressed.
5. CRT is necessarily interdisciplinary in scope and function. (Delgado; Delgado and Stefancic; Solorzano and Yosso)

These five tenets allow us to directly engage our interconnectedness as Black people.

In the 1980s, Derrick Bell, Harvard U. Professor of Law, introduced us to the theory of "interest convergence," where "the interest of Blacks in achieving racial equality will be accommodated only when it converges with the interests of whites" (Bell). The interests of Black people are always at the mercy of those of White people, which reinforces for us that we will only ever have one another to rely upon. We cannot afford to look to people who need incentive to care about our humanity for our salvation. We absolutely must look within ourselves. Hence, CRT, a body of scholarship that encompasses the many vantage points necessary to fully encapsulate the Black experience, appropriately answers to that critical mandate for Black people. Opposing CRT in its purest and most original intent construed from Derrick Bell places someone on the wrong side of history. Growing out of the Civil Rights Movement, CRT creates a paradigm for combatting anti-Blackness and addressing Black people being granted access to their human rights head on. We are at a crucial point in our nation's history, where there is growing disapproval of CRT, attacking its advocacy on behalf of our most vulnerable populations, [composed of] "lives of a people too often mistreated, too often misunderstood" (Hudson-Weems, *Africana Womanism* 130). We cannot stand idly by and allow willful ignorance to distract us from reaching our goal of weaving Blackness into the fabric of American identity. Dr. Hudson-Weems calls these critical moments in time "the Emmett Till Continuum" and any disruption to such negates everything many before us have fought for in their painful efforts to end horrific racial crimes.

If we utilize CRT in ways most beneficial to us as Africana people, we will actively dismantle White supremacy's strategic implementations that reinforce disarray amongst us. When we learn more about ourselves, our history and how together, in community throughout time, we have collectively fought against systemic racism, intellectual warfare, and strategic familial undoing, we are better positioned to inform our futures to actualize our power as a people. And isn't this, after all, what true humanity is all about, a genuine dedication emerging from "collective paticipants in making the world a better place . . . for total parity and justice for all"? (Hudson-Weems, *Africana Womanism* 130).

Bibliography

Adegoke, Y. "Aspirational—and Aggressive: Are Black Reality Shows Peddling a Problematic Narrative?." *The Guardian*, 14 Oct. 2020, www.theguardian.com/tv-and-radio/2020/oct/14/aspirational-and-aggressive-are-black-reality-shows-peddling-a-problematic-narrative.

Amiri, F., and Welsh-Huggins, A. "Recordings Show Chaos Surrounding Ma'Khia Bryant Shooting." *Associated Press News*, 2021, apnews.com/article/makhia-bryant-ohio-shooting-video-recordings-186abfbcfd1717a8c42a38021a83de4b.

Bell, D. "Brown v. Board of Education and the Interest-Convergence Dilemma." *Harvard Law Review,* vol. 93, no. 3, 1980, pp. 518–533. doi:10.2307/1340546.

Craven, J. "No Charges For Spring Valley Cop Who Slammed Black Teenager." *The Huffington Post*, 2017, www.huffpost.com/entry/spring-valley-high-school-assault_n_58792986e4b0b3c7a7b12a5a.

Delgado, R., Stefancic, J., and Harris, A. *Critical Race Theory: An Introduction*, 2nd ed., NYU Press, 2012, www.jstor.org/stable/j.ctt9qg9h2. Accessed 29 June 2020.

Esposito, J., and Edwards, E. B. "When Black Girls Fight: Interrogating, Interrupting, and (Re)Imagining Dangerous Scripts of Femininity in Urban Classrooms." *Education and Urban Society*, vol. 50, no. 1, 2018, pp. 87–107, https://doi.org/10.1177/0013124517729206.

Evans-Winters, V. E. "Flipping the Script: The Dangerous Bodies of Girls of Color." *Cultural Studies ↔ Critical Methodologies*, vol. 17, no. 5, 2017, pp. 415–423, https://doi.org/10.1177/1532708616684867.

Freeman, M. "Reality TV Gives the 'Angry Black Woman' a Bad Name. Sometimes Anger is a Good Thing." *Washington Post*, 2017, www.washingtonpost.com/news/post-nation/wp/2017/10/27/reality-tv-gives-the-angry-black-woman-a-bad-name-sometimes-anger-is-a-good-thing/.

hooks, bell. *Sisters of the Yam*. Routledge, 1993.

Hudson-Weems, C. *Africana Womanism: Reclaiming Ourselves*, 5th ed., Routledge, 2019.

———. "The Benefits of Campus Activism." *Diverse Education*. 2016. diverseeducation.com/article/82675/.

Love, B. J. "*Brown* Plus 50 Counter-Storytelling: A Critical Race Theory Analysis of the "Majoritarian Achievement Gap" Story". *Equity and Excellence in Education*, vol. 37, no. 3, 2004, pp. 227–246. https://doi-org.proxy-bc.researchport.umd.edu/10.1080/1066568049049159/.

Morris, M. *PUSHOUT*. The New Press, 2016.

Solorzano, D., and Yosso, T. "Critical Race Methodology: Counterstorytelling as an Analytical Framework for Education Research." *Qualitative Inquiry*, vol. 8, no. 1, 2002, pp. 23–44. https://doi-org.proxy-bc-researchport.umd.edu/10.1177/107780040200800103.

II. Descriptive & Prescriptive: Applications, Exercises, Questions, Implications & Challenges

1. How can we create opportunities for sisterhood & brotherhood within our communities?
2. How can you tell your counter-story?
3. Which medium could you utilize to best share your narrative?
4. How can we resist White supremacy in our own local communities while navigating it on the outside within our educational pursuits?
5. What are the commonalities between the Civil Rights Movement and Critical Race Theory?

Chapter 12

Nourish to Flourish: Maroonage–Woodsonian Philo-Praxis and the Education of Black Children

Contributed by:
Lasana D. Kazembe, PhD

Knowledge and ways of knowing derived from Africana history and epistemology have been typically marginalized, devalued, or altogether excluded from the learning landscape of students and the pedagogical vision of educators. Those tiny fragments that do sometimes get included are usually derivative, disconnected from wider Africana culture, and, therefore, fail to appropriately reflect and convey the richness, breadth, and diversity of Africana peoples' history and humanity. This essay urges a return to African-centered worthwhile ways of knowing, valuing, and meaning-making based on Africana cultural knowledge, life praxes, and deep traditions of educational excellence. The author draws inspiration from two key sources: The Maroon history that occurred for centuries throughout overlapping African Diasporas and the pedagogical and historical recovery mission undertaken by consummate historian and Master Teacher, the Honorable Dr. Carter G. Woodson. Both sources are interpreted and situated as living practice texts (philo-praxes) that stimulate and bring about several things: (1) critical resistance to and escape from harmful ideological and psychocultural models imposed by Eurocentric culture; (2) development of Africana-based aesthetic and materialist approaches that make worthwhile use of Africana cultural knowledge within educational contexts; (3) development of an apprenticeship tradition to appropriately interpret, sustain, and convey an African-centered intellectual genealogy to current and successive generations of Black educators and students.

Introduction: Taking Flight and Returning to the Source

How shall we talk flight? How shall we take flight? What shall be our means of propulsion?
   Every successive generation of African-descended people grapples with (or should in some form or another) those and other critical cultural questions. These are organic, ongoing, and ontological questions of agency, place, space, time, and ultimately, of how we construct, converse, and correspond to/with our authentic cultural selves. Such questions (and

questioning) form an important entry point and segue for how we access, interpret, and inculcate meaning, as well as construct and sustain transformative models of Black educational excellence. This essay argues for a reassessment and urges a return (*Sankofa*) to cultural ways of knowing, valuing, and meaning-making drawn from sociocultural models inspired and informed by an African-centered paradigm.

As illustrated by the courageous historical exertions of various Maroon societies, as well as the historiographical exertions of Carter G. Woodson, a return to the source is based on consistent excavating, synthesizing, curricularizing, and centering of African peoples' historical contributions and world experiences. In a compelling sense, the return can be considered a mode of ideological flight that is fluid, culturally transcendent, and effectively functions as a form of psychological *maroonage*. The complex work of reclaiming and recasting Africana cultural knowledge should be the task of committed Black educational stakeholders who possess an African-centered worldview and disposition grounded in reality and self-knowledge, and who are invested in productively serving current and successive generations of African people—especially children.

Nourishing and Flourishing: Maroons and Maroon Spaces

How shall we talk flight? How shall we take flight? What shall be our means of propulsion?

As early as the sixteenth century, kidnapped Africans—scattered throughout the Americas and away from their ancestral homes—were forced to come to terms with and confront such questions and seek solutions in a tumultuous, European-constructed world of chronic violence, confusion, systematic cruelty, and organized brutality. In response, African people drafted actionable solutions that came in varied and creative forms of stand-your-ground resistance ranging from fight back, arson, agitation, sabotage, mass uprisings, and labor slowdowns/stoppages. More often, however, Africans engaged a more expedient form of resistance: flight (i.e., running away). Many of these fugitives fled to inhospitable forests, swamps, and/or mountainous regions throughout the Americas in order to escape the onslaught of European (mainly Spanish and Portuguese) oppressors and the vicious, anti-life system of enslavement established by European mercantilists, solicitors, and profiteers. Historically, these Africans are known and referred to as Maroons.

The word "Maroon" is derived from the Spanish word *cimarron* and translates to "fugitive," "runaway," or "one living in the mountaintops." Through sophisticated political and cultural organization, Africans developed flourishing, long-lasting, stable Maroon communities characterized by their unique worldview, perspective, and intentionality and undergirded by what Kambon (*The African Personality in America*) characterized as the African Survival Thrust. Kambon described the African Survival Thrust as exertions undertaken by people of African ancestry during critical and consequential periods such as the Middle Passage, Nat Turner Revolt, Reconstruction Era, Civil Rights Movement, Black Power Movement, and Black Arts Movement. Beyond the United States, Black liberation struggles have and continue to occur throughout the world (particularly in the western hemisphere) and contextually in the wake of European-imposed formations (historically and contemporarily) such as enslavement, colonization, land theft, settler colonialism, cultural disruption, and diverse forms of anti-Black violence.

Maroons embraced and employed (physical) maroonage as protracted, revolutionary acts of defiance, agency, and cultural affirmation. As a consequence, these groups of African fugitives banded together in organized resistance to establish independent, self-regulated hybrid communities (Brazil, Jamaica, Haiti, Cuba, Suriname, Florida, North Carolina, Mexico, etc.) based on their own worldview and in resistance to the one imposed on them by European aggressors. Aptheker notes that the perhaps the most populous Maroon colony was located in between Virginia and North Carolina in the Great Dismal Swamp and likely included some 2,000 [Africans] (168). Another topographic distinction of Maroon societies is that they were developed in both borderlands and hinterlands in particular throughout the Americas. Naturally, Maroon societies adopted a militaristic social identity that served as protection for the group as well as a way for Maroons to maintain their cultural identity and autonomy. These courageous Ancestors endeavored to intentionally liberate themselves (i.e., escape) from the genocidal and terroristic context of enslavement, psychological oppression, and cultural hegemony (Lockley; Lockley and Doddington).

In short, akin to the physical flight of their Maroon ancestors, African peoples' ability to functionally utilize the processes and skills of historical recovery and reinscription can be interpreted as a form of ideological flight; a deep cultural statement and ontological expression informing how they interpret and make sense of the world. Maroon ancestors endeavored to intentionally liberate themselves (i.e., escape) from a tripartite system of physical enslavement, psychological oppression, and cultural hegemony. Maroons sought to author a new reality in/on which they could locate, apprehend, and reinscribe their own African-centered, cultural ways of knowing, seeing, and being in the world. Hence, in both a theoretical and practical sense, maroonage constitutes not only a running *from* (i.e., escape) but also a running *toward* (i.e., return).

We Must Nourish to Flourish

Efforts to deny and denigrate the history and humanity of Black people are not new. Woodson (*The Negro in Our History*) documented early efforts by scientists and psychologists to use quantitative data to depict Black youth as inherently derelict, psychologically, bereft, and/or genetically criminal. Such efforts, according to Woodson, provided the basic justification for culturally authentic, scientific investigations regarding not Black history—but Blacks *in* history. Within educational contexts, the marginalization of African history and culture is so thoroughly pervasive that it has generally come to be viewed as normal and is uncritically accepted by many educators and students. It is through such cultural hegemony (one form being curriculum violence) that the deficit values, dispositions, invisibilized dynamics, and doctrinaire of Eurocentrism is translated and reinforced through textbooks, curricula, teacher training, classroom practices, popular culture, digital media, interpersonal, and other channels.

As Woodson fully understood, it is not (nor has it ever been) enough to simply engage in endless, eloquent critiques of racist and reductive educational assaults by dominant culture. Nor is it ever enough for Black researchers, teachers, and educational stakeholders to engage in reactionary (and ultimately meaningless) praxis. Both tactics have limited shelf life and do not allow us to proactively or critically leverage the resource of Africana history, culture, and epistemology. King and Swartz have highlighted the role of Maatian values,

Nguzo Saba principles, and instructional connection as foundational pedagogical practices to locate, center, and sustain Black students in their history and heritage (107). The Kazembe ("A Mighty Love," "Curriculum Studies," "The Steep Edge") has insisted that the historical interrogations of marginalized groups take into account the fluid, symbiotic, and dynamic nature of the past and present and that they adopt philosophical stances and insurrectionist pedagogical practices that invoke and activate cultural memory. wa Muiu advocates a transformative twenty-first-century Pan-African model and approach to education that equips children with skills to survive and flourish and that is acts as an epistemological bridge between Black children, their culture, and local and wider environment.

The marginalized life praxes of Africana people represent perhaps the most understudied and underutilized of our cultural assets. Paraphrasing Woodson (*The Mis-Education of the Negro*), Asante cogently observes:

> African Americans have been educated away from their own culture and traditions and attached to the fringes of European culture; thus dislocated from themselves, Woodson asserts that African Americans often valorize European culture to the detriment of their own heritage.
>
> . . . if education is ever to be substantive and meaningful within the context of American society, Woodson argues, it must first address the African's historical experiences, both in Africa and America (170).

For people of African ancestry to research, interpret, convey, and infuse what they deem aesthetically and culturally meaningful takes on special emphasis as it usually means the infusing and centering culturally responsive content and prosocial practices that are affirming and liberatory as opposed to reductive and predatory. Baptiste-Brady relates that acts of liberation and empowerment occur when we resurrect, (re)claim, and (re)situate critical Blackness and Africana Indigenous Knowledges. She goes on to articulate seven principles (community rootedness, humility and reflectiveness, spatial and chronal reimagining of classrooms, mentorship, love and care, storytelling, bold acts of disruption) for rethinking and reclaiming curriculum as Black educator (184–90). It is the cultural and *spiritwork*, then, of serious, culturally grounded, and committed Black educators, administrators, researchers, artists, and other activist educational stakeholders to build on and resonate African-centeredness as normative.

Woodsonian Anteriors and Interiors

A consummate historian, educator, author, and publisher, Carter G. Woodson consistently urged people of African ancestry to constantly look inward and turn toward Africana cultural epistemology and historical examples. Ani frames this as the life-affirming quest for psychological consensus, complementarity, and oneness with/in African selves and culture. The inward odyssey, widely reflected throughout Woodson's scholarly corpus, is natural and necessary to nourish the hearts, minds, and souls of Black folk—especially Black children.

Woodson's impact and direction during the first few decades of the twentieth century represented (perhaps) the earliest and most consistent presentation of a critical, affirming, and authoritative Black historical perspective. Woodson's far-ranging and diverse scholarly works (e.g., biographies, oral histories, folklore, history, critical essays, correspondence, documentary) reflect his culturally insistent scholarly assertion that all aspects of the Black experience required critical, scientific reexamination, and more authentic representation. Woodson's scholarly collaborators included former students, mentees, employees, and others who shared his interest in the reinterpretation and dissemination of accurate, culturally affirming content about Black world history and experiences. In addition to Lorenzo Greene, James Hugo Johnston, and Benjamin Brawley, Woodson also collaborated with historians and scholars A. A. Taylor, Rayford Logan, Charles Wesley, and Benjamin Brawley. Several of these men were directly involved with propagating Woodson's scholarly mission and legacy for successive generations (Boehm and Goggin; Dagbovie).

Woodson's work with Black school teachers was an extension of the Black struggle for self-definition and self-determination, and a primary way of affirming Black identity and agency, nourishing the cultural appetites of Black children, and formalizing the study and recognition of Black peoples' historical achievements and contributions (Boehm and Goggin; Dagbovie). The establishment of Negro History Week in 1926 is widely considered Woodson's titular contribution to the intellectual and cultural advancement of Black people. The Association for the Study of Negro Life and History (which Woodson founded in 1915), propagated Negro History Week by producing history kits containing curriculum materials and by encouraging Black people to form history clubs within their school districts and civic associations. Undoubtedly, the widespread embrace of Negro History Week was propelled alongside the insurgence of the 1920s as the decade of the New Negro, a prodigious period of race consciousness and pride among Black Americans that also had epistemological and aesthetic connections to the global Négritude Movement. During the decade of the 1960s, Negro History Week evolved into Black History Month (specifically on many college and university campuses) and still—nearly a century after its founding—continues to be observed throughout the United States. And, as Woodson originally intended, Black people were/are supposed to use the designated period of as a way to culminate, celebrate, showcase, and deepen their life-long interrogations into Africana history and culture (Woodson, "No Study").

Woodsonian Philo-Praxis and Maroonage Sites

In addition to revitalizing and recapitulating Black/African Diasporic knowledge via curricula and popular observance, Woodson also recognized the need for publishing and disseminating information about Africana history and culture, as well as creating autonomous Black institutional structures. Throughout his life, "The Father of Black History" founded numerous organizations, journals, and associations and used those formations to organize and extend the mission of documenting, preserving and teaching a scientific and historical account of people of African ancestry.

As one of the most outstanding figures of the twentieth century, Carter G. Woodson's work in education and community engaged practice took shape across several decades and continents. From 1903 to 1907, he served as an English teacher and school supervisor in the Philippines. Later he traveled throughout Europe and Asia and studied at the Sorbonne University in Paris, where he became fluent in French. In 1908, he received his MA from the University of Chicago, and in 1912, he received his PhD in history from Harvard University.

Woodson and his colleague Jesse E. Moorland founded the Association of Negro Life and History (now called the Association for the Study of African American Life and History) in Chicago in 1915. Dagbovie shares that "Woodson's 'office-home' played a vital role in his mission to promote the scholarly study and popularization of [B]lack history" (vii). As a maroonage site, this space served as the official headquarters of the *Journal of Negro History* (founded in 1916), The Associated Publishers Press (founded in 1921), and the *Negro History Bulletin* (founded in 1937). Outside of his writing pursuits, Woodson held several positions within academia. He served as principal of the Armstrong Manual Training School in Washington, DC, before becoming a dean at Howard University and the West Virginia Collegiate Institute.

Woodsonian philo-praxis can be interpreted as an intellectual and cultural disposition, an epistemological stance, and an Africana philosophical worldview committed to the psychocultural liberation of Black people and the restoration of their history. Woodson's life praxes encourage us to actively reflect and prodigiously champion the best of Africana cultural epistemology including: (1) promoting its activist philosophy; (2) critical resistance to cultural hegemony, marginalization, or appropriation; (3) deepening inquiry into and authentic representation of its cultural antecedents and inherited traditions; and (4) conveyance to and support of younger generations of students, teachers, and artists.

As a sentient model for intellectual cultural, and pedagogical excellence, Woodson's philo-praxis is stimulated and propelled by a hydraulics of psychological *maroonage* that calls for conscious, committed, and consistent interrogation and integration of history, institutional development, and African Diasporic experiences. This, of course, includes the nuanced leveraging of Black cultural voices, realities, political language, creative expression, history, perspectives, and psychosocial phenomena. For Black folks (most especially educators and students), Woodsonian philo-praxis is culturally responsive, worthwhile, and immediately recognizes and affirms the strategic value of Africana epistemology, agency, and culturally insistent ways of knowing and being in the world. More, it indirectly functions to interrupt and dismantle inequity, cultural hegemony, and White supremacy.

Even a cursory glance of Woodson's accomplishments (most particularly his more than 30 publications authored between 1915 and 1950) reveals that his life-long efforts were rooted in resistance, struggle, and transcendence, and therefore broadly and acutely reflect the historical and social experiences of people of African ancestry. For Woodson and his Maroon ancestors, the Black struggle for self-definition (freedom) and self-determination (liberation) functioned as a life-affirming love praxis of reclaiming and recasting Africana history and culture, orienting African people to reality, and instituting revolutionary social transformation to the benefit of Africana people worldwide.

Philosophical Dimensions of Woodsonian Philo-Praxis: African *Jeli*

How shall we talk flight? How shall we take flight? What shall be our means of propulsion?

Woodsonian philo-praxis and maroonage both call for conscious, committed, and consistent interrogation and integration of Africana history, sociocultural contexts, and sociopolitical reality. This orientation includes: leveraging of Africana cultural voices, realities, political language, creative expression, history, collective memory, perspectives, and psychosocial phenomena. In these (and other ways), Woodson exemplifies Konadu's insistence that the critical work and praxeological stance of Black/Africana scholars be drawn from and guided by the lives of the very people they study. The Black struggle for self-definition (freedom) and self-determination (liberation) is a strategic method of reclaiming and recasting history and culture, orienting to reality, and instituting revolutionary social transformation.

As pedagogue and practitioner, Woodson both drew from and epitomized the *Jeli* (African oral historian) tradition during a time when very few Black U.S. educators and scholars were on the scene. Woodson's approach to emancipatory learning and liberatory pedagogy was rooted in an Africana cultural synthesis that is expansive and corresponds efforts to appropriately and effectively leverage the sentient voices, collective traditions, interpretive frameworks, and accumulated experiences of African people. Such frameworks and cultural traditions comprise fertile ground for theorizing and understanding the textual, contextual, and subtextual meanings of Africana life praxes. Woodson's life-long work, scholarly production, and institution-building praxis reflects the *Jeli* tradition of stewardship and provides critical inroads for cultural synthesis. His life and legacy were profoundly and radically informed his life-long project to document and disseminate Africana history.

Watta describes *Jalolu* (the plural of *Jeli*) as "products of culture" and the sentient memory of their people. In historical African society, the role and social responsibility of *Jalolu* was ever-expanding and shifting. At the same time, however, an essential function of the *Jeli* is to internalize, interpret, convey, and keep salient the cultural memory of the community. *Jalolu* are personally and socially obligated (in the modern context) to critically engage the world, transmit the word, and operate within the apprentice tradition to relate, represent, and [ultimately] build upon the expansive and complex cultural epistemology of people of African ancestry.

I have identified four critical assumptions for *Jeli* (such as Carter G. Woodson) that resonate across genealogy and chronology. These assumptions are in no particular order and include: (1) consistent adherence to appropriately represent, interpret, sustain, and convey the cultural genealogy and folk traditions of people of African descent; (2) consistent adherence to appropriately interpret reality (phenomena) affecting Black political and social life; (3) encourage all people of African ancestry to reflect on and act productively and responsibly on their own behalf; and (4) obligate oneself to serve humanity (particularly the vulnerable and the afflicted) productively and responsibly.

Jalolu are the inheritors of an elaborate, ethical, and long-distance legacy of resistance, struggle, and cultural interpretation/representation, shaped, characterized, and bracketed by the historical/topical implications and ongoing psychosocial challenges inherent within and posed upon the African Diaspora.

Aspect One—Critical Questioning of Established/Presented Truths (i.e., What Knowledge is Worthwhile)?

Whose notion of truth shall be expressed (that of the oppressor or oppressed)? What means have been put in place for accessing this truth? Why is this considered worthwhile? Even from within the veil, what are the various approximations and aspects of truth? The worthwhile question must be asked if we strive to encourage Black students to pursue and immerse themselves in new forms of awareness and expansiveness (vis-à-vis Woodsonian philo-praxis, pedagogy, and teachings). To be avoided at all costs is the potential for creating scenarios whereby Black students and educators exchange one form of intellectual colonization for another. An essential component of Woodson's framework involved developing of a rich pedagogy of questions about Africana legacies, musings, reactions, and subjectivities. Hence, Woodson's pedagogical stance and cultural worldview should draw attention to both broad and specific aspects of Africana lives and agency including the concern for civilization, notions of freedom and justice, questions about and reflections on identity in relation to Africana history and culture.

Aspect Two—Decolonization of Ideas, History, and Historiography

An essential thrust of Woodsonian philo-praxis involved leveraging the critical messages of Black ancestral voices and narratives in order to create a scientifically informed frame of reference to decolonize history and historiography. Woodson and his coterie of researchers, scholar-collaborators, educators, and journalists served as interpreters for this new frame of reference. Hence, having kept up with the demand for and challenge to Black education and historiography, Woodson (and by extension his Maroon ancestors) sought to de-emphasize Eurocentric interpretative modes and reference points which had for centuries been imposed on Africana people.

For now, two additional aspects to be explored relative to Woodsonian philo-praxis and important role as a *Jeli*: (1) development of a functional synthesis (ideas, expression, and interpretation) and (2) Africana people (especially educators and students) as Multi-contexual Learners. The first is a discussion of how the African concept of *Nommo* (the generative and creative power of the word) factors into Woodson's work as well as in his professional personal pedagogy. The second aspect explores how Woodson's sentient philo-praxis continues to exist and function as a critical orientation that challenges Africana people to develop their repertoire of skills to interrogate and critique the multilanguaged world of contradiction and fixed assumption. Both aspects have far-ranging implications for the education of Black children.

Aspect Four—Encouraging Students to Become Multicontextual

Woodson's professional career, diverse scholarship, and literary accomplishments may encourage Black educators and students to become multicontextual in their approach to writing, learning, and culturally responsive education. Woodson's orientation to writing and documentation go far beyond literacy treatments that simply emphasize technical aspects. Morrell et al. assert that critical literacy encompasses not only skills mastery but also a commitment to critique and eradicate cultural hegemony and oppressive societal structures. For Black teachers and students alike, a Woodsonian critical literacy stance also includes questioning assumptions and critiquing our consumption and digestion of dominant (hegemonic) ideas, status quo motifs, and fixed meanings. Black students must become multicontextual if they are to absorb and critically synthesize reality. Bakhtin and Holquist observe:

> We must interrogate the life and the behavior of discourse in a contradictory and multi-languaged world . . . Language—like the living concrete environment in which the consciousness of the verbal artist lives—is never unitary. (275)

If they are to understand and interpret social reality, Black students must be taught to see critically and to raise questions on a number of levels. As a holistic process, a multicontextual orientation encourages students to develop and evolve skills to improve communication and to encourage their return to Africana ways of knowing, achieving, and making meaning in the world. Contemporary society provides ample diversions in the form of escape hatches and seductions designed to ensure that we continue to enshrine and valorize non-Africana art forms, ideas, and spaces even as we demonize and crucify our own. Such hegemonic conditioning is designed to downplay our interest in and involvement with culturally affirming practices that tilt toward psychological liberation. Insofar as maroonage is concerned, this attempt to bring us out of hiding must be recognized for what it is and resisted. Individualism presents one of the biggest contemporary challenges. We define and engage maroonage as the antithesis of individualism. maroonage, both in thought and practice, is a collective stance that draws on people to create community out chaos. maroonage recognizes that there is strength, value, and limitless potential in unity of purpose.

Conclusion

Undoubtedly, there are numerous questions promised and posed by maroonage and Woodsonian philo-praxis that have yet to be addressed. Given that, even as we continue to engage historical interrogation and ongoing synthesis of these myriad, unexplored questions we must keep in mind that education is always messy; always a political act. A contemporary call for maroonage urges committed Black educators, artists, scholars, and culture workers to actively engage and enact the best of Africana cultural and intellectual traditions. In addition to revaluing, revitalizing, and aesthetically reinvesting in African Diasporic knowledge, also needed are critical pedagogies, committed pedagogues, and appropriate fugitive sites for *maroonage* that function to promote Africana cultural knowledge and to disrupt the structures of inequity. The related exemplars of Ancestral maroonage and Woodsonian philo-praxis epitomize the struggle for self-definition and self-determination among Africana people as a primary way of (re)affirming the Black intellectual tradition, critiquing and dismantling oppression, and plotting a course back to themselves.

Bibliography

Ani, M. *Yurugu: An African-Centered Critique of European Cultural Thought and Behavior.* Africa World Press, 1994.

Aptheker, H. "Maroons Within the Present Limits of the United States." *The Journal of Negro History*, vol. 24, no. 2, 1939, pp. 167–84.

Asante, M. K. "The Afrocentric Idea in Education." *Journal of Negro Education*, vol. 60, no. 2, 1991, pp. 170–80.

Bakhtin, M. M., and Holquist, M. *The Dialogic Imagination: Four Essays.* U of Texas P, 1981.

Baptiste-Brady, J. Rethinking Curriculum Through Critical Blackness and African Indigenous Knowledges: A Black Educator's Response. *Africanizing the School Curriculum: Promoting an Inclusive, Decolonial Education in African Contexts*, edited by A. Afful-Broni, J. Anamuah-Mensah, K. Raheem, & G. J. S. Dei, Myers Education Press, 2021.

Bennett Jr., Lerone. "Still on the Case: Carter G. Woodson, Father of Black History." *Ebony*, 1993, pp. 23–8.

Boehm, R., and Goggin, J. A., editors. *Papers of Carter G. Woodson and the Association for the Study of Negro Life and History, 1915–1950.* Black Studies Research Sources, 1999. bit.ly/3ev6lRu

Dagbovie, P. G. *"Willing to Sacrifice": Carter G. Woodson, the Father of Black History, and the Carter G. Woodson Home.* National Parks Service, 2012. bit.ly/3y0X5w2

Kambon, K. *The African Personality in America: An African-Centered Framework.* Nubian Nation Publications, 1992.

Kazembe, L. D. "A Mighty Love: Culture, Community, and Liberatory Practices Among Educators of Color." *Handbook of Research on Teachers of Color* (book chapter), 2021a, In press.

———. "Curriculum Studies and Indigenous Global Contexts of Culture, Power, and Equity." *The Oxford Encyclopedia of Curriculum Studies*, edited by M. F. He & W. Schubert, Oxford UP, 2021b. doi.org/10.1093/acrefore/9780190264093.013.1591

———. "The Steep Edge of a Dark Abyss": Mohonk, White Social Engineers, and Black Education. *Journal of Black Studies,* vol. 52, no. 2, 2021c, pp. 123–43. doi.org/10.1177/0021934720959388

King, J. E., and Swartz, E. *Heritage Knowledge in the Curriculum: Retrieving an African Episteme.* Routledge, 2018.

Konadu, K. *Our Own Way in This Part of the World: Biography of an African Culture, Community, and Nation.* Duke UP, 2019.

Lockley, T. Runaway Slave Colonies in the Atlantic World. *Oxford Research Encyclopedia of Latin American History*. 2015. bit.ly/3bwcgEf

Lockley, T., and Doddington, D. "Maroon and Slave Communities in South Carolina before 1865." *The South Carolina Historical Magazine*, vol. 113, no. 2, 2012, pp. 125–45.

Morrell, E. *Critical Literacy and Urban Youth: Pedagogies of Access, Dissent, and Liberation*. Routledge, 2008.

wa Muiu, M. "The Contemporary Relevance of Pan-Africanism in the 21st Century." *Routledge Handbook of Pan-Africanism,* 1st ed., edited by R. Rabaka, Routledge, 2020.

Watta, O. *The Human Thesis: A Quest for Meaning in African Epic.* Publication No. E5 1985 W37. SUNY Buffalo, PhD dissertation.

Woodson, C. G. "No Study and Consequently No Celebration." *The Negro History Bulletin*, vol. 13, no. 6, 1950, p. 122.

———. *The Mis-Education of the Negro*. Africa World Press, Inc., 1933.

———. *The Negro in Our History*. The Associated Publishers, Inc., 1922

Chapter 13

Be Woke! Black America and the Holy Trinity—A SERMON

Contributed by:
Rev. Debra Walker King, PhD

Carefully determine what pleases the Lord. Take no part in the worthless deeds of evil and darkness; instead, expose them. It is shameful even to talk about the things that ungodly people do in secret. But their evil intentions will be exposed when the light shines on them, for the light makes everything visible. This is why it is said,

"Awake, O sleeper,
rise up from the dead,
and Christ will give you light."

(Ephesians 5:10–14 NLT)

During my second year of divinity school, I received a graded paper filled with accolades of praise for my work, but containing one perfection-marring complaint. Without specifying the location of the flaw, my professor reminded me not to use "gendered language" in my work. As a University of Florida (UF) English professor, I knew better than to do this and was sure I had not violated this much-valued academic rule. I thumbed through the paper, seeking the culprit that corrupted what should have been a perfect submission. After pouring over every word several times, I saw it. Appearing throughout the paper was the word "He," capitalized, sometimes in boldface, but always in reference to my Heavenly Father. My violation? I had written of God in the masculine, which, for my professor, was an assault on political correctness and academic professionalism. At that defined moment, the challenge for me commenced, as gender and gender language pre-date today's debate, dating back to the very "beginning," as presented in the Bible.

In today's world of political correctness, as well as its violation, many have discarded the Holy Trinity, defined sacredly as Father, Son, and Holy Spirit. Instead, the politically correct, attempting to diminish gendered boundaries that exclude women, look at the Holy Trinity as God our Creator, Jesus our redeemer and the Holy Spirit our sustainer. Although

183

this is all true, it places limits on the honor we give our Heavenly Father. Granted, when we do this, we feel good about ourselves and our ability to see God beyond sexist and gendered frames. We overwrite memories associated with careless and dangerous male caretakers. We give those they wound a creator unassociated with the "man of the house" or "father" who assaults, wounds, or abandons. In short, we pride ourselves on our ability to free God from the structured dominion of man-made institutions and discrimination; however, herein lies the crux of the problem. God does not need our act of liberation. We need His.

God is all in all, master of every design, the unmoved mover who makes all things happen that happens yet remains the same. God is the one who gives all things that are given and the one who makes all righteousness available to us, denying His children no good thing. God is the one without whom no thing that will be can be. We are because God, the Father, is. However, many of us reject this God, this Father, claiming He is the White man's creation—a creation designed to control Black people and distort our vision of ourselves as God's "original people." In many ways, they are correct. While we dare to create a God with limitations or, rather, our history of illiteracy and enslavement has done this as well as our dedication to long defunct traditions, we still allow the image forced upon us to make us idolators of that image. Many of us have become believers of tradition and a people standing within the shadow of truth, practicing a form of godliness, but who are inheritors of nothing. In fact, some of these traditions are confusing and represent a past in which Black Americans were disfranchised spiritually.

Have you ever seen someone hold up a finger as he/she stood up and walked out of a church service, for instance? The first time I saw this, it was a woman leading a child beyond the doors of the sanctuary. I wondered if they were sick or lost. Maybe they needed help and were calling for the nursing ministry to follow them outside. Why was the woman lifting a finger toward heaven and walking out? Answer: Tradition. No one gave me any other answer to this question because I was too afraid to ask. I didn't want to be revealed as lacking in knowledge, cultural, or spiritual. As I grew older, I learned the extended finger, a practice which originated during slavery, is a sign indicating one's exit from the general body of congregates. It was a sign the slave masters commanded their slaves to use when leaving their seats during worship services—services designed especially for slaves! The White masters wanted to know where every Black body was at all times. This need to know included when slaves excused themselves for personal reasons like using whatever bathroom facilities were provided for them. Black attendees were to stay put and learn of the God their enslavers created specially to indoctrinate the enslaved to the rules of the master narrative—not the Bible.

As early as the 1800s White missionaries in the British West Indies used an abridged Bible, designed for teaching slaves about the god of the planter class, a god who wanted them enslaved. Unlike the standard Bible, which had 1,189 chapters, this abridged Bible had only 232 chapters. Ninety percent of the Old Testament was missing and half of the New Testament. You can find one of three existing original copies of this text in the Museum of the Bible in Washington, DC, (on loan from Fisk University).[1] In it you find a different god from the one we think we know, one created to maintain bondage and control of Black people, a god who said nothing of equality but commanded proslavery messages

---

[1] Martin.

Chapter 13: Be Woke! Black America and the Holy Trinity—A SERMON

such as the infamous "servants, be obedient to them that are your masters according to the flesh, with fear and trembling, in singleness of your heart, as unto Christ; not with eyeservice, as men pleasers; but as the servants of Christ, doing the will of God from the heart" (Ephesians 6:5, KJV).

This god was white, usually with blond hair and blue eyes, an idol hovering above many Black congregations on Sunday mornings even today. This god did not empower those whose skin was not peachy, creamy, and white. This god demanded only the obedience of Black people as they served, not a Heavenly Father, but the world of White masters surrounding them. This god designed a special part of heaven where "good" slaves could peep through a special opening and see their masters luxuriating in a heaven they could only enter, if lucky, at the lower gates:

> She [upper-class white woman] even thinks that up in heaven
> Her class lies late and snores,
> While poor black cherubs rise at seven
> To do celestial cores.
>
> (Cullen)

Clearly, this god did not recognize Black people as sons and daughters. This god was not "Our Father." Slaves of the master narrative (the politically correct narrative of antebellum tradition and anti-Blackness) were never told they were lights of a Heavenly Father. They were not deserving of all the good things God provides those He loves; those who love Him, trust Him and follow the model of Jesus who, while on this earth, fought for justice and the liberation of the weak, despised and disenfranchised. Of course, the master narrative would not allow stories of freedom or liberation of any kind. It would never reveal to the enslaved just how much power they had as God's people or how much it would take from the master narrative if the enslaved "sleeper" awoke and learned of God's promised gifts to His children, regardless of race, ethnicity, class, or gender.

You may shake your head asking, "all of this because of a raised finger?" Yes, all of this. But why? It is because this is how we sleep. We sleep in a vapor, thickened by a past that denies us access to truth and power. My contemplations about the raised finger made me think more deeply about other traditions, which linger in the sleeper's heart and in the Black American consciousness. What other notions of God, such as our relationship with the Holy Trinity, lie in the folds of misunderstanding or lost relevance? What other religious signs of bondage and lies of subservience do we continue to uphold and practice? What poisons lace the public and tragic masks we wear ("the mask that grins and lies; it hides our cheeks and shades our eyes"—Dunbar), withholding real power from people with dark skin? What did the ancestors, living and dead, who walked in the footsteps of a liberator named Jesus, know that we missed? I am talking about women like Harriet Tubman, Sojourner Truth, and Jarena Lee, and men, too, like Fredrick Douglas, James Cone, and Martin Luther King, Jr.—to name only a few of the "woke" who braved the waters of change and fought for our people's liberation. How did they access truth amidst lies and use its power for the sake of liberation?

To begin with, they threw off the traditions of the sleeper—from wearing our best clothes during Sunday morning services, which originates from a past when work and servitude offered no other time to dress up and display our finest; to the silencing of women in church, a Paulinian directive aimed at prostitutes who disrupted worship by announcing their availability for sexual transactions. Secondly, they stripped the idol of its white face and master narratives, realizing these things separate us and mutate our purpose, packing true freedom beneath musty and worn, old baggage. They loved the Father, Son, and Holy Spirit and, thus, entered into Spiritual relationship with the Holy Trinity—the power of creation presented to us through the first four words of Genesis, words not changed in the Bible from era to era, translation to translation: "In the Beginning God . . ."

Who is this Holy Trinity? Is this a God who supports race, class, and gender exclusions? Does this God approve of abridged Bibles and Spiritual disfranchisement? Is this a God who denies any part of creation? No! The God of the beginning is a Trinity of love offered to us as one God in three persons. That God is the one Jesus addressed as "Our Father" and a Holy Spirit that the original, ancient Hebrew text of Genesis identifies using a feminine pronoun. That God offers an image that is not a lie; it offers a "family" of power in one Sovereign Being, a Being neither male nor female, but both. To be even more specific, that God is the one who clothed the figure of its human representation in the form of a beloved son, Jesus, perhaps, because the hierarchy of sinful men would only listen to or value a son. That God is the feminine essence "hovering over the surface of the waters" at the moment of creation (Gen. 1:2). That tripartite God is the one who created human beings after saying, "Let *us* make humankind in *our* image, according to *our* likeness . . . So God created humankind in his image, in the image of God he created them; *male and female* he created them" (NLT Gen. 1: 26-27, emphasis mine). This image of the Divine offers us "a God to glorify," a liberator to follow, and a love to imitate.

This God we serve is present in each of us through the redemption price Jesus paid on the cross—not just men and not just women, but both. We were created in the image of God, not the other way around, but we, being politically correct, try to create God in our image. And we have succeeded, if only in language. We speak of the "He/She" god, the mother/father god, the "They/Them" god and the "It" god. In this way, we created the perfect and politically correct divinity in our own image. But we must realize we are not creators of God! God is not made in our image. We are God's creations made in God's image. The image God created in us is a special delivery, given freely and fully without compromise, reservation, or questionable deliberation and abridgement. Made in the image of a Holy Trinity, we are not like other creations of the earth: Cows that chew the cud, flowers that decorate the hill side, waters that rush to the shore and back into the sea, or stars that line the night's sky. We are more than all of that. We are the image of God and that does not mean we were made to look like God or ponder the hierarchal value of God's image in our physical features. When we think only of ourselves as reflections of God in appearance saved by the Blood of Jesus only, we forget to be God-like. We fall asleep and forget the image of God we were meant to be.

Awake and know we are more than that! We were made in the natural image of God to think, desire, and understand as God thinks, desires, and understands. We were made in the moral image of God to love as God loves, have compassion as God has compassion and be kind as God is kind. Because God is love, we were made to reflect God's love, receiving it continually and reflecting it back to God in obedience, prayer, praise, and works of faith, mercy, and peace. And lastly, we were made in the political image of God to govern all creation as God governs—with empathy, benevolence, and care—while transforming the valleys of despair into hills and mountains of peace and hope.[2] Our living should reflect actions of liberation, justice, and equality that mirror those of Jesus through the power of the Holy Spirit and to the Glory of our Heavenly Father.

No! God is not made in our image because we, twenty-first-century liberators, are name chasers and position grabbers. We are not reflections of God's image because we are not awakened to God's uncompromising offer of wisdom, love, justice, and liberatory care. We are not reflections of God because we have no power! We have not tapped into the path of true freedom and neither have we grasped the power of transformation given only through the Holy Spirit!

As "the religious faithful," we blame our inactivity and cloak of sleepiness on many things, beginning with "the fall" in Genesis. Yes, it is true. We learn how we lost our connection to the image we were made to reflect in the third chapter of Genesis where humanity listens to evil instruction instead of the voice of God. Pictured as a serpent, the misdirecting voice of potential annihilation spoke (as the slave master's voice spoke to slaves) to disconnect us from what we were meant to be—beings of power and warriors for justice; the poor; and those enslaved by masters and monsters, devils and drugs. Because of what is called "humanity's fall," the image of God once enjoyed by the human being, was compromised in the muddy rivers of sin and the dark decay of enslavement to iniquity, misinterpretation, and meaningless traditions. There we wallow in death, scurry about pits of despair, squirm beneath masks of demonic demise, and stumble along paths of an alienation that separate us from God. Then, we wonder why we cannot get clean. Instead of reflecting the Holy Trinity, as we were made to do, we allow the serpent of annihilation to curl around our feet and slide around our shoulders. We listen to its voice and reject the power God offers. Our spiritual connection with God stays lost and our hearts grow even more dull, our ears become hard of hearing, and we shut our eyes to sleep.

Awaken! Be woke! Get the power you need to change your circumstances and the circumstances of our people. When we seek to find God in outdated traditions and structures that alienate truth, we remain cut off from the image of God so that our spirits might not look with its eyes, and listen with its ears, and understand with its heart (Matt. 13:15–16, NLT). We think we are free, playing around with pronouns, using she/her, he/his and them/they as parenthetical tags to our names in emails and online communications while the real work lays unwitnessed and unaddressed.[3] We think we are free because many of us do not know, or cannot see, that according to 2018 statistics "58.2% of Black and African American young adults (ages 18–25) and 50.1% of adults (26–49) with serious mental illness [do] not receive treatment." We think we are free because no one talks about and few bear witness to the number of young Black mothers who die each year because they could not afford or were not offered effective prenatal care.[4] We think we are free because many of us are unaware, unconcerned or afraid of the hidden assaults ethnic and class bias, racism and Black female marginalization use to bind our flesh to hopelessness and a great need for rescue.

But long ago God saw that great need, had pity on us and decided we must see, hear, and understand, not through the lens and legacies of scriptural misdirection and

---

[2] Runyon.
[3] Mental Health America.
[4] Chuck.

anti-Blackness, but through the Spirit. Long ago, God decided we must be *born again* (John 3:3). This birth is not of flesh and bone, which fall away and turn to dust, but of Spirit and, like the person of God whom Jesus called "Father," it is full of power, grace and mercy. It is a birth that once again gives us access to the image of God we were meant to be—a birth given by agreement and acceptance. When we accept God's gift of redemption, our misdirection and blindness dissolves beneath the presence of God's Spirit who leads us on the path where truth, understanding, and clear vision reside. This is the part of the Holy Trinity living inside the reborn, those regenerated children of a loving and faithful Father. It is the part of God moving inside all who are woke fully. In this rebirth, the gendered slough of political correctness and our enslavement to evil idolatry and unnecessary traditions that mislead and bind us to a past of detriment and trauma, also dissolves.

We worship a God who is our Father, not a goddess of political correctness or a lord of racial captivity. "Amen?" We worship a God who loved us so much He dressed His son in a human body and provided a way out. Through that son, God the Father, offered us adoption and a Spirit of empowerment. He cared for us so much He decided to provide a way we can become more than creations once again. He offered us adoption and a Spirit, the Holy Spirit, of empowerment, rescue, and light. And because we are the adopted children of the one Jesus called "Father," and only Father, more than 160 times in the New Testament, we can cry out, "Abba, Father" and be heard. Because we are heard, we can do the necessary things to transform the pressures of oppression and anti-Blackness into promises and change—if only we are awake enough and concerned enough to act in concert with that glorious power.

No matter the tasks before us, God in Heaven is our partner, a Holy Trinity of power. Have faith in Him and all we put our hearts and minds to do will be done in perfect grace and favor. Awaken to your life and recognize that as reflections of God, we have an obligation to expose injustice, bias, disparities, and disfranchisement wherever we find it. Move your work of faith beyond the doors of the church into the marketplace. That is, move it into your jobs, your daily interactions, your expressions of love, and your witness for those living beneath various banners of suffering and distress. For our God is not just any god made of small things and personal human desires, hierarchies, and exclusions. Our God is the director of all that happens in our lives and all we dare dream to become. Seek the face of God before submitting to any task or claiming a solution to any concern. Lay claim to the power a daughter or son of God has the right to inherit. Our Heavenly Father wants us to have it or the Holy Trinity would not have provided a way for us to receive it. "Amen?"

Know this and understand: God created all, but God is not the Father of all. God is the Father of the redeemed, and of those who are answering redemption's call moment by moment. God is the Father of those who accept full membership into the family of the Almighty and claim boldly the inheritance due a child of God—not an inheritance offered only in the everlasting future, but also an inheritance provided by the Holy Trinity here, now, today! When we engage as God empowers each of us—as God anoints us individually—we are truly "woke," knowing we have the right to walk as lights filled with the Spiritual wonders and power of an adoption that flesh, the "master" narrative, and political correctness cannot begin to understand or receive.

So, awake! Take hold of your inheritance and experience true freedom! Acknowledge with great joy your position as sons and daughters of an omnipotent and sovereign Father.

Stand in it with your heads held high, knowing no darkness can possess that which the Holy Trinity claims, unless we give it permission.

> Be woke! Rise and wash in the sweet vapors of God's love, the wonder of the Lord's saving grace, and the gentle guidance of the Holy Spirit while embracing God's blessings.
>
> Be woke! Rise and see with Spiritual eyes, hear with Spiritual ears, as the power of God moves in your life.
>
> Be woke! Rise and accept God's gift of redemption within your spiritual heart, knowing who you are and claiming all that being endowed with the Spirit of God means.
>
> Be woke! Rise knowing you are a bona fide, qualified, worthy, and justified member of God's Holy family.
>
> Be woke and *Stay Woke!* Live *empowered* as the images of God you were made to be.

Bibliography

Chuck, Elizabeth. "The US Finally has better maternal Mortality Data: Black Mothers Still Fare the Worst." *NBC News Online*, 30 Jan. 2020. www.nbcnews.com/health/womens-health/u-s-finally-has-better-maternal-mortality-data-black-mothers-n1125896. Accessed Mar. 2021.

Cullen, Countee. "For a Lady I Know." *All Poetry*, 1920s, allpoetry.com/For-A-Lady-I-Know. Accessed 24 Mar. 2021.

Dunbar, Paul Laurence. "We Wear the Mask." *Poetry Foundation*, 1895, www.poetryfoundation.org/poems/44203/we-wear-the-mask. Accessed 24 Mar. 2021.

Martin, Michel. "Slave Bible from 1800s Omitted Key Passages That Could Incite Rebellion." *NPR*, 9 Oct. 2018, www.npr.org/2018/12/09/674995075/slave-bible-from-the-1800s-omitted-key-passages-that-could-incite-rebellion. Accessed 2 Mar. 2021.

"Black and African American Communities and Mental Health." *Mental Health America*, www.mhanational.org/issues/black-and-african-american-communities-and-mental-health. Accessed Feb. 2021.

Runyon, Theodore. *The New Creation: John Wesley's Theology Today*. Abingdon Press, 1998.

Conclusion

For My People, #FortheCulture:
A Contemporary Remix of Margaret Walker's poem

For my people in places experiencing police brutality & the mothers mourning
For my code switchers living in double consciousness daily;
For my hoteps who know the truth and don't trip on the negative connotation of the term;
For my Activists doing work in the streets & behind the scenes becoming urban legends;

For my communities emerging & shifting into villages constantly dreaming of a Black Wall Street;
For my people bringing back the Renaissance—art crawls & spoken word jazz at brunches, day parties, echoing the Niggerati at Niggerati Manor or the Cotton Club listening to modern day Lady Days, Counts, Dukes & Dizzys;

For My People in bondage but in jail cells enslaved by a system of unfairness within a pseudo free society where black folk do time, but white folk get money off the exact same product;
For my people in a school system that keeps their minds unfree;
For my people trying to free their minds, build their wealth but imprisoned by student loans;

For my people living life & making dollars outta change just to survive the day & push again;
For my people who live to be the best dressed in any room;

For my people who relate to HBCU experiences & use their education everyday in many ways;
For my people teaching youths, preparing leaders with limited resources—a way outta no way;

For my people who are lawyers fighting the fight; in Congress telling the truth, or in the courthouse fighting to seek the truth for the race—The reincarnations of Houston and Marshall;
For my people defying the statistics and proving black love exists and is endearing;

Let a new society rise. Let another community be born. Let a second generation full of courage issue forth; let a people loving freedom come to growth. Let a race of men and women rise and take control.

—Keena Day, MA/PhD Candidate

The above poem by educator and freelance writer, Keener Day, gives an excellent overview of the critical issues that have prohibited the proper and full ascendence of the African American. In this "Contemporary Remix" of Margaret Walker's 1942 celebrated poem, "For My People," Day, as did Walker some 80 years earlier in anticipation of the rise of the civil rights activists and supporters in every arena of life of the 1950s, 1960s, and 1970s, resounds that clarion call, the evolution of a "new generation," courageously promoting love, respect, and justice for all. These concerns and more are only some of the very issues that the astute contributors in this volume have put forth, as they also successfully debunk the pervasive, negative assigned connotations and denotations of what "Woke," (Eyes open to truth) "Reparations" (Economic Returns), and "Critical Race Theory" (A Civil Rights Continuum) really means in order to successfully forge our way in securing our future. Other issues pursued in this volume include further clarifications and explications of other ideas relative to positive and accomplished Black life such as *Afrocentricity* and *Africana Womanism/Africana-Melanated Womanism*, as we strive to at last take our "seat at the *Grand* table" for securing necessary "Generational Wealth" for the ultimate security and true survival of Africana life, history and culture. Importantly, these concepts can serve as foundational in future engagements and conversations of another important realism of life today—*AfroFuturism* and *AI*.

Whether one agrees with the Constitutional Rights of all or not, given that the dominant culture had excluded Blacks, designated as only 3/5 human being, from this privilege, it is the responsibility of the people to uphold that law, an assignment for which today's African Americans are compelled to hold white US citizens accountable. The denial of "the inalienable rights" of all humankind, which should naturally include Blacks, commands a clarion call today for a corrective, based upon the legal mandates explicated in the July 4, 1776 Declaration of Independence, although originally designed "for whites only":

> "We hold these truths to be self-evident, that all men are created equal, that they are endowed, by their Creator, with certain unalienable Rights, that among these are Life, Liberty, and the pursuit of Happiness.

> That to secure these rights, Governments are instituted among Men, deriving their just powers from the consent of the governed, That whenever any Form of Government becomes destructive of these ends, it is the Right of the People to alter or abolish it, and to institute new Government, laying its foundation on such principles, and organizing its powers in such form, as to them shall seem most likely to affect their Safety and Happiness.
>
> Prudence, indeed, will dictate that Governments long established should not be changed for light and transient causes; and accordingly all experience hath shewn, that mankind are more disposed to suffer, while evils are sufferable, than to right themselves by abolishing the forms to which they are accustomed. But when a long train of abuses and usurpations, pursuing invariably the same Object, evinces a design to reduce them under absolute Despotism, it is their right, it is their duty, to throw off such Government, and to provide new Guards for their future security."
>
> —Thomas Jefferson, et al., *The Declaration of Independence*

And we must demand that the original decree, demanding the respect and recognition of all, rightfully include African Americans, many of whom have, in many ways, contributed significantly to the overall civilization of this homeland.

During the last year and a half, 2020 to 2021, there have been massive upheavals, including both global demonstrations against racism, and the formidable Coronavirus. On the matter of the former, the image of 14-year-old Emmett Till is forever evoked, a vivid lynch victim, all because he whistled at a white woman. On-going murders of Black men and women, too, has fueled the flames, as these "Emmett Till Continuums" make it virtually impossible to forget the past. And nor should we. The global sweep of raging Coronavirus, too, has made it impossible to ignore its presence, as millions the world over are dying daily, as they painfully succumb to a mysterious invasion, also never to be forgotten. With these nemeses, particularly the obvious events that scream out "racism," there must be serious commitments to creating models for improving our diverse world, commanding an interdisciplinary/intercultural focus, tailored and disseminated for ultimate human survival. The mission of diverse scholars/mentors herein, dedicated to transforming our world, guided by a genuine appreciation of True Cultural Diversity in the Du Boisean sense, will satisfy that demand, as we ultimately foster a diversity in not only color/ethnicity, but also in thought and action! Herein lies a more humane society, characterized by **True Cultural Diversity**, not assimilation, which we witness in this book, to some degree,

1. Truth via unveiling contributions of Blacks, relegated to "hidden figures."
2. Love and a sense of empathy and kindness in an overall sense of human decency.
3. A respect for and celebration of all cultures and their uniqueness, ultimately enhancing our society.

In creating a positive inclination for the entire body, for example, these guidelines could be enhanced wherein all are asked

1. To insist upon Accountability for all acts to dissuade injustices.
2. To eliminate White Privilege for ultimate true equality.
3. To debunk total Racism via unveiling historical, and current truths.

With interdisciplinary and intercultural scholars such as those presented in this textbook, collectively offering useful Africana theoretical concepts and acts, it could stand as a model for informing our minds for advancing a better worldview. Admittedly, we need more plausible/workable ideals, particularly relative to racial dominance and how that plays out culturally, socially, politically, economically, and spiritually. Thus, meaningful scholarly activities, relative to the dynamics of a valued justice system for all, demonstrating an intellectual movement—from the faculty, staff, administrators, and student body—will lead the day. And so, as we advance to a harmonious world wherein all can enjoy the benefits of True Cultural Diversity, with a diverse population, imbued with unique collective beliefs and practices, a positive is virtually inevitable. Indeed, as we "*Strive Toward Freedom,*" the very title of Dr. Martin Luther King Jr.'s 1958 signature book, our initiatives and efforts will expectedly be manifested into the powerful fruition of a long due racial healing wherein racial harmony resides forever.

Commentary on the benefits of appreciating True Cultural Diversity in the quest for human parity is often mirrored in literature, an artistic creation reflecting the grandeur of life itself. And what better literary figure than Pulitzer Prize-Winning author, Toni Morrison, the first African American female to win the Nobel Prize for literature (1993), representing in her massive contributions, powerful materials that graphically demonstrate, in so many ways, how the American and African American cultures represent an unacknowledged merger of experiences wherein the identities of both are miraculously dictated by the other. This truism is not only unacknowledged by the dominant culture, but moreover, blatantly denied, as whites find it virtually impossible to imagine Blacks playing the role of defining them via their acts and mindset, which can only be so via the presence of Blacks in their lives. Thus, their very character is shaped and molded by the existence of Black life in their world of white privilege and white superiority. Indeed, the role of Blacks is seminal in these literary pieces, not minor characters who can easily be dismissed as if they never existed. In fact, there could not be such a personality as in the white persona were it not for Black presence, in an interesting twist, made possible in their privileged statue. For example, the novels reputed as American masterpieces, like William Faulkner's *The Sound and the Fury* and Ernest Hemingway's *The Sun Also Rises*, have memorable white characters whose very essence is shaped by African Americans and their reality as their "slaves." These characters and many more validate Morrison's perception of Black characters as major, rather than minor in her brilliant analysis of Black and white life, depicting true reality, featured in her seminal collection of essays in *Playing in the Dark: Whiteness and the Literary Imagination*. Truth reigns here.

While the references to literary reflections on life is endless, I will close with a reminder of the impressive multidisciplinary chapters herein, including Africana perspectives from those identified as cultural theorists, economists, historians, theologians, anthropologists, entrepreneurs, as well as activists, to name a few. As we gather ideas and opinions about how we respond to life today in quest for a better world, hearing what the contributors for this volume have to say, which is very important, is priceless and hence, should be taken as utmost critical information, thus, eliminating the false meaning/defintion of Critical Race Theory (a Civil Rights Movement continuum), introduced by prominent Harvard University Law Professor, Derrick Bell, thereby discouraging the unjustifiable need for its removal from academic and otherwise circles. Truth and facts are critical and should not be concealed, but instead, remembered:

REMEMBER-

Colfax, LA (1873); Wilmington, NC (1898); Atlanta, GA (1906); Elaine, AK (1919); Tulsa, OK (1921); Rosewood, FL (1923), among **a thousand more** - all victims of racist massacres, white violent terrorism, based upon fear of economic competition and pretense protection of white womanhood initiated by the dominant culture!

REMEMBER *TULSA*, OKLAHOMA!!!
(100 Year Anniversary—1921)

Coda

SANKOFA—Learn the lessons of the past in order to move forward for a successful future

Reflections on Our Past, Present, and Future Possibilities:

From Film Script: *Liberating Emmett/Whitten's Atonement*; Defining Moments and Endorsements

What better way to close a comprehensive body of research on the critical matter of centuries of the dehumanization of a people, all in the midst of current raging coronavirus. Symbolizing what Hudson-Weems calls "the true ugliness of American racism staring us in the eye" is the bloated face of Till. Highlighting that infamous case of the 50s, the inception of the modern massive public demonstrations against abject racism and discrimination, following the 1954 Brown versus Topeka Board of Education Supreme Court Case a year before, is, indeed, appropriate. The first Black Supreme Court Justice, Thurgood Marshall, successfully litigated the case, rooted in the 1896 "Separate but Equal" Plessy versus Ferguson Jim Crow Law. In that case, he established the unconstitutionality of segregation. As we consider where we are today with race relations, the rampant brutal murders of countless Blacks throughout this country graphically evoke the brutal lynching of Emmett Louis Till, thus, representing "the Emmett Till Continuum" and national/international demonstrations contesting such abominable, dehumanizing acts. The rest is history, calling

197

for a halt once and for all for true human justice. The years 2020 and 2021 have presented the most challenging times for people globally due to the formidable Coronavirus, which has killed millions of people worldwide. Moreover, in the midst of this global disaster, we in the United States have experienced even more turmoil, particularly stemming from racial strife, resulting from centuries of boundless racial dominance, which at last is now being challenged more than ever. National demonstrations have ensued, following countless murders of African Americans. International communities, too, have joined in their support of the demands of African Americans for long-overdue racial justice. In this global movement, what is so powerfully evoked is the visceral 1955 brutal murder of Emmett Louis Till, a 14-year-old Black Chicago youth, lynched for whistling at a 21-year-old white woman, Carolyn Bryant of Money, Mississippi.

The infamous murder case is told via the lives of four: **Dr. Clenora Hudson-Weems**—The first to establish Emmett Till as the true catalyst of the Civil Rights Movement of the 1950sa and 1960s; **Mamie Till-Mobley**, the passionate mother of Emmett, who spent her life sharing the tragic saga of her only child, Emmett, at the hands of two southern racists, 24-year-old Roy Bryant (husband of Carolyn Bryant) and his 36-year-old half-brother, J.W. Milam; **Rayfield Mooty**, Mamie's advisor and strategist who accompanied her throughout the ordeal; and **Attorney John Whitten, Jr.** the redemptive spirit, evolving from his remorse and atonement via legally representing Black Mississippians *pro bono*, thereby offering, through a radical change of heart, a possible racial healing.

In reviewing the Civil Rights Movement and Till as catalyst, we witness it as, indeed, an ongoing tragic and senseless phenomenon, "The Emmett Till Continuums," with modern day symbols like 46-year-old George Floyd and 26-year-old Briana Taylor, among many more like victims. In anticipation of the future of Africana people and people in general in the midst of the global pandemic, we must work toward making a better tomorrow on all fronts, one which must include also ways of enhancing the financial status of all, too often dismissed as insignificant—"it's not about the money" —in securing the long-deserving legacy for all children and their children, thus, General Wealth!

In order to better understand where we stand today, we can begin with the appreciation of the totality of the Emmett Till Legacy, including how his name has today become a household word. To do this, there must be a fuller understanding of not only *what* happened to young Emmett, but moreover, *why* it was for too many years swept under the rug, *how* it was finally unearthed after 33 years of silence—though a true international *cause célèbre* during the inception of the Civil Rights Movement—and finally, *where* do we go from here—all Critical Keys for ending Racism!

The Great Debate

Act Eight

SCENE ONE

(University of Iowa—2:00 p.m. (September 1986)—Jefferson Bldg.—Proposal Debate. Clenora, with briefcase, waits in the hall by conference room.)

(Dr. Walton, 40s, opens the door.)

DR. WALTON   "Clenora. The committee is waiting."

(Clenora enters. Her DOCTORAL COMMITTEE of five in their 40s and 50s—four males (two blacks and two whites) and 1 female (white)—are seated at oval table. She places briefcase on table in front, retrieves the stack of papers from briefcase.)

DR. WALTON   "Your Proposal, Clenora?"

CLENORA   "Thanks, everybody. But I'd like to first advise you that I'm changing my topic from Black Women Writers to Emmett Till and The Civil Rights Movement."

DR. WALTON   "Did I hear you correctly, Clenora? You're not going to do Black Women Writers, but instead Emmett Till and the Civil Rights Movement?"

CLENORA   "Right. Remember final paper for your class last semester—'The Lost Chapter in the Civil Rights Movement?' Rayfield Mooty was right—'Historians will talk about the good and the bad, but they don't want to deal with the ugly.'"

(Clenora pauses a moment, then continues in a strong voice.)

CLENORA   "I've been having recurring dreams of Emmett since childhood. That's why I'm here, requesting your approval for this dissertation topic."

(Committee listens tentatively.)

DR. WALTON   "So, exactly where are we now, Clenora?"

CLENORA   "I plan to document everything leading up to the Movement, beginning right after the lynching of 14-year-old Emmett of Chicago for whistling at Carolyn Bryant, 21, in Money, Mississippi, AUG 28, 1955."

DR. WALTON   "Clenora, have you reviewed the literature on this?"

CLENORA   "That's just it. There is no full-length study with this position from established historians."

DR. WOODARD   "We're listening, Clenora."

CLENORA   "For example, Benjamin Quarles, great 20th century black historian, never once mentioned Till in his book, *The Negro in the Making of America*."

(The committee appear a bit surprised. Clenora continues.)

CLENORA   "He cites Rosa Parks' DEC 1, 1955 demonstration as the Movement's inception. Then there's Vincent Harding's *The Other American Revolution* in which doesn't mention Emmett Till either."

(Committee begins to nod.)

CLENORA	"Finally, there's John Hope Franklin with only one reference to Till in his book, *From Slavery to Freedom*. And he's not even indexed."
DR. WOODARD	"Well, that alone speaks volumes, Clenora. You really have your work cut out, as the catalyst of the Movement had long been established."
DR. WALTON	"Yet and still, Clenora, changing the established position from Rosa Parks as catalyst of the Movement to Emmett Till is virtually impossible."

(The committee nods in agreement.)

CLENORA	"I am not taking away from Rosa Parks. She will always be the Mother of the Movement, and Dr. King, the Father of the Movement. But the Child of the Movement is Emmett. Somewhat of a trilogy."
DR. RAEBURN	"Although that makes sense, still traditional interpretation of the Movement sounds logical enough and legitimate as it stands."
CLENORA	"Logic and legitimacy do not make it true. When you look at the public rallies, out-cries against this, Emmett Till was the catalyst."
DR. WOODARD	"Rosa Parks as catalyst of the Movement has been very effective, hasn't it?"
CLENORA	"Of course, but even she admitted that when asked why she refused to go to the back, she said she thought about Emmett and couldn't go back."
DR. WOODARD	"So there you have it. Emmett's a backdrop."
CLENORA	"Much more. I want to set the record straight. Emmett's lynching occurred 3 months and 3 days prior to Rosa Parks' demonstration."

(She steps toward the panel).

CLENORA	"Fact is, the incident set the stage for the Montgomery Bus Boycott, galvanizing the Black community."
DR. WOODARD	"Well, I must say, when you think about it, she's correct."
CLENORA	"People were incensed and demanded changes, especially for our kids, the heart of the matter."
DR. RAEBURN	"Must the Emmett Till case be the catalyst? Can't you say that Till was a very significant factor in the rise of the Civil Rights Movement?"

(Dr. Kirber smiles as she nods in agreement).

CLENORA	"Not really, because he was far more than that. He was the impetus!"

DR. RAEBURN	"Is it really that important?"
CLENORA	"Yes, it is. I believe that it probably would have probably placed us at a more advanced stage."
DR. WOODARD	"It would be interesting in seeing how you work these dynamics out later."

(The room is silent. Dr. Raeburn then speaks softly).

DR. RAEBURN	"Are you serious, Fred? Iowa is a top Research One Institution! This thesis is extremely problematic!"
DR. HORWITZ	"Yes, and what about those who have invested in your career—Ford Foundation?"
DR. KIRBER	"And historians, who have established their careers on those findings, including Dr. John Hope Franklin?"
DR. WALTON	"Clenora, what happens if you can't defend your dissertation?"
CLENORA	"Then, I don't get the PhD and I'm willing to take that chance."

(The expression on the committee's faces was that of shock.)

DR. WALTON	"Give this some thought, Clenora."
CLENORA	"I have. And if I can't get a supportive committee here because my thesis may disrupt the status quo, then I guess I'm done here."

(She starts putting her papers in her briefcase, then stops).

CLENORA	"Don't you get it? Everything was predicated upon this: 1957—Little Rock desegregation; 1961—Freedom Riders; 1962—James Meredith's enrollment at Ole MS; 1963—Medgar Evers' murder; 1964—The murder of the 3 civil rights workers."

FLASHBACK—Remembering the Birmingham Church Bombing

BACK TO PRESENT:
(In tears, Clenora flinches for a brief moment.)

DR. WOODARD	"Clenora. Clenora. Are you okay?"
CLENORA	"It's our kids again. The 4 little girls in the 1963 Birmingham Church bombing. We have to protect them."

(Dr Kirber stands up, now taking a supportive position.)

DR. KIRBER	"Clenora's absolutely right. And if we don't support her now, we may later regret it."

(Dr. Walton leans over to Dr. Woodard, whispering something. Dr. Woodard nods. Dr. Walton then addresses the committee).

DR. WALTON	"If she's willing to risk her whole career, then let's do it."

DR. WOODARD	"To be quite frank, we really have nothing to loose. She does. And it could be a possibility for us to gain recognition if it works."
DR. WALTON	"The University of Iowa has a reputation for supporting pioneering research like this. I really think we should."

(The committee pauses, reviews notes, then nods in consent.)

CLENORA	"I really appreciate your support and I promise, I am going to get the PhD."
DR. RAEBURN	"Clenora, I'm sure you know that this is not going to be easy. It could jeopardize your career later."
DR. HORWITZ	"Indeed, this is just the start of the kind of opposition you will get with such controversial research."
DR. KIRBER	"Yet it should be interesting, seeing historians in general respond to this new perspective."
DR. WOODARD	Your position here anticipates the role of the murder of Emmett Till as a hotly contested commodity. I Look forward to it.
DR. WALTON	"Be careful, Clenora. This subject is a lot to put on the shoulders of anyone, especially a female."
CLENORA	"I accept this assignment from the Almighty. Liberating Emmett as the true catalyst is to live for. And I project others will later follow."

Clenora and Doctoral Committee of five

1. Dr. Jonathan Walton, Prof. of History (University of Iowa)—Chair
2. Dr. Fredrick Woodard, Dean (University of Iowa)
3. Dr. Richard Horwitz, Department Chair, American Studies (University of Iowa)
4. Dr. John Rayburn, Department Chair, English (University of Iowa)
5. Dr. Linda Kirber, Professor of History and National Chair, American Studies (University of Iowa)

(A copy of the Iowa City Press Citizen Newspaper dated September 27, 1986. Caption on the front page reads, "University of Iowa Student gets $10,000 Ford Grant for Lynch Trial Study.")

CLENORA (V.O.)	It started that way: The Proposal, The Challenge; The Facts, The Conflict; The Audacity, The Tradition!

Following the MAY 1988 Commencement at the University of Iowa, where Clenora Hudson received her PhD, she was commissioned by the university to write the story of why and how she had chosen the Emmett Till saga for her Ford Doctoral Dissertation—"Emmett Louis Till: The Impetus of the Modern Civil Rights Movement." The article she wrote, "The Unearthing of Emmett Till: A Compelling Process," was published in the Fall issue of *The Iowa Alumni Review* (OCTOBER 1988: 18–23). Four months later

(FEBRUARY 1989), she was interviewed on *Midday News* in Salt Lake City, where she offered the first televised coverage on Till as catalyst of the Civil Rights Movement. Below, she captures defining moments of the four key players identified in her research, wherein they demonstrate their seminal roles in the infamous Till murder case:

The Four (4) Key Players

SCENE 23—*Mamie & Mooty*—S Bend, IN

MOOTY—"Historians will talk about the good and the bad, but they don't want to deal with the ugly. The ugliness of racism is not a white man's telling a Black woman to give him her bus seat—bad as it is—but the confident home-invasion, kidnapping and murder of a fourteen-year-old black youth and the exoneration by jury of the youth's apparent killers."

MAMIE—"Let me just say that until my dying day, I'm going to be fighting this thing. So help me God I will. I'm not going to be fighting color. I'm not going to be fighting creed. I'm not going to be fighting anyone's beliefs, so long as they're safe and sound, so long as they don't reach out and destroy me or someone else."

SCENE 53——*Whitten* at Home

CLENORA—"When I first met you in the summer of 1986, you said that you always knew from the beginning that the brothers were either directly or indirectly involved and that your mission was to defend them at any cost and you did that. So what do you think about Emmett Till today?" (A long silence)

WHITTEN—"Misery! Misery! Absolute Misery! I've always felt nothing but Misery. From the very beginning I've felt nothing but Misery. You know, you're not always committed to what you do. Sometimes you do what you do to earn a living. I did what I did to earn a living... [But] I'm truly sorry [now] for the verdict and I hope my lesson will change the hearts of others."

Defining Moments

1. CLENORA

   But why weren't we told that Emmett Till's death is what started the Civil Rights Movement? It was at the heart of the matter!

   RAYFIELD MOOTY

   Don't rightly know, mam. You're the historian. I'll tell you the story. You tell me the why.

2. CLENORA

   I'll show them. Downplaying Emmett is the very reason the Movement did not start on a higher note.

   MIKE

   What do you mean, babe?

   CLENORA

   The Movement started from the cruel murder of a child and our response which was Rosa Parks and the bus boycott. Connecting them would have taken us to a more advanced level of commitment. It's about the children; don't you agree?

   MIKE

   I see. Then our demands for equal rights and protecting our children would have been one and the same?

   CLENORA

   Exactly. There was no Movement without Emmett. Even Rosa Parks admitted it, though much later. You see, Mike, unearthing truths is truly priceless. Liberating Emmett from being an embarrassment to the catalyst of Movement is my goal.

3. INT. CHICAGO, Illinois—GOVERNOR'S OFFICE—DAY

   Rayfield Mooty is seated at the desk, right across from GOVERNOR WILLIAM J. STRATTON.

   RAYFIELD MOOTY

   Governor Stratton, you gotta get the Mississippi officials to release Bo's body so we can bring him back home.

   GOVERNOR STRATTON

   Are you referring to that Chicago boy they found in the river in Mississippi?

RAYFIELD MOOTY
That kid is my family. Emmett Till. Please, Governor Stratton. Force them to return Bo's body to his mom. They plan on burying him there. We need him here.

GOVERNOR STRATTON
How can we justify such a demand?

RAYFIELD MOOTY
Governor, he's a resident of the state of Illinois, not Mississippi.

GOVERNOR STRATTON
He resided here with his mother and attended our public schools here?

RAYFIELD MOOTY
That's right, sir.

GOVERNOR STRATTON
Still, I feel there will be some strong resistance from that state.

RAYFIELD MOOTY
Not if you do your part as the Governor of his home state. Emmett has the right to come home for a proper burial. Every citizen has that right. Don't you agree?

GOVERNOR STRATTON
Yes, and as the governor, I will do everything in my power to make that happen.

RAYFIELD MOOTY
Thanks so much. I felt sure that you as Chief Executor in the state of Illinois would uphold your duties.

GOVERNOR STRATTON
Well, that's my mission.

RAYFIELD MOOTY
And that's what we entrusted you to do when we put you in office. I'm sure you won't disappoint us now, not in this time of grief and urgency.

GOVERNOR STRATTON
Mooty, you can tell Emmett's mother that I'll contact the officials in Mississippi to demand that body!

RAYFIELD MOOTY

Thank you, Governor. The family will be very pleased to hear this.

4. Chicago—Rayner Funeral Home

RAYFIELD MOOTY

I don't care bout instructions on that box. Mamie paid a thousand bucks to bring that kid home.

MR. RAYNER

Ms. Mamie?

RAYFIELD MOOTY

She's got to see what's in that box. It could be dirt in it. You've got to open that box and I mean now!

MAMIE

Please. I've got to see Emmett again for myself. I've got to know it's him, my baby, my only one.

MR. RAYNER

For God's sake, Ms. Mamie don't look. I'm a family friend, and I'm telling you, don't look.

MAMIE

If you can't open it, Mr. Rayner, just give me a hammer. Please! So help me God's, I'll do it!

RAYFIELD MOOTY

It'll be okay, Mamie. That won't be necessary. Don't worry. I think Mr. Rayner can take care of that, and if he can't, then I will.

5. Mamie's Home—Our first Interview (1/6/88)

MAMIE

Why, Clenora, you seem to know everything about Emmett. Why did it take you so long to get to me?

CLENORA

Because you're the icing for the cake, Mamie, and that comes last.

MAMIE

So, what can I tell you that you don't already know?

CLENORA

I want to know more about Emmett the boy, his hobbies, his dreams, his overall character.

MAMIE

He was a good boy who loved his family. He often talked about building his grandmother her own church and, of course, he helped me around the house in so many ways. As for his dreams for his future, he had a passion, and said time and again that he wanted to be a professional baseball player. And I'm sure he would have been had things been different.

CLENORA

It seems that you, your son and Mr. Mooty played a key role in the Civil Rights Movement.

MAMIE

Yes, but there is one thing I wish you would do for me, Clenora.

CLENORA

And what's that, Mamie?

MAMIE

You said Bo whistled. I wish you would say Emmett "allegedly" whistled. You see, Bo had a speech impediment and stuttered. That was to free his words.

CLENORA

I understand, Mamie. But I can't. All my research confirms that Emmett did whistle at Carolyn. You see, in saying that he "allegedly" whistled is to suggest that his lynching was a mistake: They thought he whistled and killed him. Their act was a crime, Mamie, not a mistake. They had no right to kill him. Why, I can almost hear Emmett now saying, "Thanks, Ms. Hudson. I did whistled, but that didn't make me a bad boy."

MAMIE

Indeed, Emmett was not a bad boy. And the Emmett Till Players proudly bear his name.

CLENORA

I understand that you have them recite Dr. King's

speeches. Can you now help me spread the word about Emmett's real significance, as catalyst of the modern Civil Rights Movement?

MAMIE

I'll try to, Clenora. I have to get used to saying that because I have never said that before.

GENE Mobley (Mamie's husband)

Good point, Clenora, and I can certainly help her with that. But for now, since Mamie spent hours preparing this great meal for us—Salad, Shrimp Creole & Rice, Green Beans, Ice Tea, Pound Cake & Ice Cream—I say it's time to eat.

(They laughed and adjoined for a late lunch before Clenora's departure around 5, back to Iowa.)

6. University of Iowa

Two days before Clenora's Dissertation Defense on April 25, 1988, she received an important letter in mail from Mamie:

MAMIE (VO)

". . . I feel that you have the background and the sensitivity to help me with my own story of Emmett as I knew him. And how my life has been directed as a result of losing him. So I am asking you now, to set aside the time to help me write this book. I feel that time is of essence, because much time has already passed."

7. University of Iowa—Dissertation Defense

AUDIENCE MEMBER #4, A WHITE PROFESSOR

Clenora, you seem to have established credence in what may one day become an awesome debate in the Academy throughout the world.

CLENORA

Please note that society does have a tendency to select truths, rather than expose them all.

AUDIENCE MEMBER # 4

Then are you ready for a lifetime commitment to upholding your position, even if it means losing a lot of career opportunities?

CLENORA

Indeed, even though I must admit that I never thought about the risks I may be taking concerning my career.

DR. WALTON

Well, that's something to think about, Clenora, because it's true. With that, I thank you, Doctor, for such an enlightening and prophetic question. Are there any more questions? It's been a lengthy and intense defense, and it's time for the committee to cast the vote.

. . .

DR. WALTON

Well, that wasn't too long, Clenora. And now, with the committee, I am proud to report our unanimous decision and say that you have successfully completed the PhD. Congratulations, Dr. Hudson.

(The committee members smile and shake her hand.)

CLENORA

Yes! Thank you, Jesus! With the endorsement of the Academy, Emmett is liberated at last!

(A staff member interrupts with a telegram from Mooty just received by the American Studies receptionist for Clenora.

INSERT:
She reads the TELEGRAM aloud, as Mooty's voice takes over)

RAYFIELD MOOTY (V.O)

"Many stories have been written about Emmett, but none have told it like it was. The materials I gave you, Clenora, was the experience I lived through and watched during the court trial in Sumner, Mississippi. I still have my press card. I am glad I found someone to tell it like I saw it. Since I cannot find the words to express my feelings of appreciation, I will just say, thanks, thanks, thanks."

8. INT. ROB AND CLENORA'S ROLLS ROYCE—Robert pulls out from the curb. Mooty peers out the window, pensive, smiling as he views all enroute to the hospital.

RAYFIELD MOOTY

A Rolls Royce! A Rolls! Ha! This must be my last ride!

Clenora reaches back to touch Mr. Mooty as she speaks.

CLENORA

We've only just begun, Mr. Mooty. Let's just get you to the hospital so we can ride this story together. I love you.

(Sadly, Mooty dies a few days later in intensive care.)

9. CLENORA

Mr. Whitten, there's always something new, a new angle, like your twist from supporter of White Supremacy to empathizer for Blacks.

ATTORNEY JOHN WHITTEN

Well, Clenora. It hasn't been easy. I just couldn't shake that kid. Now, I find myself running across one story after another.

CLENORA

What kind of stories, Mr. Whitten?

ATTORNEY JOHN WHITTEN

Something that reminds me of something I read in your book. You know I read it from cover to cover. So have you seen that recent story in *The Washington Post* about Emmett's father?

CLENORA

I can't say that I did.

ATTORNEY JOHN WHITTEN

Well, it was written by this gentleman who was researching the controversy surrounding the 1945 execution of Louis Till in Italy.

CLENORA

Yes, and how the Mississippi press tried to use it against Emmett—"Like Father, Like Son."

ATTORNEY JOHN WHITTEN

Now they're revisiting that case and some pretty interesting things are coming out. I'll get it to you.

CLENORA

No bother, Mr. Whitten. I already covered that controversy in my dissertation/book. Remember? Anyway, I'm leaving today for my engagements at Swarthmore and Bryn Mawr Colleges.

10. Till Banquet—Ebony and Ivory

CLENORA

Thank you, Mamie, for Emmett, and for your children here, the Till Players. And now, I have a special invitation for you, given by Representative Louis DeBerry.

REPRESENTATIVE LOIS DEBERRY

Mrs. Till, you are here now invited to join the platform guests as speaker, with Mrs. Rosa Parks, at the SEPT 1995 Congressional Black Caucus in D.C.

MAMIE
Oh, my Lord. I would be honored. And Emmett, too. Thank you so much Representative DeBerry. And thank you, Clenora. It's happening. At last it's really beginning to happen.

(*DeBerry, a platform guest, nods and waves her hand. The Audience applauses. With teary eyes, Mamie smiles.*)

11. Grand Finale—Whitten's Home
CLENORA (V.O.)

No more recurring dreams. Oh, there were times when I, like Mamie, asked questions; like Mooty, fought fearlessly, and like Whitten, had regrets. But at the center of it all, it's still Emmett.

CLENORA (V.O. CONT.)

Emmett, you gave your life. Mamie, you gave deep love. Mooty, you gave commitment, and Whitten, you gave atonement.

12. Rappers
Till Poem put to Rap Song/Music

13. Today's Emmett Till Continuums:

George Floyd

Briana Taylor

My'Khia Bryant

More Victims before and after these three Symbols (i.e., Trayvon Martin, Sandra Bland, all which Must End NOW!)

Endorsements for the first and fourth Emmett Till Books

From *Emmett Till: The Sacrificial Lamb of the Civil Rights Movement* (1994)

Dr. John Blassingame, Yale University—"I found *Emmett Till* to be an usually revealing & exciting narration of an important twentieth century event, crucial in the origins of the CRM. When you really think about it, Hudson-Weems is absolutely right. We historians missed it."

Dr. C. Eric Lincoln, Duke University—"She [Hudson-Weems] challenges the most sacred shibboleths of the origins of the Civil Rights Movement. . . . And she says a lot America needs to hear again right now."

Mamie Till Mobley, mother of Emmett Till—"Hudson-Weems has dug relentlessly into Southern justice, revealing the stench and ugliness of race hatred, American style. She has captured the essence of Emmett, the Sacrificial Lamb, . . . trapped in a web of hate."

To *Emmett—Legacy, Redemption and Forgiveness* (2014)

Dr. Delores P. Aldridge, Emory University—"Clenora's *Emmett* vividly details the story of the Till Murder Case. As it unfolds, we witness a change in heart of a racist to an empathizer for the oppressed."

Jonathon Van Maren, Radio Host, *The Bridgehead*, Toronto, Canada—"*Emmett*, a significant story that demands our collective attention, tells of our past wicked prejudice and possibilities of creating a more just society. . . . [inspiring] moral revulsion needed to spur people to action."

Barry Morrow, Oscar Award-Winning cowriter of Rain Man—"*Emmett* could greatly curtail racial domination thus, escalating to racial healing. Coming on the heels of *The Butler*, *12 Years a Slave* and *Selma*, *Emmett*, no doubt, is both timely and urgent!"

The Chronicle of Higher Education

Professor Seeks to Make Film About Lawyer Who Defended Racist Murderers

By Jennifer Ruark
Published May 30, 2003

Columbia Daily Tribune

The Civil Rights Movement, then and now: Anti-Racism to stop the Emmett Till Continuum in a 5-step solution

By Clenora Hudson-Weems
Published June 20, 2020

Epilogue

Contributed by:
Maurice Green, PhD
Evangelist Dr. Alveda C. King
Kamika Lynette Bell, M.Ed.

While the definition of racism as a race-based systemic operation of producing outcomes across every sociopolitical stratum is soberingly clear, racism in practice and at its core is also an admission. Its presentation as a mode of control via declarations of superiority and support systems of privilege mask a much more salient truth. This truth is that its founders, practitioners, and supporters remain unwilling to entertain ideals that suggest the concepts of fairness and equality as true objectives. Whether it is the creation of biased exams that are presented as "objective measures" of academic potential, and subsequently afford disproportionate opportunities or those who have been acutely prepared via resources beyond the means of those born into the lower economic rungs of society to the level of maternal care provided to expectant mothers in hospitals situated in the poorest of communities. The benefactors of this system will not allow the comforts of their privilege to be disturbed in a way that would impact advantages, both direct and ancillary that their offspring enjoy. They say "no." Of course, this stance is not new.

Bible scholars often refer to the story of the prophet Moses leading the children of Israel out of the oppressive regime of Egypt. They speak of Moses' request of Pharaoh to release the oppressed people so that they could live their own lives. These people were the slave labor responsible for generating an economic benefit to his house and kingdom. He also said "no." Interestingly, he only relinquished when the price he and his people paid for his position cost more than he could afford. Indeed, racism has a long and storied global history.

The end of racism is akin to the proverbial carrot that is held in front of the horse to invoke movement. Every step the animal takes makes it believe that it's one step closer to the desired goal. This chase leads to frustration and fatigue, while the only reward received is by the man on the horse tricking the animal into labor. This analogy is not to suggest that we as a people should discontinue our fight for a fair and equitable society. It is meant to invoke a reorientation of thought. Is our progress invariably linked to another people's moral awakening that inspires their commitment to making amends? Is that the end of

215

racism that we expect? We have asked for that end for four hundred years and they still say "no," not yet or someday. Is it possible that the end of racism is manifested through our complete acceptance of their consistent four centuries of, "no"? Could the actual end of racism be our people turning inward—intellectually, financially, educationally, politically, and spiritually—to finally neutralize the intended effect of a system geared toward the complete subjugation of our present and future generations? Should we no longer view ourselves through the eyes of our oppressor, as W.E.B. Du Bois posited—". . . the sense of always looking at one's self through the eyes of others, . . . [with their] amused contempt and pity." (*Souls*, 1903)? The end of the impact of racism must be our goal. It is achievable, but within the sphere of our influence and control. We do not have another four hundred years of hoping these benefactors will change their answer. They already gave us four hundred years' worth of "no."

Admittedly, racism is as old as sin, and without question, it is, indeed, sinful. But we must consistently pray that the divisiveness of racism be broken down and that the systemic lie that empowers racism in America will be not only exposed, but eradicated. We are one blood, one human race, and should be regarded as equal, "from the womb to the tomb." The American Dream, The MLK Dream, the dreams of every hopeful human being, can never be realized until racism is eradicated. As Rev. Dr. Martin Luther King, Jr. stated time and again, "Injustice anywhere is a threat to justice everywhere."

But now, I believe America is waking up. I think the water is boiling so rapidly now that people are realizing that their families are interwoven with all of this. People now are having to wake up, for we have a responsibility. People now say, "Maybe this is going too far." Racism, a major culprit in the upheaval, not only rears its ugly head in situations such as the twenty-first century George Floyd tragedy. Racism is deeply rooted in the socioeconomic systems of America even now in 2021. Meantime, while America is "grateful" for the justice for George Floyd, Planned Parenthood, on the other hand, is telling us the organization now recognizes that racism is bad, while assuring us its attempts to annihilate the Black community will continue unhindered, but now with a veneer of wokeness. Maybe now is the time to connect the dots. Maybe justice for George Floyd should become a gateway to justice for all.

Granted, African Americans have fought for centuries for our Civil Rights. It has been a fight that stems primarily from the simple fact that we are Black. The biggest disadvantage that African Americans faced in the search for racial equality dates back to the time when we were forcefully enslaved on white farms and plantations. It was only after Lincoln's 1863 signing of the Emancipation Proclamation, which was a declaration made from a need to save the union, and not to free the Blacks, though a positive outcome, that African Americans were legally freed from slavery. The limited freedom ushered in a new kind of fight, characterized as Jim Crow Laws. Fast forwarding to the 1960s and the 1970s, a number of African American intellectuals worked cohesively to form Black Studies Programs and Departments in a bid to include our information in the curriculum. It is from these studies that Africana paradigms, like Afrocentricity and Africana Womanism, and a multitude of others, later emerged. The authors in this edited volume are herein continuing the dialogue on these concerns relative to real Black freedom, with a particular emphasis on the ongoing racial climate in the United States.

African Americans have spent four hundred years of trying to be understood, and maybe have a place of their own in a world dominated by racism. The urge to return and reclaim African-centered values and African meanings, however, is very vital for the Black race, which is a goal that can be achieved through the adoption of an African-centered curriculum as well. It is our responsibility to pave the way for the next generation, but we must first pass on to them tools for their advocacy in terms of their demands for authentic paradigms and perspectives on Black life. We can be sure that as we continue to move forward, our move need be a collective one, one by which we embrace true "sisterhood" and "brotherhood," knowing that at some time in some way, we are our ancestors! Pass it on!

Afterword

Contributed by:
Gail F. Baker, PhD

If you have arrived at this Afterword for "Africana Paradigms, Practices and Literary Texts: Evoking Social Justice," you have already gained clarity and a better understanding about the tumultuous experiences of Africana people. Despite your thoughts when you began this book, you are now left with a greater appreciation for what has been missing, and what is still needed in order to bring wholeness, peace, and justice for all humankind.

The scholarly dream team assembled for this text serves as a testament to the powerful influence of editor Clenora Hudson-Weems, who has devoted her career to chronicling and uplifting the lives of black people. All authors were asked to bring their true selves into the work—rather than viewing the subject matter from a purely theoretical framework. In so doing, they have provided a richness to the text that is often lacking from so many general works.

The book takes readers through a perilous and complex journey, established first through a framework of Afrocentricity and Africana Womanism. Part 2 provides a more historical perspective, supported by literary exemplars representing those life experiences, both past and present. The culminating section, Part 3, deals with the evolution of the movements, and through accepting and utilizing the lessons from the past, we are able to, then, avoid repeating those mistakes in future endeavors—*SANKOFA*.

Through the text, several key themes emerged. There is the notion that racial awakening will come from a recognition of that past—no matter how painful. There is the audacious use of authenticity as a premise for studying racial constructions; however, there is much more to come from such an initiative, for the book also embraces the role of social justice as a consequential means of advancing racial progress, a major goal that is sorely needed today. The illusive universal goal of peace, security, and happiness—sought by governments, theologians, and societies worldwide—made its appearance here, as well. The efforts of the talented authors herein with their informative contributions were designed to shed light on truths that should be uncovered in order for changes to be made, while simultaneously offering ways by which those changes can be better realized for the coexistance of a truly harmonious future for all.

The fact of the matter is that the idea of workable solutions is one of the most compelling ideas covered in this edited volume. The authors were not simply content to dwell solely on the problems. They sought much more, which consequently evolved into a special book that left its readers with some sense of hopefulness that progress is, indeed, a conceivable possibility.

Granted, the goals of this book were vastly ambitious, and the authors have unquestionably exceeded them. Hence, this laudable work, perfected by an array of amazing thinker-activists, has rendered something from which all can truly benefit, a something that is projected to bring victory, at last, for all, particularly for African Americans, who have long sought after this powerful quest in their aspiration for true Social Justice.

Abstracts

PART I   Africana Theories: Inter-Cultural and Inter-Disciplinary Perspectives

1   Afrocentricity and Transformation: Understanding a Movement

Molefi Kete Asante, PhD

Chapter 1 gives a thorough historical overview of the concept of Afrocentricity, which is an intellectual perspective deriving its name from the centrality of African people and phenomena in the interpretation of data. Maulana Karenga, a major figure I the Afrocentric Movement, says "it is a quality of thought that is rooted in the cultural image and human interest of African people." The Afrocentric school was founded the late twentieth century with the launching of the book *Afrocentricity*, where theory and practice were merged as necessary elements in a rise to consciousness. Early influences included Kariamu Welsh, Abu Abarry, C.T. Keto, Linda James Myers, J. A. Sofola, and so on. Psychologists who argued along lines included Bobby Wright, Amos Wilson, Na'im Akbar, Kobi Kambon, Wade Nobles, Patricia Newton, and so on. African American scholars trained in Political science, history, and sociology, such as Leonard Jeffries, Tony Martin, Vivian Gordon, Kwame Nantambu, Barbara Wheeler, James Turner, and Charshee McIntyre, greatly influence by the works of Yosef Ben-Jochannan and John Henrik Clarke, had already begun the process of seeking a non-European way to conceptualize the African experience prior to the development of Afrocentric theory.

2 Africana Womanism: Authenticity and Collectivity in Securing Social Justice

Clenora Hudson-Weems, PhD

Chapter 2 gives a clear definition of Africana Womanism as an authentic family-centered paradigm, showing how it reflects the prioritization of **Race, Class, and Gender** in the daily experiences of Africana women on every level of their existence worldwide. This is evident, for our ultimate success, including our social, economic, religious, and political persuasions, calls for a **Collective Movement**, one which includes **Men, Women, and Children**. The 18 distinct elements of Africana Womanism define how this goal can be best realized in bringing to fruition, via loving each other, our God-given birthright as human beings for the survival of our future generations. As validated by two Namibian writers, Angela Cowser and Sandra I. Barnes, in "From Shack Dwellers to Home-Owners," practicing the Africana Womanism features daily, is one way to elevate one's life via mandating collectivity. Therefore, in order to create and secure a better society, one wherein love and happiness co-exist, security and friendship reside, as well as an overall good will for all reigns, we must put in place ways by which these realities can prevail, united forever as a fierce support system, resolute in bringing our dreams to a final state of actuality.

3 Black Women Adult Educators—The Utterers of Black Leadership Preparation: Africana Womanism and the Afrocentric Praxis

Jacqueline Roebuck Sakho, EdD

Eurocentric view has monopolized the theoretical development of adult educational leadership preparation in American Higher Education, Prek-20 at the exclusion of Afrocentric theories broadly defined and specifically, Africana Womanism. Using the theoretical underpinnings of Africana Womanism and Afrocentric praxis, this chapter discusses future leadership preparation utilizing Nommoic, Sankofan, and Maatic Afrocentric reasoning wherein we come together and work together—"In it together"—to bring forth a harmonious world of peace, happiness, and ultimate success for all humankind.

4 The African American Literary Tradition

Clenora Hudson-Weems, PhD

The African American Literary Tradition beautifully reflects Black life, beginning with American Slavery and Antislavery (1619–1865), to The Civil War (1861–1865), to Post-Civil War, Reconstruction, and Reaction (1865–1920), to The Harlem Renaissance (1920–1930), to Social Changes (Early 1930 to 1950), to Black Nationalism, Black Aesthetics, and the Black Arts Movement (the searing 1960s), up to the Contemporary Era (1970 to the dawn of the new millennium). This literary chronology of Black life in America, marking key events in our "stride toward freedom," effectively delivers literary responses to those defining moments in the African American literary traditions, imbued with verbal pictures reflecting memorable moments in time. As we move further into a next millennium, African American literature continues to build on the foundation established at the beginning of the African Americana literary tradition, with the oral tradition and the slave narrative depicting Blacks in the quest for freedom. African American literature has recorded the defeats and the triumphs, the fears and the dreams. Its strength lies in its ability to present the truth—the good, the bad, and the ugly. Indeed, our literature gives voice to the eternal spirit of American Americans and the legacy of Black life.

5 The Essential James Baldwin: Life and Literature, At Home and Abroad

Pamela D. Reed, PhD

Few American authors have written and spoken as unreservedly, unapologetically, and presciently about America's racial dysfunction as did James Arthur Baldwin, the celebrated, yet controversial, artivist who routinely held up a mirror to American society. The present study seeks to mine the former child preacher's canonical prose, both fiction and nonfiction, to gain insight into the philosophies espoused therein. From some one of his earliest and most seminal essays, to the poignant poetry volume, *Jimmy's Blues*, to his film-adapted novel, *Go Tell It on the Mountain*, to his groundbreaking play, *Blues For Mister Charlie*, as well as myriad interviews, and scholarly volumes analyzing his catalog, his works and words are closely examined to pinpoint recurring themes and motifs that, even now, more than three decades since his passing, continue to resonate with—and inspire—generations of thinkers to study and build upon his ideas. As such, his writings have become a mainstay in the canons of both American and World Literatures.

Keywords: religion, Baldwin canon, racism, antiracist, protest fiction

6 Stories of Empowerment: The Benefits of Academic and Social Experiences at HBCUs

Sharon H. Porter, EdD

Historically Black Colleges and Universities (HBCUs) are institutions of higher learning founded before 1964. The purpose of HBCUs was to educate African Americans, who were legally denied a right to education and to provide them with trades and skills that would improve the quality of their lives.

HBCUs today are destinations for not only African American students, but international students as well. The National Center for Education Statistics reports that one in four students enrolled at HBCUs are non-Black; this population matriculates to the HBCU for its strong academic programs, inclusive academic advising, and avant-garde course offerings and majors.

HBCUs are still considered a safe haven for African American students today. This chapter identifies the personal accounts of graduates of Howard University, Kentucky State University, St. Augustine University, North Carolina A&T State University, and Winston-Salem State University. The chapter will further explore the significance of HBCUs and how they are still relevant today. To be sure, the HBCU experience goes far beyond academics, for the benefits of the social experiences, too, are boundless.

7 Africana Studies and Economics, In Search of a New Progressive Partnership

James B. Stewart, PhD

The scope and meaning of terms like African American Studies, Black Studies, and Africana Studies have evolved continually since the field was established in schools, colleges, and universities in the late 1960s. Discourse about the economic conditions of people of African descent has always constituted an important dimension of the Black intellectual tradition that Africana Studies seeks to preserve and extend. Significant barriers exist, however, to collaboration between economists and Africana Studies specialists. Opportunities to collaborate across the disciplines arise in addressing issues such as hyper-unemployment, pervasive poverty, environmental racism, Black land loss, and the plight of Black farmers. The author suggests that efforts by Africana Studies specialists to understand many of the current dynamics could be enhanced through collaboration with those economists attempting to develop the subfield of stratification economics.

8 When Will We Learn? It's Not Their Heads, It's Their (Broken) Hearts

S. Renee Mitchell, EdD

Weaving theory, research, and original poetry, this chapter is a personal journey of one Black female educator, author, and former newspaper journalist in Portland, Oregon, with a less than 3% Black population. Shifting from being emotionally trapped and spirit-murdered by schools and society, Black youth learn to embrace their emotional emancipation, evolving to become entrepreneurs, paid workshop facilitators, and social change agents. This chapter discusses how Hudson-Weems' Africana Womanism has allowed the author to shape a simple mentoring program into a comprehensive, award-winning, youth-leadership development organization that uses a signature, three-step process. I Am MORE (Making Ourselves Resilient Everyday) is now the first and only Oregon-based organization to win several national awards for its social-emotional learning (SEL) curriculum. Based on Africana Womanism, Ubuntu and other culturally relevant concepts, this educator stopped expecting youths' behavior to change and, instead, changed her own. Her role evolved from (play) Momma to Master Gardener, who tills the ground of her students' potential by nurturing them with profound love, raising their critical consciousness, and tapping into their innate creativity. The essence of I Am MORE's evidence-based theory of change is ***When I am grounded in my own power, I am then inspired to empower others.***

PART III Evolutionary Ideas, Trends, and Movements

9 Networks of Steel: How Reparations for European Enslavement of Africans Unite the African Diaspora

Raymond A. Winbush, PhD

> *If you are the son of a man who had a wealthy estate and you inherit your father's estate, you have to pay off the debts that your father incurred before he died. The only reason that the present generation of white Americans are in a position of economic strength ... is because their fathers worked our fathers for over 400 years with no pay ... We were sold from plantation to plantation like you sell a horse, or a cow, or a chicken, or a bushel of wheat ... All that money ... is what gives the present generation of American whites the ability to walk around the earth with their chest out ... like they have some kind of economic ingenuity. Your father isn't here to pay. My father isn't here to collect. But I'm here to collect and you're here to pay.*

(Malcolm X on Reparations, November 23, 1964, Paris, France)

The struggle for reparations resulting from the European Enslavement of Africans (EEA) is history's greatest crime against humanity. Beginning in 1441, when 12 Africans were stolen from their homeland of Cabo Branco (now Mauritania) by captains Antão Gonçalves and Nuno Tristão and enslaved in Portugal[1] and ending in 1888, when Brazil officially outlawed slavery, some 60 million Africans[2] were kidnapped, transported, raped, enslaved, hanged, maimed, sold, and burned. It is common for researchers to count the Africans transported during the Middle Passage, the horrendous two and a half to three months journey aboard ships, as the *total* number of Africans arriving in the so-called "new world." Once reparations are achieved for the *global* African community, it will liberate them economically, psychologically, and spiritually but will also begin the long and arduous process of liberating the descendants of Europeans from a false sense of superiority over their accomplishments, long thought to be of their ingenuity rather than their violence.

10 The Modern Civil Rights Movement

Clenora Hudson-Weems, PhD

> *Remarkably, however, no historian has ever fully gauged the impact on the American conscience of the widely publicized lynching on August 28, 1955 of a 14-year-old black Chicago youth, Emmett "BoBo" Louis Till, & the subsequent mock trial of Till's assailants as the genesis of the*

---

[1] Robinson, Randall. *The Debt: What America Owes to Blacks.* New York, Plume, 2001.
[2]

Civil Rights Movement. The incident shocked & stunned some; yet instilled absolute terror in countless others. (Emmett Till: The Sacrificial Lamb of the Civil Rights Movement, 8 & 11)

Chapter 4 is a powerful study that firmly establishes the 1955 brutal lynching of 14-year-old Emmett Till as the true catalyst of the Civil Rights Movement. Having occurred three months and three days prior to Rosa Parks' demonstration—her refusal to relinquish her bus seat to a white man in Montgomery, Alabama on December 1, 1955—Emmett's tragic saga and the subsequent public outcry contesting the crime became an indisputable national/international *cause célèbre*. In fact, it set the stage for the 1956 year-long bus boycott, although it was soon buried and remained so for some 33 years, until the 1988 Ford Doctoral Dissertation, "Emmett Louis Till: The Impetus of the Modern Civil Rights Movement" (University of Iowa), unearthed and documented the failure of noted historians—Benjamin Quarles, John Hope Franklin, John Blassingame (who later endorsed the book), and so on to recognize its impact on American society as catalyst of the true ugliness of American racism.

11 End Emmett Till Continuums: Beyond George Floyd, Breonna Taylor, and Ma'Khia Bryant

Ngeri Nnachi, JD, MPPL

Black intellect, Black smiles, Black joy, Black creativity, gone in moments. Trayvon Martin wanted to work with airplanes. Sandra Bland had just completed her new employee forms at her alma mater, Prairie View, to start her position as a Community Outreach Coordinator. A Google search will explicitly tell you how those dreams were extinguished with their violent murders. What those searches fail to acknowledge is that they dreamed at all. Fathers, mothers, brothers, sisters, so violently taken from their families . . . from us, leaving voids that no measures of justice or accountability can ever fill. All we are left with is our words, and our attempts to uphold their memories. In this chapter, we honor that they dreamed, they loved, they hoped. We honor the lives of all of our Black bodies that dream to see another day in the hopes that we make this reality manifest for us all.

This chapter provides tools for combatting the pervasiveness of anti-Blackness and its impact upon the lives of Black boys and Black girls. This chapter discusses how Africana Womanism and Critical Race Theory can be instrumental and advocating for the humanity of all Africana people. The Emmett Till Continuum continues and with the right tools, we can effectively curtail its impression to where it ceases.

12 Nourish to Flourish: Maroonage—Woodsonian Philo-Praxis and the Education of Black Children

Lasana D. Kazembe, PhD

Knowledge and ways of knowing derived from Africana history and traditions have typically been marginalized, devalued, or altogether excluded from the learning landscape of Black students. Those tiny fragments that do sometimes get included are usually derivative, disconnected from wider Africana culture, and, therefore, fail to appropriately reflect and convey the richness, breadth, and diversity of Africana peoples' contributions throughout history and to the forward march of human development. This essay urges a return to African-centered worthwhile ways of knowing, valuing, and meaning making based on Africana cultural knowledge and life praxes. The author draws inspiration from two key sources: the Maroon history of the African Diaspora and the pedagogical mission undertaken by historian and Master Teacher, the Honorable Dr. Carter G. Woodson. Both sources are interpreted and situated as living practice texts (philo-praxis) that stimulate, nourish, and bring about several things: (1) critical resistance to and escape from ideology and psycho-cultural models imposed by the dominant culture; (2) development of Africana-based aesthetic and materialist approaches that make worthwhile use of Africana cultural knowledge within educational contexts; and (3) development of an apprenticeship tradition to appropriately interpret, sustain, and convey an African-centered intellectual genealogy to successive generations.

Keywords: Africana history, African-centered paradigm, African Diaspora, Woodson

13 Be Woke! Black America and the Holy Trinity—A Sermon

Debra Walker King, PhD

"Wake up, for our salvation is nearer now than when we first believed."

(*Romans* 13:11b, *New Living Translation*)

In this sermon, Rev. Dr. Debra Walker King, an ordained African Methodist Episcopal Church Elder, offers the popular phrase, "be woke," as not only a call to sociopolitical awareness and justice, but also as a Biblical directive. She suggests humanity, Black Americans specifically, can never be woke fully until a personal relationship with the Holy Trinity and God's Truth opens the believers' eyes. Reflecting on the persistence of outdated traditions and beliefs, as well as the corruptible currency of today's insistence on political correctness, this chapter explains how Black Americans continue to sleep even as we issue the call for an awakening. The essay solicits attention to how outdated traditions and semantics block, or subvert, the Black Christian's path into a true relationship with Godly power, engagement, and social change. She suggests that the only way to "be woke" fully and intentionally is to stand in acceptance of our inheritance as children of God and the accompanying charge to be social, political, and loving images of God. This must be our primary focus, King argues, as we engage the fight for America's social transformation, a transformation that moves us all beyond the enslavement of closed eyes into liberation, from the persistence of race and gender-based oppression and violation to illuminating power, effectiveness, and endurance.

Conclusion Opening

For My People, #FortheCulture: A Contemporary Remix of Margaret Walker's poem

Keena Day, MA/PhD Candidate

For my people in places experiencing police brutality & the mothers mourning
For my code switchers living in double consciousness daily;
For my hoteps who know the truth and don't trip on the negative connotation of the term;
For my Activists doing work in the streets & behind the scenes becoming urban legends;

For my communities emerging & shifting into villages constantly dreaming of a Black Wall Street;
For my people bringing back the Renaissance – art crawls & spoken word jazz at brunches, day parties, echoing the Niggerati at Niggerati Manor or the Cotton Club listening to modern day Lady Days, Counts, Dukes & Dizzys;

For My People in bondage but in jail cells enslaved by a system of unfairness within a pseudo free society where black folk do time, but white folk get money off the exact same product;
For my people in a school system that keeps their minds unfree;
For my people trying to free their minds, build their wealth but imprisoned by student loans;

For my people living life & making dollars outta change just to survive the day & push again;
For my people who live to be the best dressed in any room;
For my people who relate to HBCU experiences & use their education everyday in many ways;
For my people teaching youths, preparing leaders with limited resources—a way outta no way;

For my people who are lawyers fighting the fight; in Congress telling the truth, or in the courthouse fighting to seek the truth for the race—The reincarnations of Houston and Marshall;
For my people defying the statistics and proving black love exists and is endearing;

Let a new society rise. Let another community be born. Let a second generation full of courage issue forth; let a people loving freedom come to growth. Let a race of men and women rise and take control.

Coda

Reflections on Our Past, Present, and Future Possibilities: From Film Script: *Liberating Emmett/Whitten's Atonement*; Defining Moments and Endorsements

Clenora Hudson-Weems, PhD

What better way to close a comprehensive body of research on the critical matter of centuries of the dehumanization of a people, all in the midst of current raging coronavirus. Symbolizing what Hudson-Weems calls "the true ugliness of American racism staring us in the eye" is the bloated face of Till. Highlighting that infamous case of the 1950s, the inception of the modern massive public demonstrations against abject racism and discrimination, following the 1954 Brown versus Topeka Board of Education Supreme Court Case a year before, is, indeed, appropriate. The first Black Supreme Court Justice, Thurgood Marshall, successfully litigated the case, rooted in the 1896 "Separate but Equal" *Plessy v. Ferguson Jim Crow Law*. In that case, he established the unconstitutionality of segregation. As we consider where we are today with race relations, the rampant brutal murders of countless Blacks throughout this country graphically evoke the brutal lynching of Emmett Louis Till, thus, representing "the Emmett Till Continuum" and national/international demonstrations contesting such abominable, dehumanizing acts. The rest is history, calling for a halt once and for all for true human justice.

About the Editor and Contributors

Molefi Kete Asante, PhD—Creator/Advancer—*Afrocentricity*; Professor/Founding Chair, Department of Africology, Temple University; General Editor, *Journal of Black Studies*; author of *The Afrocentric Idea* and *The History of Africa: The Quest for Eternal Harmony*

Gail F. Baker, PhD—Provost and Vice President of Academic Affairs, University of San Diego; coauthor of *Exploding Stereotypes*

Kamika Lynette Bell, MEd—Executive Director, Catalyst for Change, Inc & Girls with Pearls

Judge Joe Brown, JD—TV Personality of CBS 15-year Syndicated Court Show—*Judge Joe Brown* (Hollywood, California), the worldwide longest-running TV Court Show during its time (1998–2013)

Keena Day, MA—Doctoral Candidate, University of Dayton; Director of Humanities Instructions & Fine Arts, DSST Public Schools; author, poet, freelance writer

Maurice Green, PhD—Founding Manager and Director, Black PhD Network and Black Doctoral Network

Clenora Hudson-Weems, PhD—Creator of *Africana Womanism*; Establisher of Till as Catalyst of the Civil Rights Movement; Professor of English, UMC; author of *Africana Womanism: Reclaiming Ourselves*, Fifth Edition; *Emmett Till: The Sacrificial Lamb of the Civil Rights Movement*; coauthor (Wilfred Samuels, PhD) of *Toni-Morrison*

Jamica Jacobs—Biological Sciences, Senior, McNair Scholar, MU

Benjamin Jones—Medical Student, University of Kansas

Lasana D. Kazembe, PhD—Executive Director, Third World Press; Assistant Professor, Indiana University–Purdue University Indianapolis; editor of *Keeping Peace*

About the Editor and Contributors

Alveda C. King, HonDr. h.c.—Evangelist & Niece of Dr. Martin Luther King, Jr., Pastoral Associate, Priests for Life; Leader of Civil Rights for the Unborn; author of *King Rules: Ten Truths for You, Your Family, and Our Nation to Prosper*

Debra Walker King, PhD—Professor of English and UF Term Professor (2019–2022), University of Florida; author of *African Americans and the Culture of Pain*

S. Renee Mitchell, EdD—Award-Winning 25-year Former Newspaper Journalist; national award-winning program for Black youths—*I Am M.O.R.E.* (Making Ourselves Resilient Everyday); two-time nominee for *The Pulitzer Prize*

Ngeri Nnachi, JD, MPPL—Doctoral Dissertator, University of Maryland–Baltimore County; author of "Our Father Didn't Show Up to Court for the Child He Ruined" (*The Atlantic*, 2016)

Sharon Hargro Porter, EdD—Executive Director, Next in Line to Lead Aspiring Principals Leadership Academy (APLA); Editor-in-Chief, *Vision & Purpose LifeStyle Magazine*

Pamela D. Reed, PhD— Founding Executive Director of Africologic Institute, Associate Professor of English, Virginia State University; Featured Blogger, *Diverse: Issues in Higher Education*

Jacqueline Roebuck Sakho, EdD—Assistant Professor of Educational Leadership and Administrator; Director, Principal License, Lewis & Clark College, Graduate School, Department of Leadership Studies & Audlt Education, School of Education, North Carolina A&T State U

James B. Stewart, PhD—Past President National Council of Black Studies; Vice Provost (ret.) and Professor Emeritus, School of Labor and Employment Relations, Penn State University; author of *Flight: In Search of Vision*

Raymond Arnold Winbush, PhD—Research Professor and Director of the Institute for Urban Research, Morgan State University; author of *Should America Pay? Slavery and The Raging Debate on Reparations*

Appendix

SYLLABUS—African Diaspora Literature & Theory—*ZOOM*

English 2400/Black Studies—Theorizing Africana Literature
Professor—Clenora Hudson-Weems, PhD
Class: Tuesday and Thursday-12:30-1:45
Phone: 573/882-2783 (o); 310.984.9423 (c)
Websites:

    http://web.missouri.edu/~hudsonweemsc/

or

    www.africanawomanism.com

Course Description

Theorizing Africana Literature is an undergraduate course designed to introduce students to Africana Literary Theory, Thought and Action. Dating back to American Slavery up to today's moments during the trying experiences surrounding global demonstrations contesting racial dominance in the midst of a global coronavirus, the materials for this course allows for a reflection on past defining moments, as well as present experiences, as we search for meanings in life in order to move forward for solace and victory for all humankind.

    The main objective of the course is to introduce students to Africana literary and theoretical constructs as an authentic way of interpreting Africana life with possible solutions to issues impeding progress for Africana people. Much of this can be found in the mirroring images in literary texts, evolving from some of the most powerful representations of life challenges for Africana people – Unspeakable American Slavery experiences; Emancipation, Reconstruction & Jim Crowism; The Civil Rights Movement & Its Sister, the Black

234 Appendix: SYLLABUS—African Diaspora Literature & Theory—*ZOOM*

Arts Movement; up to today's Human/Civil Rights Movement. Yet, in the words of the father of the Civil Rights Movement—Dr. Martin Luther King, Jr., who apply names his celebrated book, Stride Toward Freedom is the way, "till Victory is won!" This is the goal in James Weldon Johnson's "Lift Every Voice and Sing," later adopted as the Negro/Black National Anthem.

The topics and literary works shift back & forth, from a thematic to a chronological structure. Learn and Enjoy!

Textbooks and Course Materials:

Baldwin, James. *If Beale Street Could Talk*. Dial Press.

Hudson-Weems, Clenora, Editor. *Africana Paradigms, Practices and Literary Texts: Evoking Social Justice*. Kendall Hunt, 2021.

Morrison, Toni. *Home*. New York: Alfred A. Knopf, 2012.

All *Videos* (You Tube or on-line, etc.) must be viewed outside class period, followed up by class discussion.

Grade Criteria:

Class Participation—15%

Oral Report—15%

Quizzes—20%

Mid-Term Exam—25%

Final Test/Exam—25%

Attendance is mandatory; 3 or more unexcused absences will result in lowering class grade a minimum of 1 grade level—Periodic Role Call.

> *(If you anticipate barriers related to the format or requirements of this course, if you have emergency medical information to share with me, or if you need to make arrangements in case the building must be evacuated, please let me know as soon as possible.)*

Weekly Schedule:

1. **Course Overview**

   Students will introduce themselves (their classification, major & what their expectations are for this course)

   Course Requirements and **Assignments**; Review **Syllabus**

   Discuss Oral Reports & what is expected from them.

2. **Part II: Africana Moments & Persuasions in Re-Shaping Our Lives** (*Africana Paradigms, Practices & Literary Texts—APPLT*)

   Chap. 4 "The African Am. Literary Tradition"—Hudson-Weems

Appendix: SYLLABUS—African Diaspora Literature & Theory—*ZOOM*

A careful reading of the chapter, with further commentary on noted literary selections, i.e. the samples below:

FROM

"On Being Brought from Africa to America" – Phillis Wheatley 1773

'Twas mercy brought me from my *Pagan* land,
Taught my benighted soul to understand
That there's a God, that there's a *Saviour* too:
Once I redemption neither sought nor knew.
Some view our sable race with scornful eye,
"Their colour is a diabolic die."
Remember, *Christians*, *Negros,* black as *Cain*,
May be refin'd, and join th' angelic train.

TO

"We Wear the Mask"—Paul Lawrence Dunbar 1896
We wear the mask that grins and lies,
It hides our cheeks and shades our eyes,—
This debt we pay to human guile;
With torn and bleeding hearts we smile,
And mouth with myriad subtleties.

Why should the world be over-wise,
In counting all our tears and sighs?
Nay, let them only see us, while
    We wear the mask.

We smile, but, O great Christ, our cries
To thee from tortured souls arise.
We sing, but oh the clay is vile
Beneath our feet, and long the mile;
But let the world dream otherwise,
    We wear the mask!

TO THEN

3. Chapter 9—Emmett Till & "The Civil Rights Movement"
   Quiz on Till; The poem, "The Truth of Till"
   Video Discussion—*Eyes on the Prize—TheAwakening/Ain't Scared*
   ORAL REPORT(S)—The Coda (Toward the End of Book)

TO

4. **The Black Arts Movement**

   ORAL REPORTS—Amiri Baraka, Sonia Sanchez, Haki Madhubuti

   AND NOW

5. PART I: Africana Theories: Inter-Cultural/Inter-Disciplinary **Movements** (*APPLT*)
   Chapter 1—"**Afrocentricity** & Transformation: Understanding a Movement"—Molefi Kete Asante
   Discuss Questions, etc. at the end of the chapter.

6. Chapter 7 The Essential James Baldwin: Life and Literature—*Pamela D. Reed*
   The Book & the Film—*If Beale Street Could Talk*
   "Blues for Mr. Charlie" Monologue by Ronnie Rowe (**YOUTUBE**)

   ORAL REPORT(S)

7. **ORAL REPORTS** on activists/orators:

   Malcolm X

   Martin Luther **King**, Jr

   Stokely **Carmichael**

8. REVIEW

   MID-TERM EXAM

9. Chapter 2—**Africana Womanism**: Authenticity & Collectivity in Securing Social Justice—Clenora Hudson-Weems
   Discuss Poems & Orations covered in the Selection.

10. Discuss questions, etc. at the end of the chapter.

    ORAL REPORT(S)

11. Chapter 8—Networks of Steel: How Reparations for European **Enslavement of Africans Unite the African Diaspora**— Raymond A. Winbush

    ORAL REPORT(S)

Appendix: SYLLABUS—African Diaspora Literature & Theory—*ZOOM*

12. Chapter 10—Ending the Emmett Till Continuums: Beyond **George Floyd, Breonn Taylor, My'Khia Bryant**—*Ngeri Nnachi, JD/MPP; Kamika Lynette Bell, M.Ed*

ORAL REPORTS

13. Where Do We Go from Here?
    More Questions, Commentaries, & Solutions
    (Suggestions from authors of the book's Foreword, Preface, Introduction, Conclusion, Epilogue & Afterthought)

14. Chapter 12—Be Woke! Black America & the Holy Trinity: A SERMON—Debra Walker King

ORAL REPORT(S)

15. Toni Morrison's *Home*
    Wrap Up Discussion
    Course Evaluations

Index

A

Abarry, Abu, 23, 24, 26
Abel, I. W., 158
Abiola, M.K.O., 144
Abraham, Willie, 24
Abrahms, Stacey, 94
Adams, Olive Arnold, 157
Adegoke, Y., 164
Adult Education leadership, 33
    Africana Womanist, 37–39
    Africana Womanist Adult Educator, 36
    Maatic Argumentation, 45–47
    Nommoic Creativity, 43–45
    reframing CAE, 34–36
    Sankofan approach, 40–43
    three initiation journeys, 39–40
aesthetics, 30
afrarealism, 40
Africa, reparations and struggle for, 143–144
African Americans, 148
African American literary tradition
    American slavery and antislavery, 69–72
    Black Nationalism, Black Aesthetics, and The Black Arts Movement, 82–84
    Civil War, 72
    contemporary era, 84–86
    Harlem Renaissance, 76–79
    post-Civil War, reconstruction, and reaction, 72–76
    social changes, 79–82
African Diasporas, 171
African *Jeli,* 177–179
African Knowledge Program, 142
African Survival Thrust, 172
Africana Studies, 105
    collaborative reconceptualization of race, 110–111
    current opportunities, 109–110
    economic research, unrealized opportunities to, 107–108
    ideology, the sociology of knowledge and potential for, 106–107
Africana theories, 1
Africana Womanism, 3, 33, 46, 164, 192
    and Africana-Melanated Womanism, 9
    feature of, 11
    interconnectedness of Africana, 7
    intersectionality, 8
    literary tradition, 8
    in modern-day struggle, human rights, 6
    research and commentaries, 13
    theory of, 9
Africana Womanist, 37–39
Africana Womanist Adult Educator, 36
Africana Womanist Literary Theory (Hudson-Weems), 10

239

Index

Africana-Melanated Womanism, 9, 18, 192
Africology, discipline of, 30
Afrocentric Adult Educational Leadership, 34, 40
Afrocentricity, 23
   Africology, discipline of, 30
   as corrective and critique, 29
   Diopian influence, 28
   emergence, 25–26
   five distinguishing characteristics, 26–27
   objectivity-subjectivity, 27–28
   principal concepts, 29–30
   school of thought, 24–25
Afrocentric, 25
Afrocentric Movement, 23, 25
Afrocentric theories, 33
Afrocentricity, 1, 10, 192
Akbar, Na'im, 23
Allen-Smith, Joyce, 110
American Advertising Federation (AAF), 164
American Association of Adult Education (AAAE), 34
American Revolution, 139
American slavery and antislavery, 69–72
Amutefi Publishing Company, 25
Anderson, Doug, 159
Andrews, William L., 70
Angelou, Maya, 64, 83
Anglo French, 34
Angry Young Man, 56
Ani, Marimba, 24
Ansa, Tina McElroy, 86
Armah, Ayi Kwei, 26
art, 126–127
Asante, Molefi Kete, 10, 25, 26, 30, 33, 38, 43, 44, 57
ascendent, 116
Ashe, Arthur, 63
Association for the Study of Negro Life and History, 175
The Associated Publishers Press, 176
audience transformation, 126
axiology, 30

B

Babangida, Ibrahim, 144
Baker, Houston Jr., 86
Baldwin "Amen" 111, 62–64
Baldwin, James Arthur, 53–64
Bambara, Toni Cade, 85
Bankole, Katherine, 26
Banneker, Benjamin, 70
Baraka, Imamu Amiri, 63, 82
Barkley, Naomi Pleasant, 95
Barksdale, Richard K., 69, 77, 86
Barnes, Sandra I., 4
Barton, Rebecca C., 72
Bell, Derrick, 46, 47, 168
Ben-Jochannan, Yosef, 23
Bennett College for Women in Greensboro, 98
Bergman, Peter M., 155
Berry, Mary Frances, 156
Bett, Elizabeth "Mum," 143
Biden, Joe, 94
Blacks, dehumanization/brutalization of, 16
Black Adult Educationist, 40
Black Aesthetics, 82–84
Black Africans, 28
Black American struggle, 147
Black America, 156, 183–186
   and Holy Trinity, 183–189
Black Arts Movement, 55, 63, 76, 82–84, 172
Black Critical Theory, 122
Black Culture and Black Consciousness (Levine), 75
Black Economic Development, 107
Black Economic Research Center (BERC), 108, 109
Black girls, 164
Black Greek Letter Organizations (BGLO), 94, 98
Black leadership, 154
Black National Anthem, 3
Black Nationalism, 82–84
Black Panther, 55
Black Power Movement, 25, 55, 83
Black womanism, 85
Black Women Adult Educators, 33
Black women educators, 38
Black/African Diasporic knowledge, 175, 179
Blackness and the Adventure of Western Culture (Kent), 77
Blackshire-Belay, Aisha, 24, 26
Black-White Wealth Gap, 145

Blassingame, John, 156
Blaustein, Albert P., 155
Blyden, Edward Wilmot, 24
Bone, Robert, 78
Bonner, Marita, 78, 79
Booker, Simeon, 157
Bottoms, Keisha Lance, 94
bproud, 126
Bradley-Mobley, Mamie, 159
Brawley, Benjamin, 175
Brent, Linda, 8
British West Indies, 184
Brookfield, Stephen D., 36
Brooks, Gwendolyn, 83
Brotherhood of Sleeping Car Porters, 158, 160
Brown v. Topeka Board of Education, 94, 148, 155
Brown, Elsa Barkley, 44
Brown, Sterling, 78
Brown, Theodore, 159
Brown, William Wells, 72
Bruce, Dickson D. Jr., 73, 75
Bryant, Ma'Khia, 164
Bullins, Ed, 83
Burnham, Louis E., 157

C

California State University, 6
Campbell, Bebe Moore, 86
Campbell, James Edwin, 74
Caribbean, the Caribbean Community (CARICOM), 138, 140
Caribbean, struggle for, 140–143
  African Knowledge Program, 142
  cultural institutions, 141
  full formal apology, 140
  illiteracy eradication, 142
  indigenous peoples development program, 141
  psychological rehabilitation, 142
  Public Health Crisis, 141
  repatriation, 140–141
  technology transfer, 142–143
Carter, Joelle Davis, 96
Center for Positive Thought, 25
Charles, Ray, 62

Chestnutt, Charles Waddell, 74, 75, 76
Cheyney University, 94
Childress, Alice, 83
Chinweizu, 24
Christian, Mark, 8, 19
Civil Rights Act, 94
Civil Rights Movement, 19, 55, 135, 167, 168, 198
Civil War, 15, 34, 72, 93, 147
Clarke, John Henrik, 23
classism, 18
Cleaver, Eldridge, 55, 83
Clifton, Lucille, 82–83
Collective Movement, 4
Community Outreach Coordinator, 163
Condition-Effects-Alleviation Complex, 29
Cone, James, 185
The Conjure Woman (Chestnut), 74
Constitutional Rights, 192
Cook County Industrial Union Council, 159
Cook, Mercer, 83
Cooper, Anna Julia, 14, 15, 24, 72, 76, 78
Cooper, J. California, 86
cooperative economic behaviors, 111
Corrothers, James D., 74
Cosby, Bill, 62
cosmological, 30
counter-storytelling, 166
Cowser, Angela, 4
Cox, Oliver, 108
Craig, Rictor, 95
Creative Revolutionist™, 129
Crimes Against Humanity (CAH), 141
Critical Adult Education (CAE), 33–36, 40
Critical Race Theory (CRT), 166–168, 195
Critical Youth Empowerment (CYE), 122
Crummell, Alexander, 24, 73
Cullen, Countee, 76, 77
cultural information, 44
cultural institutions, 141
Cummings, E. E., 27

D

Dagbovie, P. G., 176
Daniels, Lee, 63
Davis, Angela, 85
Davis, Frank, 108

Davis, Miles, 62
Day, Keena, 192
debt cancellation, 143
Declaration of Independence, 192
Delaney, Lucy A., 72
Delaney, Martin, 24
Delaware State University, 6
Dent, Tom, 83
dialect poetry, 74
Dillard, C. B., 116, 120
Diop, Cheikh Anta, 24, 28
Divine Nine, 98
Dorson, Richard, 69
double consciousness, 75
Douglas, Frederick, 8, 185
Douglas, Paul, 159
Douglass, Frederick, 70, 83
Dove, Nah, 24
Dovidio, J. F., 117
DuBois, Eugene E., 34, 45
DuBois, W. E. B, 24, 27, 63, 75, 106, 107, 147
Dumas, Henry, 86
Dumas, M. J., 117
Dunbar, Paul Laurence, 74, 75
Dunbar-Nelson, Alice Moore, 79
Durr, Clifford, 154
Duster, Dan, 15

E

Ebonics, 30
economics knowledge transfers, 106–107
Educational Effectiveness of Historically Black Colleges and Universities Briefing Report, 93
Edwards, Paul, 70
Ellison, Ralph, 63, 78
Emancipation Proclamation, 15, 147, 149
Emergency Land Fund (ELF), 110
emotional emancipation, 122–124
empowerment, HBCUs
 experience, 94–96
 history of, 93–94
 significance of, 94
 support of faculty, 96–97
epistemological, 30
Equiano, Olaudah, 8, 70

established/presented truths, critical questioning of, 178
ethnographic poetics, 129
European Enslavement of Africans (EEA), 137, 139
Evans, Mari, 82
Evers, Medgar, 56

F

family centrality, 5, 9
Fanon, Frantz, 24, 29, 83
Farm Service Agency, 110
Faulkner, William, 194
Fauset, Jessie, 77
fear beneath, 150–151
Federation of Southern Cooperatives, 110
feminism, mainstreamed narratives of, 165
fictive kinship, 121
Finch, Charles, 24
First Pan-African Conference on Reparations, 145
Fisher, Dexter, 86
Flexible Role Player, 5
Floyd, George, 163
Franklin, John Hope, 155
Fred Whit, 95
French at the Paris Conference, 139

G

Gaertner, S. L., 117
Gaines, Ernest, 83
Gallup-USA Funds Minority College Graduates Report, 95
Garvey, Marcus, 24, 76–78
Gayle, Addison Jr., 82
George Washington Bridge, 58
Gilliam, Doris, 13
Giovanni, Nikki, 82, 84
Glaude, Eddie S. Jr., 54
God, 184, 186–188
Gonçalves, Antão, 137
Goode, Kenneth G., 155
Gordon, Charles, 83
Gordon, Vivian, 23
Gray, Lasimba M., 15

Great Migration, 76, 77
Green, Joy, 96
Greene, Lorenzo, 175
Grimke, Angelina Weld, 72
group identities, 111
Gumbo ya ya, 44

H

Haley, Alex, 83
Hammon, Briton, 70
Hammon, Jupiter, 71
Harlem Renaissance, 15, 16, 76–79
Harper, Frances Ellen Watkins, 72
Harper, Michael, 86
Harris, Joel Chandler, 73, 74
Harris, Kamala, 94
Harvard U. Professor of Law, 168
Hayden, Robert C., 34
Hayes Compromise, 148
Hayes, Rutherford Birchard, 148
Heard, Josephine D. Henderson, 72
Hemingway, Ernest, 194
Hemton, Calvin, 150
Henderson, Errol, 24
Henderson, Stephen, 83
Herman, J. L., 126
Hernton, Calvin, 156
Hierarchy of Human Needs, 121
Hine, Darlene Clark, 107
Historically Black College or University (HBCU), 34, 93
  experience, 94–96
  history of, 93–94
  significance of, 94
  support of faculty, 96–97
historiography, 178
Holocaust of Enslavement, 42
Holy Spirit, 183, 186
Holy Trinity, 183, 185–189
  Black America and, 183–189
Home to Harlem (McKay), 77
Hopkins, Pauline E., 76
House, Callie, 143
Howard University Alumni Club of Atlanta, 95
Howard, James H. W., 73
Howard, T. R. M., 157
Howells, William Dean, 74

Hubbard, Larese, 14, 15
Hudson-Weems, Clenora, 1, 3, 8, 9, 10, 13–15, 26, 36, 43, 47, 78, 85, 115, 120, 165, 167, 197, 198
Huggins, Nathaniel Irvin, 79
Hughes, Langston, 63, 77
Huie, William Bradford, 150
Hunhuism, 45
Hunter, Kristin, 82
Hurd, Brian, 96
Hurston, Zora Neale, 42, 77

I

I Am M.O.R.E. (Making Ourselves Resilient Everyday), 120–122, 125, 126, 128
illiteracy eradication, 142
indigenous peoples development program, 141
individualism, 179
Infants of the Spring (Thurman), 77
inside-out, 123
Institute for Colored Youth, 94
intellectual dislocation, 33
interconnectedness of Africana, 7
Interesting Narrative of the Life of Olaudah Equiano, or Gustavus Vassa, the African (Equiano), 70
internal colony model, 108
International Africana Womanism Conference, 6
intersectionality, 8

J

Jackson State University in Mississippi, 97
Jackson, Angela, 86
Jalulu, 177
Jamaica, 142
James, Kevin, 97
Jefferson, Thomas, 71, 193
Jeffries, Leonard, 23
Jeli, 177–179
Ji Yuan, 27
Jim Crow laws, 147, 149–150
Johnson, Abby Arthur, 77
Johnson, Charles, 84
Johnson, Georgia Douglas, 78

Johnson, Helen, 77
Johnson, James Weldon, 3–19, 73, 77
Johnson, Lyndon B., 149
Johnson, Ronald Maberry, 77
Johnston, James Hugo, 175
Jones, Gayl, 85
Jones, Jacqueline, 107
Jordan, June, 82, 85
Jordan, Winthrop, 150

K

Kambon, Kobi, 23
Karenga, Maulana, 23, 24, 25, 30, 83, 105, 106
Keckley, Elizabeth, 72
Kelley, William Melvin, 83, 86
Kennedy, Adrienne, 83
Kent, George, 77
Kentucky State University (KSU), 95
Kershaw, Terry, 24, 26
Keto, C. T., 23, 26
Kincaid, Jamaica, 85
King, Debra Walker, 16
King, Martin Luther Jr, 19, 56, 61, 153, 185
Kinnamon, Kenneth, 69
Kiswahili, 144n16
Knight, Etheridge, 82
knowledge, sociology of, 106–107
Komunyakaa, Yusef, 86
Kunstler, William M., 63

L

laissez-faire policy, 148
Lam, Aboubacry Moussa, 24
Land Assistance Fund, 110
Langley, April, 8
Larsen, Nella, 76–77
Laurence, Paul, 76
Lee, Don L., 82
Lee, George W., 152
Lehman, Cynthia, 26, 27
Lester, Julius, 83
Levine, Lawrence, 75
Lewis, David Levering, 77
Lewis, Hugh, 159
Lincoln University in Pennsylvania, 94

Literary Movement, 85
Little, Maxwell, 167
Living Wage Movement, 109
Locke, Alaine, 34, 76–78
Logan, Rayford, 175
Loggins, Vernon, 70
Lomax, Michael L., 98
long-lasting mental impact, 117–120
Lorde, Audrey, 85
Louis, Henry, 86
lynching, 148
Lyon, Cecil B., 61

M

Ma'afa, 34n1, 42
Maatic Argumentation, 39, 45–47
Madhubuti, Haki, 25, 84
Madondo, Gracious, 12
Malcolm X, 24, 56, 83
male compatibility, 5
Malveaux, Julianne, 107
marginalization, 144
Markham, Pigmeat, 78
Maroon spaces, 172–173
maroonage sites, 172, 175–176
Maroons, 172–173
The Marrow of Tradition (Chestnut), 74
Marshall, Paule, 83
Marshall, Thurgood, 197
Marshall, William, 61
Martin, Tony, 23, 78
Martin, Trayvon, 163
Maslow, A. H., 121
Mason, Charlotte Osgood, 77
Massachusetts Constitution, 139
Mazama, Ama, 10, 24, 26
McDonald, David J., 158, 159
McDougald, Elise Johnson, 78
McDowell, Calvin, 14
McIntyre, Charshee, 23
McKay, Claude, 15, 16, 76–78
McKnight, Reginald, 86
McLemore, Richard Aubrey, 152
McMillan, Terry, 84
McPherson, James, 86
Mercer, Mae, 61
metropolitan sprawl, 109

Mezroe, Mezz, 61
Middle Passage, 137
Miller, May, 78
Mo'hges, Miriam Maat Ka Re, 26
Modern Civil Rights Movement, 135, 147–148
   fear beneath, 150–151
   Jim Crow laws, 149–150
   labor unions, 158–160
   ranking Till with established leaders, 152–154
   sacrificial lamb, 157
   Till and traditional history, 155–157
   Till case and, 151–152
   from 1877 to 1965, 148–149
Modupe, Danjuma, 24, 25, 26, 29
Money, Frank, 17
Montgomery Bus Boycott, 155
Moore, Queen Mother, 143
Moorland, Jesse E., 176
Mooty, Rayfield, 147, 148, 157–159, 198
Morris Brown College, 97
Morris, Monique, 166
Morrison, Toni, 13, 17, 62, 64, 194
Mosely, Walter, 86
Muhwati, Itai, 6
multicontextual, 178–179
Murdock, Clotye, 157
Murray, Albert, 86
Myers, Linda James, 23
Myrdal, Gunnar, 150, 156

N

Nantambu, Kwame, 23, 24
National Association for the Advancement of Colored People (NAACP), 75, 76, 152, 159
National Labor Union, 160
National Science Foundation, 97
National Urban League, 76
Naylor, Gloria, 85
Neal, Larry, 24, 82, 83
Negritude Movement, 25
Negro History Week, 175
The Negro Author: His Development in America to 1900 (Loggins), 70
Negro in American Fiction (Brown), 78
"Negro Problem"
   Baldwin's critics, 55–56
   Baldwin "*Staggerlee Wonders*" 33, 57–58
   Baldwin "*Staggerlee Wonders*" 48, 54–55
   life and literature, at home and abroad, 58–62
Nelson, J. D., 117
New Negro movement, 77
Newson-Horst, Adele, 10
Newton, Patricia, 23
Nigger Heaven (Van Vechten), 77
Nile Valley civilizations, 25
Nobles, Wade, 23
Nommoic Creativity, 39, 43–45, 47
noneconomic behaviors, 111
North Carolina Agricultural and Technical State University (NCAT), 95
Ntseane, 34

O

O'Neale, Sondra, 71
Obama, Barack, 145
Obenga, Theophile, 24
Okur, Nilgun Anadolu, 26
Old Testament, 184
Omolade, Barbara, 38
Osofsky, Gilbert, 70
outside-up, 123

P

Parks, Rosa, 152
People of Color (POC), 121
Perkinson, James W., 41
Perlow, Olivia N., 38
personal transformation, 126
Plato, Ann, 71
Plessy v. Ferguson, 94, 149
Poitier, Sidney, 62
policy advocacy, 109–110
post-Civil War, 72–76
Predominantly White Institutions (PWI), 93
psychological rehabilitation, 142
Public Health Crisis, 141

Q

Quarles, Benjamin, 156

R

racial microaggressions, 117
racism, 11, 18, 167, 193
    collaborative reconceptualization of, 110–111
Rampersad, Arnold, 63
Randall, Dudley, 82
Randolph, A. Philip, 158, 159
Rashidi, Runoko, 24
Reconstruction, 72–76
Reed, Ishmael, 84
reparations, 138–140
repatriation, 140–141
research-based theories, 121
researcher-voiced poetry, 129
resilience, 126–127
Richardson, Willis, 78
Rivers, Conrad Kent, 82
Robeson, Paul, 24, 78
Robinson, Jackie, 63
Robinson, Jo Ann, 153
Rodney, Walter, 24
Rosamond, J., 3
Rose, Arnold, 150
Royall, Isaac, 139
Royall-Sutton, Belinda, 143

S

Saba, Nguzo, 23
sacrificial lamb, 157
Samuel, Wilfred D., 70
Samuels, Rich, 157
Sanchez, Sonia, 82
Sankofan approach, 39–44, 47
Savage, Gus, 157
schools, 116–117
Scott, Beauregard, 17
Scott, Hazel, 61
Second Morrill Act in, 94
Semaj, Leachim, 24
Semmes, Clovis, 26
sexism, 18
sexual aggression, 150
Shange, Ntozake, 85
Shuman, Michael, 109
Simms, Margaret, 107
Simone, Nina, 62

Slim, Memphis, 61
Smith, Barbara, 85
sociology, of knowledge, 106–107
social justice, 14
social transformation, 25
social-emotional learning (SEL), 118, 122
Sofola, J. A., 23, 24
South America, 13
Spellman, A. B., 82
spirit-murder, 116
St. Augustine's University, 97
State System of Higher Education as Cheyne University of Pennsylvania, 94
Steel Workers' Union, 159
Stepto, Robert, 85
Stewart, William Henry, 14
Stovall, David, 34, 39, 40
stratification economics, 111
"*Staggerlee Wonders*" 33, 53–58
Stuckey, Sterling, 71

T

T'shaka, Oba, 24
Taylor, A. A., 175
technology transfer, 142–143
Ten Hills Plantation, 139
Terry, Lucy, 71
Theatre Owners Booking Association, 78
Thiong'o, Ngugi wa, 24
Thompson, Betty Taylor, 17
Thurman, Wallace, 77
Till lynching, 149
Till, Emmett Louis, 57, 135, 151–152, 157, 163
Tillis, Antonio, 13
Till-Mobley, Mamie, 198
To Tell a Free Story: The First Century of Afro-American Autobiography (Andrews), 70
Tolson, Melvin B., 78
Toomer, Jean, 76
Toure, Askia Muhammad, 86
Townsend, William S., 158
Transactional Association of Christian Colleges and Schools (TRACS), 97
transformation, 124–126
Tristão, Nuno, 137
Trotter, William Monroe, 75
Troupe, Quincy, 86

True Cultural Diversity, 193, 194
Truth, Sojourner, 11, 12, 82, 83
Turner Foundation and Ford Foundation, 109
Turner, James, 23
Tutu, Desmond, 121

U

U.S. Department of Agriculture, 110
U.S. Small Business Administration, 97
Ubuntuism, 45
umfundalai, 25
The Uncalled (Dunbar), 74
Uncle Tom, 56
United Automobile Workers, 159
United States, 15, 18, 62, 143
   struggle for, 138–140
University of Botswana, 6
University of Florida (UF), 183
University of Missouri, 6
University of Oklahoma, 6
University of South Africa, 6
University of Zimbabwe, 6
up and beyond, 124
Up from Slavery (Washington), 75

V

Van Vechten, Carl, 77
Victorian conservatism, 73
Voting Rights Bill, 149

W

Wagner, Shanikka, 95
wakimbizi, 115
Walker, A'Lelia, 77
Walker, Alice, 85
Walker, Margaret, 83
Wallace, Phyllis, 107
Ward, Douglas Turner, 83
Washington, Booker T., 72, 75, 83
Weaver, Robert, 107

Wells, Ida B., 14, 15, 24, 72
Welsh, Kariamu, 23, 25, 26, 30
Wesley, Charles, 175
West Coast, 143
West, Dorothy, 77
The Wife of His Youth and Other Stories of the Color Line (Chestnutt), 74
Wheatley, Phillis, 71
Wheeler, Barbara, 23
When Harlem Was in Vogue (Lewis), 77
Whitaker, Fred, 95
White, Paula Childress, 86
Whitten, Attorney John Jr., 198
Whitten, John C., 150
Wideman, John Edgar, 86
Williams, Desmond, 95
Williams, George Washington, 72, 73
Williams, Jacynda P., 96
Williams, Juan, 153
Williams, Robert L., 12
Williams, Shirley Anne, 85
Williamson, Joel, 73
Wilson, Amos, 23
Wilson, Boyd L., 158, 160
Wilson, Harriet E., 72
Wilson, Tywauna, 96
Winston-Salem State University (WSSU), 93
Woodson, Carter G., 24, 107, 119, 171, 172, 173, 174, 175, 177
Woodsonian anteriors and interiors, 174–175
Woodsonian philo-praxis, 175–176, 178
   philosophical dimensions of, 177–179
Wright, Bobby, 23

Y

Young, Al, 86
Youth of Color (YOC), 121, 127
Youth Participatory Action Research (YPAR), 165

Z

Zangrando, Robert L., 155